Facilitating Language Learning

A GUIDEBOOK FOR
THE ESL/EFL TEACHER

Facilitating Language Learning

A GUIDEBOOK FOR THE ESL/EFL TEACHER

Fraida Dubin
American Language Institute
University of Southern California

Elite Olshtain
Department of Linguistics
Tel-Aviv University

McGraw-Hill International Book Company

New York   St. Louis   San Francisco   Beirut   Bogotá   Düsseldorf
Johannesburg   London   Madrid   Mexico   Montreal
New Delhi   Panama   Paris   San Juan   São Paulo
Singapore   Sydney   Tokyo   Toronto

Facilitating Language Learning
A Guidebook for the ESL/EFL Teacher

Editorial Development
Winifred M. Davis
Design
Anne Canevari Green
Production
Dennis Conroy

1234567890   783210987

Library of Congress Cataloging in Publication Data

Dubin, Fraida.
  Facilitating language learning.
  Bibliography: p. 237.
  Includes index.
  1. English language—Study and teaching—Foreign
students. I. Olshtain, Elite, joint author. II. Title.
PE1128.A2D767   428.2'4   77-2394
ISBN 0-07-017877-1

Foreword

When teachers seek information and guidance to help make their work more rewarding, it is always reassuring to receive that assistance from those who have a thorough understanding of what teaching is all about. Fraida Dubin and Elite Olshtain brought just such experience to the preparation of this book. Coupled with that experience, which has been at many levels in many parts of the world, these teacher-scholars have strong academic preparation in theoretical linguistics, psycholinguistics, socio-linguistics, and education. This preparation has permitted the authors to synthesize the most viable findings of experience, experimentation, and theorizing, and to present them to practicing or prospective teachers in terms that are precisely relevant to their immediate teaching responsibilities.

A striking example of the authors' understanding of the real concerns of teachers is found in the introduction to this book. Included here are a number of questions that teachers consistently raise as they plan for their teaching assignments. These questions relate to fundamental relationships that pertain between teachers and students, between teachers and teaching materials, and between teachers and theoreticians. But whereas many others who have prepared methodology texts have had a tendency to avoid, hedge, obfuscate, or retreat into technical jargon in responding to these kinds of questions, Dubin and Olshtain have presented clear, reasoned, usable answers that teachers can comprehend in terms of authentic teaching and learning situations.

Fortunately Dubin and Olshtain have not dedicated this volume to the resolution of the theoretical issues that beleaguer the research scholar in psychology and linguistics. Rather, they present a framework within which teachers can make defensible instructional decisions that correspond to their own teaching situations. The authors encourage teachers to define the variables in terms of their own teaching responsibilities. They guide their readers to make their own decisions through carefully considering *who* are the students, *what* is the content of the course, and *how* can this content be implemented in the classroom. This practical approach, I feel, will be of great value to teachers of students at all levels under a very large number of teaching-learning conditions.

From my point of view, among the many commendable features of this book is the authors' recognition of teachers as people who facilitate learning rather than as the source of all knowledge, the formers of all questions, and the resolvers of all problems. Teachers are seen as participants with the students in the teaching-learning context. The latter are permitted to assist in the definition of goals and in the forming of strategies that are devised to attain them. This recognition of the teachers' role puts Dubin and Olshtain on the frontiers of modern language teaching.

Russell N. Campbell,
Vice-chairman
Dept. of English (TESL)
University of California
Los Angeles

Preface

Why Another Book on Language Teaching?

Why, indeed, produce another book on language teaching when the field already appears to have an overabundance of theories, methods, and approaches? Why provide teachers with more information when, in many cases, they are already weighed down with ideas from experts? The answer is that weight by itself does not equal useful information. Overabundance does not answer specific problems which teachers themselves pose.

There is an essential need today for teachers to work with a flexible approach, a framework to plug in new ideas. The primary purpose of this book is to provide language teachers—highly experienced or just entering the field—with such a framework, one which will help them to make effective decisions for themselves. Our aim throughout is this: we want teachers of language to be able to say: "Based on my understanding of my student's needs, I feel secure to choose the approach which brings success to the learners I work with." We want teachers of language everywhere to gain confidence in their ability to cope with the difficult task they undertake each school day.

Throughout the pages of this book the teacher is viewed as a facilitator. The term "facilitator" is used to describe the role of the teacher in the learning process. A facilitator helps other people develop their own capabilities and inner resources in order to perform tasks successfully. In this view, the teacher's main concern is to *facilitate* the learner's accomplishment of the difficult job of learning a new language. The facilitator helps, but does not tell. The facilitator encourages but does not criticize. Educators throughout the world today are finding that the facilitating attitude can be an effective motivating force in the classroom.

Why do we advocate "facilitating" rather than "teaching" in the traditional sense? Because we have observed that although it is possible to tell someone else how to do something, yet the results are slight if that someone is not interested in accomplishing the task. Real learning only takes place when students accept responsibility for themselves. The following words of a song tell the tale.

> You can lead a horse to water,
> But you can't make him drink.

You can put a child in school,
But you can't make him think.

It is our strong belief that the most important task that teachers take upon themselves is to help pupils become better learners. This goal is best accomplished by creating a classroom atmosphere which allows learners to do their best in their own way. Teachers who see this as their prime objective are *facilitating* the learning process rather than teaching in the old-fashioned meaning of the word.

A number of specific classroom strategies which embody the concept of facilitating are discussed in the pages of this book. Among them are techniques such as the following: (1) planning for individualized instruction, (2) providing a humanizing classroom atmosphere, (3) encouraging interaction among students, (4) devaluating mistake counting, (5) fostering creative use of the new language, and (6) adopting alternatives to frontal teaching such as team instruction and cross-age tutoring.

The Overall Plan

The book is divided into three parts: The Introduction is Clearing the Air, summary discussions of most commonly raised questions. Part One is Beginners and Those Beyond; Part Two is Intermediates and Advanced. Throughout, the authors have carefully differentiated the ESL and the EFL points of view. For although there is a common subject matter for all— teachers in a second language frame-of-reference as well as those in a foreign language frame-of-reference—there are still vital differences between the two.

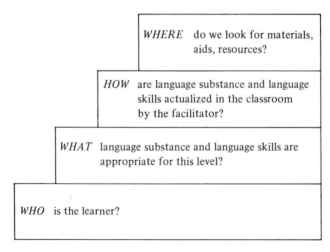

The Overall Plan of **Facilitating Language Learning**

The organization of the book into separate parts for beginners and advanced is original. Too often the field has been presented as a monolithic whole. In practice, instructors realize full well that it is not possible to utilize the same procedures with different levels of students, let alone with different age groups. For this reason, within the part Beginners and Those Beyond (typically programs for children) a special section is devoted to the adult beginner in a language course. Since all divisions into levels represent, at best, convenient fictions, the terms used to designate the two basic sections convey the view that levels of proficiency belong along a continuum rather than at exact stages.

Within each of the two main divisions, Part One dealing with Beginners and Those Beyond and Part Two, Intermediates and Advanced, problems are organized within an identical framework. Question words are used to head parallel chapter parts: (1) WHO is the learner? (2) WHAT language substance and language skills are presented at this stage? (3) HOW are language substance and language skills actualized in the classroom by the facilitator? and (4) WHERE do we look for materials, aids, and resources? Clearly, however, the answers or solutions to these questions are quite different for the separate levels. So, although the guiding themes for the chapters are parallel, the ideas which are developed diverge.

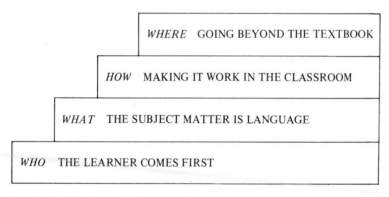

Part One: Beginners and Those Beyond

The figure on page viii gives an overview of the design of Parts One and Two. The model is in the form of steps. The first building block is the answer to the WHO question, the nature and needs of the learner. Parts One and Two pose the same questions; they then set out appropriately different answers to these questions. The figures above and on page x summarize these answers by listing the titles of the separate chapters of each of the two Parts. The four parallel chapter headings are not water-tight compartments. Their essential relationship is that each rests on what is beneath it, like steps. Each is, structurally speaking, supporting the next, and all others above it.

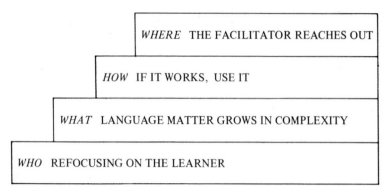

| WHERE THE FACILITATOR REACHES OUT |
| HOW IF IT WORKS, USE IT |
| WHAT LANGUAGE MATTER GROWS IN COMPLEXITY |
| WHO REFOCUSING ON THE LEARNER |

Part Two: Intermediates and Advanced

The Audience

FACILITATING LANGUAGE LEARNING has been planned for a wide audience. It can be used, to a considerable extent, by *all* teachers of language. However, the specific examples and specific problems are exemplified in terms of teaching the English language. Since the book has been conceptualized as an overview of the field of language pedagogy, it should provide guidance for teachers who are entering the field for the first time, as well as for people who are updating their professional expertise by attending in-service workshops and special courses. It is intended, too, for people preparing for language teaching careers at universities and pedagogical colleges. Even though the emphasis is on classroom affairs, many of the ideas incorporated in these chapters can be used by teachers who work with pupils on a one-to-one basis as tutors.

Workshop Activities

There are workshop activities at the end of each section of each chapter in Parts One and Two. They have been prepared as aids to teacher training. The goal of the questions is to stimulate discussion, *not* to test people on their reading of the text. Often the questions are hypothetical problems found in everyday teaching situations. They will call upon the participants to think creatively rather than to answer with passages learned by rote from the text. In all instances, the chapters provide the necessary background information rather than specific answers.

Different workshop participants may well come up will different solutions to the same questions. The mere fact that the solutions are different does not mean that each may not have a high degree of validity. The discussion should concentrate on examining analytically and thoroughly these different responses to the same questions.

Bibliography

As an additional feature for teachers-in-training, the bibliography has been organized around the central disciplines which contribute to language pedagogy. The bibliography is not intended to be exhaustive. Its real purpose is to provide a helpful next step for those who have newly entered the language teaching profession. As a further aid, entries have been limited to books since professional journals are not always easily obtainable. (For a list of journals in the field, the reader is directed to Part Two, Chapter 8, WHERE.)

ABOUT THE AUTHORS

Fraida Dubin, Ph.D., has worked in both ESL and EFL settings. Her degree in linguistics is from the University of California at Los Angeles (UCLA). Under the U.S.-sponsored Fulbright program, she trained Greek teachers of English in Athens. In the U.S., she has directed Peace Corps training for volunteers preparing to teach in Africa and Latin America. Through UCLA Extension, she has conducted a variety of in-service workshops for ESL teachers at all levels. She has also taught English to foreign students at UCLA and is a graduate of the UCLA TESL program.

Currently, she is a member of the faculty of the American Language Institute, University of Southern California (USC), where she has also taught sociolinguistics through the Department of Linguistics. Most recently, she has served as the director of ALI/USC's English language program in Tehran for National Iran Radio-Television.

Elite Olshtain teaches Linguistics and TEFL methodology at Tel Aviv University in Israel. She is in charge of a team of writers preparing textbooks for elementary and secondary level schools, teaching English to speakers of Hebrew. She is also acting as Linguistic Consultant to the Instructional Television Centre in Israel. Through these varied activities she has gained a vast experience in both textbook preparation and teacher training.

Elite Olshtain received her linguistic and ESL training at UCLA.

ACKNOWLEDGMENTS

The present book is the result of years of work in the field of learning, teaching, teacher training, and material construction in both EFL and ESL. The ideas and suggestions offered here have inevitably developed thanks to collaboration with a great number of people. Their explicit and implicit contributions have certainly affected our work. Our sincere appreciation goes to all, and we hope that they will forgive this general expression of thanks.

We must acknowledge special indebtedness to Joan Rubin who at an early stage set us in the direction of a practical rather than a theoretical approach, and to Jacqueline Schachter whose research (See 'An Error in Error Analysis' *Language Learning* v. 24: n. 2) suggested the discussion in Part II, Chapter Six on avoidance errors. Andrew Briggs' article on teaching English in Jamaica appeared in the *Los Angeles Times,* January, 8, 1974; it is quoted with his consent.

Special thanks go to Nancy Cott, Raphael Gefen, Heni Kneller, and Ruhama Kulbersh for their invaluable comments on the manuscript.

Many teachers' creative ideas have been incorporated in these pages. We want to specially cite those of Lorna Auerbach, Rita Cogswell, Janet Fisher, Paul Hamel, Grover Hudson, Linda LaMacchia, Nancy Lonke, Charles Lotte, George Papcun, Janet Porter, and Fred Rosensweig in the ESL field and Sheila Been, Ruth Benziman, Lenora Goell, Estelle Friedman, Siona Kronfeld, Rena Lavie, and Rivka Shapiro in the EFL field.

F.D.
E.O.

Contents

Foreword   *By Russell N. Campbell*   **v**

Preface   Why Another Book on Language Teaching?   **vii**

Introduction   Clearing the Air   **1**

A. Basic Questions Which Puzzle Many Language Teachers   **2**

B. Questions Frequently Asked by Native Speakers of English about English Language Teaching   **7**

C. Non-Native Speakers Ask   **10**

PART ONE   **BEGINNERS AND THOSE BEYOND**   **17**

Chapter   1. Who: The Learner Comes First   **18**

A. The Learner in the Classroom   **20**
1. The Traditional Classroom   **20**
2. The Modern Classroom   **20**
3. The Individual Learner   **21**
Workshop Activities   **22**

B. The Young Beginner   **23**
1. Within the School System   **24**
2. Peer, Parental, and Societal Pressures   **25**
3. Motivation   **27**
4. Outside the School System   **29**
Workshop Activities   **30**

C. The Adult Beginner   **30**
1. Motivation and Goals Are Already Established   **31**

	2. The Adult Beginner Needs Support, Too	**32**
	Workshop Activities	**33**
Chapter	2. What: The Subject Matter Is Language	**34**
	A. Language Substance	**36**
	1. Goals	**37**
	2. Grammatical Structures	**38**
	3. A Sample Grammar Sequence	**44**
	4. Sounds and Pronunciation	**47**
	5. Words, Words, Words ...	**49**
	Workshop Activities	**50**
	B. Language Skills	**51**
	1. Goals	**52**
	2. The Listening and Speaking Skills	**56**
	3. The Reading and Writing Skills	**58**
	4. Planning a Reading Program	**59**
	5. Combining the Language Skills	**64**
	Workshop Activities	**66**
Chapter	3. How: Making It Work in The Classroom	**68**
	A. Selecting the Approach	**70**
	1. The Inductive and the Deductive Approaches	**70**
	2. The Aural-Oral and the Cognitive Approaches	**72**
	Workshop Activities	**75**
	B. A Framework for Planning Activities	**75**
	1. Grammatical Structures	**76**
	2. Pronunciation	**83**
	3. Lexical Items	**87**
	4. Reading	**89**
	5. Writing	**100**
	Workshop Activities	**103**
Chapter	4. Where: Going Beyond the Textbook	**104**
	A. Teacher-Made Aids	**106**
	B. Programmed Instruction	**110**
	C. Instructional Television	**113**
	D. The Language Laboratory	**118**
	E. The Multi-Media Classroom	**120**
	F. Assessing Achievement	**121**
	Workshop Activities	**124**

PART TWO   INTERMEDIATES AND ADVANCED   **127**

Chapter   5. Who: Refocusing on the Learner   **128**

A. The Learner in a Social Context   **130**
1. Societal Goals   **131**
2. School Goals   **133**
3. Student Goals   **135**
Workshop Activities   **136**

B. Accounting for Individuals   **136**
1. Diagnosing Levels   **137**
2. Modes of Learning   **141**
3. Individualized Instruction   **145**
Workshop Activities   **148**

Chapter   6. What: Language Matter Grows in Complexity   **150**

A. Developing Grammatical Sensitivity   **152**
1. Selecting the Grammatical Contents   **153**
2. Interference and Interlanguage   **154**
3. Giving Explanations   **157**
4. The Textbook Is for Reference   **157**
5. Important Grammatical Topics for This Level   **158**
Workshop Activities   **163**

B. Unfolding Broader Facets of Meaning   **163**
1. Contextual Meaning   **164**
2. Situational Meaning   **168**
3. Lexical Meaning   **169**
4. Paraphrase and Meaning   **171**
5. Social Meaning   **173**
Workshop Activities   **175**

C. Enlarging the Scope of the Language Skill Areas   **175**
1. Expanding Each of the Skills   **177**
2. Linking the Skills in New Relationships   **178**
Workshop Activities   **181**

Chapter   7. How: If It Works, Use It   **182**

A. One Step at a Time   **184**
1. The Organic Plan   **185**
2. The Facilitator and the Learner Share Responsibilities   **186**

     3. Steps in the Intermediate Level Plan   188
     4. Steps in the Advanced Level Plan   189
   Workshop Activities   190

   B. Our Greatest Resource   190
     1. The Radio and the Tape Recorder   191
     2. TV and Motion Pictures   194
     3. Newspapers, Popular Magazines,
        Paperbacks   196
     4. Pop, Rock, and Folk Music   198
   Workshop Activities   200

   C. Language Is for Communication: Talking
      within the Classroom   201
     1. Activities for Reacting   202
     2. Activities for Interacting   206
     3. Activities for Sharing and Discussing   211
     4. Activities for Improvising   215
   Workshop Activities   220

   D. Broader Opportunities for Communica-
      tion   220
     1. Talking Outside of the Classroom   221
     2. A Unit for Everywhere   223
   Workshop Activities   225

Chapter   8. Where: The Facilitator Reaches Out 226

   A. Involving Other People   228
     1. Team Teaching   228
     2. Cross-Age Tutoring   230

   B. Shopping for Textbooks   231
     1. Vital Statistics   232
     2. Audience   232
     3. Language Structure and Language
        Skills   233
     4. Pedagogical Principles   233

   C. Helpful Information   234
     1. Publications   234
     2. Professional Organizations   235
   Workshop Activities   236

Epilogue   **236**

Bibliography   **237**

Index   **241**

INTRODUCTION

Clearing
the
Air

All of the political, economic, and social trends of this century indicate that our world will continue shrinking in the coming decades. People travel farther, migrate more frequently, and interact wih greater numbers of strangers than ever before in the history of mankind. As communication distances diminish, world languages become more necessary. English has risen rapidly as a leading world language during the past forty or fifty years; all predictions point to its growth as a shared language among people in many parts of the world.

English, of course, is the first language of people in numerous places beyond its home ground in Great Britain and North America. But in countries where people acquire other languages first, the need for adding English as a communicative tool is widely recognized as a necessity of modern life. With this developing world-wide audience for English language instruction, the numbers of trained people who will be required to fill language teaching positions are bound to keep on increasing.

Of the English language teachers today, many have themselves learned English subsequent to the language which they first acquired as very young children, at home within the family. Others, native speakers of English, may or may not have shared this experience of learning a new language either in childhood or adulthood. But all teachers, native and non-native speakers of English, frequently ask similar questions about language and about methods of language instruction.

This corps of practitioners includes people who are in colleges, universities, and other institutions of higher learning preparing for teaching careers. It includes seasoned teachers, people who want to broaden their background and update their understanding of the field of language pedagogy. Frequently, too, experienced teachers move into the job of English instructor after specializing in other languages. In the United States, many workers in bilingual education programs are faced with new responsibilities as teachers of ESL (English as a second language). English language teaching takes place on the para-professional level as well as through instruction offered by means of individual tutoring. Nor is it unknown for a motivated, adult language learner to want to gain an analytical understanding of the second language learning process.

The varied settings for English language teaching include learners of all ages, from children who first enter school at age five or six to adults who must make their way in a new culture with a new language. Although teachers often seem to focus their interests on one particular group, there are enough shared problems at all levels of language pedagogy to warrant the primary teacher's attention to adult needs and vice-versa. At the same time, despite the diversity among the groups of English language teachers and learners there are still a number of common questions and uncertainties voiced by all. Some of these questions are asked by both native-speaker and non-native-speaker teachers. Other queries reflect the special concerns of one group or the other.

A. BASIC QUESTIONS WHICH PUZZLE MANY LANGUAGE TEACHERS

The field of language teaching has developed markedly in the past two or three decades. One reason for this growth has been the great activity in all disciplines which study human language. Many fields have contributed to our increasing appreciation of the tremendous complexity of all languages. In recent years, English has been a primary target for scholarly research by linguists, psychologists, and other social scientists. But too frequently teachers must make their way through elaborate claims and counter-claims put forth by technical specialists. It is no wonder that many are left puzzled by the esoteric debates which have characterized a good deal of the professional literature in the field.

Is there a difference between ESL and EFL? Why are these two terms used? Do they refer to different types of language instruction?

The terms ESL (English as a second language) and EFL (English as a foreign language) are sometimes used to differentiate between the teaching of English as a subject area alone (EFL) as contrasted with the teaching of English as a language along with its use as a medium of instruction (ESL). It is important to realize, however, that the terms do not represent any real conflict as far as language pedagogy is concerned.

To further blur the contrast between ESL and EFL, many people use the expression "second language" when English is considered a language of widespread use in a particular country, even though in the schools it is taught as a foreign language and is not used to instruct in other subject areas. Another aspect of the confusion over the terms arises in places where English is a "second" language in terms of its use as a world language, but it may be the third or fourth language learned by the people of that particular country. In India, speakers of Bengali, Gujerati, or Tamil, for example, must also learn Hindi at school, the country's second or national language. In Ethiopia children study the national language, Amharic (often not the child's mother tongue), and English as well. In ordinary references English is often spoken of as a vital "second" language, in India and Ethiopia, as well as other places.

Is there one best method for teaching English as well as other languages? Is there a right and a wrong method?

A belief in the existence of one, best method is based on pure myth—an unfortunate fact for those who look for easy paths to quick success. Language is so interwoven with so many facets of human life, the needs and goals of learners of a new language are so diverse, and all languages present such differences in their surface structure that the only one-best-method is to put aside forever the idea that one approach can ever be found which will answer every problem in every situation.

Fortunately for teachers today there is a palette of approaches to sample, the result of cyclical attention over the decades to one or another of various doctrines in language pedagogy. But the researchers in the field have yet to produce formulae which will provide teachers with computerlike answers for all possible circumstances. The best faith for a teacher is to believe in his or her own ability to make decisions based on a sound acquaintanceship with as many approaches as possible, and by becoming familiar with as many sources of materials as possible. In the final analysis, it can be a teacher's option to fit the approach and the materials to a particular set of student and societal needs and goals.

Many teachers have discovered that by expanding their views of the nature of language and by expanding their understanding of how people learn and use language they are able to sharpen their abilities at making practical decisions in the classroom.

Why do language teaching methods seem to follow such fads? We had just convinced our education ministry that students should do more than read and translate Shakespeare in English courses. Now we've begun to hear that choral drilling is not the whole answer either.

If a student's goal is to learn to read and understand the writings of great literary artists such as William Shakespeare, then the grammar translation method is quite to the point. Students who sit through second and foreign language classes which focus on one particular skill, or one activity, learn just that one skill which they have spent hours practicing—if they are motivated to learn anything.

If students need to be able to communicate in English, if they need to interact with people whose native language is English, then they must work on listening-comprehension and speaking skills. Choral practice seems to be one useful activity which does give students in large classes an opportunity to practice speaking skills. However, this one activity alone is not sufficient to enable a second language learner to advance in an essential language skill—aural comprehension.

In recent times, too many language classes have spent quantities of time repeating sentences without giving enough consideration to whether or not the meaning of the message had been understood. Or even whether the meaning was vital enough to students' interests to have mattered to them in the least. Parrots, too, can listen and repeat. But human beings can listen, understand, and continue to create sentences of their own. A good motto for learning a new language might well be: listen/comprehend/communicate.

Why is there so much concern over methods of language teaching? Why don't we teach languages in a natural way, the way children learn their first language? All people seem to be able to learn their native language painlessly.

It is perfectly true that all human beings everywhere who have normal physiological and mental abilities learn their native language seemingly without effort. All that appears to be necessary to trigger the acquisition mechanism is exposure to human language. Further, it does not matter what type of society or culture a child is born into for first language development to take place because all human languages are alike in their essential properties. There are no simple or primitive languages spoken by human beings any place on this planet.

Recent research by psycholinguists has concentrated on neurophysiological aspects of language acquisition. The capacity for acquiring a communicative system as complex as human language seems to belong uniquely with the human species. Moreover, there is a strong innate, developmental character to the acquisition of first language. But there are very specific differences between the first language acquisition process and second language learning. For as vital and important as the understanding of how people everywhere learn their native language is for the field of language pedagogy, the two take place under very separate circumstances. Essentially, the second language and all subsequent languages are learned when the slate is no longer clean. The brain has already been imprinted with the code of the first language.

Second language courses which purport to teach in a natural way by recreating the conditions under which people learn their first language, hold out quite false claims for success. Human beings cannot turn back some sort of time machines in their heads and reproduce the circumstances under which first language acquisition took place.

Which of the language skills should receive the most prominence—listening, speaking, reading, or writing?

When literate people want to learn languages for communicative purposes, the skills of reading and writing definitely belong within the scope of language courses. (Remember, too, children in primary grades who can read in their native language are literate.) The specific course objectives determine whether or not the skills of reading and writing—one or the other or both—receive special attention. Students' needs and goals must always be considered first. For many learners, English is a medium through which to obtain access to information in specific areas of knowledge. This objective can often be carried out with the skill of reading alone, particularly if the student only has time to concentrate on reading skills.

Approaches which rigidly deny learners the opportunity to use their ability to read and write in their native language as aids in the process of learning a new language have serious limitations. Metaphorically speaking, why tie learners' hands behind their backs when you want them to touch their toes? By compartmentalizing language skills, the utility of using one skill in the practicing and strengthening of another is completely overlooked.

The slogan which emphasized as "natural" the sequence, listening-speaking-reading-writing failed, too, to realize the deeper meaning of listening. When listening is tied to comprehension and to understanding, then the essential cognitive function of language is brought into focus. Given this view of the listening skill, listening-comprehension and reading are linked to each other since they both represent language understanding at deep levels of cognition.

Newer approaches are pointing out that the productive language skills of speaking and writing mutually complement each other, just as listening-comprehension and reading are related. It is quite possible that language teaching texts in coming years will make more use of the link which connects the receptive skills of listening-comprehension and reading as opposed to the productive skills of speaking and writing.

What should be my primary responsibility as an instructor? Should I try to teach all of the grammatical structures?

In the majority of places in the world today where English language teaching takes place, a recognized goal is for learners to internalize the basic grammatical skeleton of English by controlled presentation of small chunks of useful phrases at a time. Vocabulary, too, needs to be carefully controlled so that learners are not overwhelmed by too many items to master all at once.

An important result of recent linguistic studies into the nature of language has been a new awareness on the part of teachers that they can feel more relaxed about the language matters which they present to learners. Linguistic research has brought forth a clearer appreciation of the tremendous complexity of language. All of a language can never be learned in a classroom, just as all of a language can never fit into a classroom textbook. Despite the great amount of work on the English language in recent years, there remain many subtle areas that have not been analyzed by linguistic scholars.

Is it considered poor practice to teach rules of grammar in second language courses?

Not in the least. Even primary school children need to be able to gain insights into the structures which are embedded in the language patterns presented for practice. For adults, the need to understand the systematic nature of language is even more important. For many years there was a certain stigma attached to the idea of teaching so-called grammar rules in language classes. This negative view came about as a result of at least two factors: (1) The traditional approach of the grammar-translation method often gave more attention to teaching rules than to helping people learn to speak and use a language. Obviously, good language pedagogy calls for both strategies. (2) The rules which too often had been taught in the context of English language pedagogy reflected usage rules or rules of language etiquette. They frequently dwelt on *do's* and *don'ts* which failed to reflect deeper, structural patterns in the language.

Recent emphasis in linguistic and psycholinguistic research into the cognitive function of language is enabling language teachers to understand the importance of having learners grasp both the meaning of new sentences in the target language and also the grammatical rules which the sentences illustrate. Rules are certainly called for in second language teaching. But they should be rules which reflect accurate, concise statements of how the processes of language operate.

Successful second language learners probably form their own rules based on accurate observations of the data which is presented to them. Being able to sense the structure of language, being able to see patterns and relationships—these qualities have a great deal to do with an individual learner's innate ability for adding second languages to his or her linguistic repertoire. Why not put this faculty to use in the teaching process?

If I have some ability to speak the students' first language, should I use it in the classroom?

The history of methodology has gone through drastic changes: there have been periods during which only the pupils' native language was spoken in the classroom (the grammar translation method) and periods where the native language was completely banned from the classroom (the direct method). The first approach, which did not expose the pupils to the spoken target language, resulted in a high level of proficiency in the literacy skills and often zero proficiency in the spoken language. From the experience of the opposite approach, however, the teacher who is not allowed to utter a word in the native language has to go to the greatest pains to explain words, expressions, and grammatical structures in the target language—often at the expense of true comprehension on the part of the pupil. Thus, after repeating a long list of sentences with the word "chalk," always demonstrating the object, a teacher found that half the class thought they were being taught the word "white." Wouldn't it have been simpler and safer to give the equivalent of the word "chalk" in the native language and then still continue the same amount of drilling and demonstration but this time with full comprehension by the pupils?

How then is the teacher to make a useful decision as to when to use the native language and when to use the target language only? The best policy is the use of "common sense." Let us always remember that precious classroom time should be devoted almost totally to the target language so as to provide maximum exposure to that language. Therefore, the lesson must always be conducted in the target language. However, there is no good reason to forbid the use of the native language when this can simplify or clarify matters. To explain a difficult lexical item or a complex grammatical rule, it may be much more economical to use the native language. In fact, trying to limit oneself to the target language may really waste time and cause lack of clarity. Pupils should be guided to use the target language all the time, but when the native language is more economical and safe it should be allowed.

B. QUESTIONS FREQUENTLY ASKED BY NATIVE SPEAKERS ABOUT ENGLISH LANGUAGE TEACHING

Is it an easy assignment? No, simply by knowing a language because it was the first one to be acquired does not necessarily mean that a person can easily teach it to others. Aside from classroom skills per se, providing instruction regarding a language which we know natively can be a difficult and frustrating experience. It's so hard to slow down, to realize that we are crowding in too much—and the answer does not lie in just slowing down our rate of speaking. For by doing so we sound unnatural and are distorting the language which we are trying to teach. No matter how hard we try, English seems like the air we breathe. We take it for granted until we have to try to teach it to someone else.

What is the difference between teaching "English," which all students take throughout elementary and secondary school, and ESL? Can I easily move into ESL teaching from a background in "English" and "Language Arts"?

When children who have grown up in English-speaking homes first enter kindergarten at age five or first grade at age six, they have already mastered a large part of the sound system and most of the basic grammatical structures of their native language. So, in fact, have children everywhere, no matter what language environment they happen to be born into. The primary task of the elementary school is to teach literacy—reading and writing—to those children who already *know* the English language. The same is clearly not the case for the ESL student. In ESL instruction, at no time can the teacher assume that the student understands the content of the lesson when it is presented in English only.

Another goal in language-arts programs for native speakers is to foster an increased sensitivity to language through exposure to literature. But here again, the content of the curriculum for children who know and who use automatically the complex systems which make up the grammar of the language can in no way be the same as the curriculum for ESL. Learning to speak clearly, to convey ideas, to use language for self-expression—all of these objectives of language arts are for ESL students like working on the tenth decimal point before they have even mastered the first one. Beginning ESL students need to assimilate a small amount of language at a time, basic sentences, questions, responses. They need a great deal of practice using vocabulary which is related to their everyday life and needs.

Undoubtedly, English teachers in both the lower grades and in secondary schools who have an interest in the forms and structure of language can, with training, become excellent ESL teachers as well. But since the training and college preparation of English teachers has traditionally been heavily slanted in the direction of literature, with here and there a composition course, considerable re-tooling is often necessary. Only in recent years have four-year colleges and universities been able to offer course work in the structure of the English language or in general linguistics directed at prospective teachers' interests.

Public school administrators would do well to look to the foreign language teachers on their staffs as potential talent for ESL assignments. These people are already sophisticated in some of the techniques of language pedagogy. Most important, they see themselves as *language* teachers. They are professionally equipped to look at language analytically and structurally. They have some first-hand experience in the painful process which all second language learning entails and they are likely to have cultural empathy with students who come from other parts of the world and from non-English speaking backgrounds.

How does bilingual education fit into the ESL curriculum?

Today, more and more communities are becoming aware of the special language needs of newcomers. The most dynamic trend in ESL within the United States has been a growing acknowledgment of the advantages of bilingual education. In no way is bilingual education an approach which is contrary to ESL. Rather, the two are simply part of the larger field of second language pedagogy. But in those places where a bilingual-bicultural approach has been adopted, there is a belief that the first language can serve as an important link through which to gain competence in the new language. Bilingual education is an important development in the United States because it recognizes the benefits of maintaining a pluralistic society. A pluralistic society is one which recognizes the need of people to feel pride and respect for their first language and culture.

In the early 1960's, Dade County, Florida, experimented with one of the first bilingual education programs to accommodate the large inflow of children from Cuba. Since that time, the right of children to be schooled in their mother tongue has been legislated by Congress into law in the Bilingual Education Act of 1968 and affirmed by the U.S. Supreme Court in a case involving non-English-speaking Chinese children in San Francisco (Lau v. Nichols). Most bilingual education programs are to be found in the elementary school grades today. However, the trend is beginning to reach into secondary schools as well.

Our attention has focused too in recent years on the barrier language represents in limiting success in school for sizeable groups of native-born American children. For there are significant numbers of people, members of ethnic groups in the United States, who speak a language other than English in the home. For example, the thousands of American Indian children, particularly in the southwest; Mexican-American children, many of whom live in the western states; Puerto Rican children in eastern cities; and Eskimo children in Alaska. When many minority group children enter school, they must use a new language together with acquiring the dominant culture's modes of learning and behaving. That large numbers of American children from minority groups are not receiving equal educational opportunities is reflected in the fact that so many do not graduate from secondary school, let alone go on to higher education.

English has always seemed like such an inconsistent language. I've often heard people say that it has no grammar.

It is a widespread misconception among native speakers and a very false one that "English has no grammar." The notion is usually based on a misunderstanding of what "grammar" means. The model of grammar which some people look for in all languages is the one which grammarians 100 years ago, and for hundreds of years before that, used for describing Latin. This model, or outline of what to look for in a language, fortunately fits pretty well for French, Italian and Spanish, which, of course, are descendants of Latin.

Experts today who write technical descriptions of languages (e.g., linguists), use entirely different and much more sophisticated models of linguistic description. During the past few decades a tremendous amount of research effort has been concentrated on the English language with the result that some very excellent technical grammars of aspects of English are available. These are of significant value in the preparation of materials for teaching ESL. English certainly has a grammar, or native speakers could not talk with each other.

Another misunderstanding has to do with what it means to "know" a language. All human beings know their native or mother tongue. They use it effectively without being conscious of how it works. However, it takes a different kind of knowing to be able to take that language apart and look at it analytically. It does fall under the ESL teachers's responsibility to be able to talk about how the English language works—though not all the time! It is both a fascinating and a challenging experience for native speakers to learn about the processes which operate in their own language. But the experience takes time and effort. For that reason, ESL teachers should have courses that study the structure of the English language, its phonology, morphology, and syntax, as well as courses in semantic change and history of the English language.

Is it necessary to know the learner's first language in ESL teaching? How can a teacher manage a class which is made up of people from many language backgrounds?

Experience and realism in ESL teaching indicate that in both the United States and Great Britain it is more likely the case that classes will be composed of students who come from a variety of language backgrounds. This is true in all levels of ESL instruction. In fact, most textbooks for ESL are designed for speakers of all languages. But in these typical classes of many language backgrounds, it is still the responsibility of the teacher to seek out information about the specific language backgrounds represented in the group. This information helps the teacher understand some of the errors which students tend to make.

Although the ideal may seem to be the class made up of one language background, there are some positive values in mixed language classes. One such advantage is that the students must use English to communicate among themselves. Wise teachers, after students have become acquainted with class procedures, suggest that students who speak the same first language should not sit next to each other.

C. NON-NATIVE SPEAKERS ASK:

I feel a great disadvantage when I compare myself with a teacher who is a native speaker. Is this feeling justified?

Native speakers teaching their own language to pupils who don't know that language have a very important advantage: using the language which they teach comes naturally to them. What they say is always "correct" even if they can't explain why. What they say provides the "perfect" model for their pupils and they can always tell those students, "Listen carefully to the way I say it." This advantage of the native speaker becomes the biggest disadvantage of non-native speakers—they themselves can never be a perfect model; they must constantly check and question. But this is most probably the only significant disadvantage the non-native speaker has. From here on, most of the other differences will be advantages rather than disadvantages.

Native speakers know their language very well, but they are not conscious of "what" it is that they know. They have probably never stopped to question various structures or ways of expressing things in their own language since these have always come naturally to them. When they are faced with the problem of teaching a particular structure or form in their language to people who don't know the language, they do not even realize what difficulties are involved in learning that structure. Obviously most native speakers of English are aware of the difficulty in learning the irregular forms of verbs in the past, since many can remember having been corrected in the use of these forms as children. But the same native speakers may not be aware of the fact that the following three uses of the question word "what" may turn out to be three different words in another language: "What is this?", "What are you eating?", "What color is your shirt?".

In many ways, the non-native speaker has a great advantage over the native speaker. Non-native speakers have learned to question and investigate every teaching element since they are never entirely sure that they know the right answer. By questioning and investigating language forms they are, in fact, doing their own, though limited, linguistic work. Constant questioning and investigating come naturally to the non-native speaker but require careful learning on the part of the native speaker. Native speakers must train themselves to question and look into structures and grammatical forms that they take for granted in their own language. The effective language teacher, whether a native or non-native speaker, must be "a bit of a linguist" at heart. Both must try to analyze every topic of language that is presented to pupils as part of the new language course.

Another important advantage that the non-native speaker may have, although this may not occur in every instance, is knowing the pupils' first language very well (often being a native speaker of that language). Knowing the pupils' first language is very important especially in a situation where the learners form a homogeneous group. It can save considerable time and effort during the teaching process if the teacher truly understands the way in which pupils use similar structures in their first language. This knowledge is, however, not limited to linguistic features only but should include an understanding of the pupils' culture. The native speaker who teaches a homogeneous group of learners must make the effort to learn the pupils' first language or at least find out as much as possible about the structure of that language. To a certain extent this can and should be done for a heterogeneous group of learners as well. The language teacher must try to find out as much as possible about each of the native languages and respective cultures of all the various pupils. Fortunately for the teacher of heterogeneous groups, knowing something about the structure of the student's language is an easier task than is having communicative facility in that language. Thus, many teachers know enough "about" the language to anticipate certain mistakes without actually speaking the language themselves.

Both the native and the non-native speaker have certain advantages and certain disadvantages when teaching language. The most important thing is for native speakers to learn to question each form and each expression in their own language and for non-native speakers to take full advantage of their understanding of the learning process, and their understanding of the difficult structures in the language that they teach. As for the model of pronunciation, non-native speakers can avail themselves of recorded material. Thus, teachers of both types can take full advantage of their own capabilities and improve themselves where they have certain disadvantages.

Which should I teach, British or American English? What are the main differences? Which will most students need to know?

Any teacher, whether a native speaker of English or not, if teaching in a non-English speaking environment, may have to ask this question. Thus, the native speaker of American English might be teaching in an African country with a British tradition and may have to ask "Should I teach my American English or should I force myself to teach British English?" The answer to the native speaker is always: "You must teach the kind of English that you speak natively but at the same time be aware of the differences." It may often be necessary to draw the pupil's attention to the differences. But what about the non-native speaker? What will the answer to this question be?

The decision as to which kind of English is to be taught depends primarily upon the needs of the society within which we teach. If the major need of that society is to "communicate" with the rest of the world and not necessarily with one particular English-speaking country, then it does not, in fact, matter whether we teach English as the British speak it or English as the Americans speak it, but rather a kind of English that all people will understand. In such a situation the societal goals may dictate some kind of American-British mixture that is sometimes called "Branglish" or "Mid-Atlantic English." If this is the case, the situation allows for using either American or British English interchangeably. There may, however, be need for certain practical decisions: for instance, should we teach the main verb "have" in its British or American form? Since the American form with "do" in the negative and interrogative is simpler than the British "have you ... ?" the decision may very well be to teach the American form which will be accepted by all speakers of English in the world and yet is easier to teach.

In such a situation, the teacher must be aware of both the American and the British dialect, and must know what decision has been arrived at by local authorities on each point of conflict. However, both the native and the non-native speaker must be aware of the differences.

Before we can make any methodological decisions as to American or British English, let us see how serious the differences really are. Let us refer specifically to differences in the following linguistic areas: grammatical structures, pronunciation, spelling, vocabulary. It will soon become clear that the least differences are to be found in the area of grammatical structures and the most in the area of vocabulary.

In the area of grammatical structures, it is easy to enumerate the major differences since they are not so many and not very serious. The most common difference between the two dialects has already been mentioned: in American English, "have" acts like any other regular verb taking "do" in negative and interrogative sentences while in British the equivalent form is "Have you a match?" In British English, the two forms of the negative have a slightly different meaning: "This shop hasn't any shirts" is understood as a permanent state—it doesn't carry shirts, versus "They don't have any shirts" which means that they are simply out of stock. Also, the use of "have got" is very common in Britain as in the following: "Have you got a match?" and "No, I haven't got any." The use of the present perfect aspect of the verb is much more frequent in British English than in American English. The use of noun compounds like "entry behavior" or "education ministry" which is very common in American is less common in British.

There are other less important points of differences in the area of grammar; for instance, linking verbs like "look, sound," etc., take only adjectives in American English. "She looks nice. This sounds good." But in British English these verbs are quite common with noun phrases as well: "She looks a nice person. It sounds a good idea." The American speaker would tend to insert the word "like" in such sentences to make it acceptable: "She looks like a nice person. It sounds like a good idea." Such minor differences do not interfere with communication and are of relatively little importance; however, all English teachers must be aware of these differences so as not to consider a form that is common in one of the dialects as "incorrect" simply because it does not happen to be common in their own dialect.

In the area of pronunciation, although the differences are more numerous than in the area of grammatical structures, they can be organized in useful groups. Words like: class, past, fast, are pronounced with an /æ/ in American but with /a/ in South British English. There are, however, other British dialects where the pronunciation of such words is like American pronunciation. Most words, however, having the letter a in medial position are pronounced with the vowel /æ/ in both American and British dialects: cat, cap, tan; and both dialects have /a/ in words like father, car, etc. The quality of these vowels might be slightly different in each of these two dialects, but this does not constitute a serious problem in communication. There are definite differences in vowel quality of the English back-low vowels between British and American and here teachers must definitely teach the dialect with which they feel most at home. What is important is to arrive at some sort of distinction between words like law, low and hot—since there are three different vowels in these words in both dialects.

Another well-known difference between American and British pronunciation is the post-vocalic /r/ which is fully pronounced in American but expressed as vowel lengthening in British: American /car/ becomes British /cah/. Perhaps the differences in intonation and word stress are the ones the layman picks up right away as "strange sounding" in the other dialect. A very common example of different word stress is the word "laboratory" which is pronounced in American as LABoratory and in British laBORatory, which shows a difference in the main stress but also illustrates a difference in the stress on the other syllables. The same word sounds, therefore, very different in the two dialects but except for being "strange," this would not interfere with communication. Sentence and question intonations have typically different nuances in the two dialects but again do not constitute serious differences.

In the area of spelling, there are a number of specific differences that can be listed easily. Words like labour, harbour, favour, colour, keep the u in British spelling but drop it in American spelling. Other examples of differences are traveled/travelled, center/centre, program/programme. The first item in each pair gives the American spelling which is obviously closer to the pronunciation of these words, a fact which is true about all differences in spelling between American and British spelling. American spelling is therefore basically simpler for the foreign learner but often for various reasons certain countries might still prefer British spelling.

In the area of lexical items and idiomatic expressions, the difference has to do with meaning and applicability of the item in question. This might cause misunderstanding or miscommunication. Most native speakers are aware nowadays of many of these differences, thanks to the mass media of communication in the world. Therefore, examples like elevator/lift, truck/lorry, napkin/serviette and other subtle differences are not very surprising to most people. There are, however, cases where miscommunication may result from rather different usage. When an American says "presently" he means "right now" for example, "He is presently employed." When a British speaker says "presently" he means "soon": as, "She is arriving presently."

The above listing of some of the differences between American and British English was given just as an example of the type of questions one might have to consider when deciding to teach American or British English. What methodological decisions can we make on the basis of such differences? Such decisions must also be suited to the level of the pupil's knowledge. Thus, the decision may be different for the beginner as opposed to the more advanced pupil. Let us assume that the country in which we are teaching has accepted some kind of a mixed version of American and British English as the language that they are aiming for. This is a decision taken by the educational authorities and implemented by the teacher in the classroom. But what about the learner? How soon should he be alerted to the problem? Obviously the beginner should not concern himself with differences between dialects. In fact, the materials used in the classroom, as well as the teacher's presentations, should adhere more or less to an accepted norm of a mixed dialect. However, as the pupils progress in their knowledge of English, they need to be made aware of the two main dialects. Whenever the opportunity arises, the differences should be pointed out to them. Thus, the pupils will have less difficulty in reading with comprehension both American and British literature, which is often the overall objective of teaching English in many countries.

In any event, the most important factor in any kind of decision-making concerning the British and American dialects is awareness of these differences so that no teacher or examiner will mark an accepted form as incorrect or tell the pupil that one dialect is better than the other. On the other hand, the learner must share the responsibility of knowing some of these differences so that he will not confuse differences between dialects with ungrammatical forms due to interference from his own language, and excuse his own mistakes by pinning them on to "the other dialect."

I am not always sure of my own pronunciation, but I am very fluent in English. Is it all right for me to be the only model in the classroom?

The English-speaking world comprises such a variety of dialects that a pupil who has been exposed to only one model might find it rather difficult to communicate with speakers of various other dialects. It is important to expose the learner to a variety of dialects, if possible. Today audio-visual materials, tapes, records, radio programs, and other such facilities can bring different types of speakers into every classroom. This exposure to various speakers of English is important in any classroom situation, but is invaluable in a class where the teacher is not a native speaker of English.

In spite of the facilities that the non-native speaker can take advantage of, it is never too late to work on the improvement of one's own pronunciation. A pronouncing dictionary should be a constant companion for the teacher of English who is not a native speaker. Such a dictionary is invaluable in providing the teacher with correct word stress and vowel quality. Often words are mispronounced by non-native teachers not because of language interference but because of a false idea based on pronouncing a word in the way in which it is spelled.

It is important that young beginners be exposed to native speech whenever possible. Effective teachers who are not sure of their own pronunciation will not hesitate to tell the pupils to imitate the model on the tape rather than themselves. This can gain the teacher only real respect. It will allow teachers to be freer with their own speech in the classroom even if they know they are not near-native. They will know that the pupils accept their speech and yet have ears open for any native models available.

My students are only interested in learning to read the target language. Why should I spend time on grammatical rules, structure drills, and pronunciation practice?

It is true that in many courses students in their last years of study feel that the only thing they want to concentrate on is the skill of reading for comprehension. In many countries in the world this is the most urgent need for all students—ability to read texts in English. Modern methodology today believes that even students whose final aim is reading for comprehension would do better in the end if they have done sufficient work in grammatical structures and aural-oral skills throughout the entire course of study. The ability to understand the natural flow of the foreign language in either spoken or written form requires considerable competence on the part of the learners even if they never have to utter one word, but it takes time to achieve this degree of competence. The only way to help pupils reach a high level of proficiency in reading for comprehension is to also help them acquire a recognition grammar.

What role does literature play in the teaching of a new language?

The teaching of literature should never become an aim in itself in the foreign language course of study. It usually constitutes a certain stage of progress reached by the advanced learner. At that point, literature is just a vehicle. In fact, it is only one of various media which are available for practicing the full use of the new language. Literary criticism and analysis are the aim of literature courses given at the university level but should not be the aim of the foreign language course of study, even if often they might be pleasant by-products.

PART
ONE

BEGINNERS
AND THOSE
BEYOND

1

WHO

The
Learner
Comes
First

OVERVIEW

People have always looked for magic paths to quick success. Early explorers looked for a so-called fountain of youth, a potion that would ensure everlasting life. Similarly, teachers have viewed "method" as the magic word which would solve problems encountered in the classroom. If we could only find the right method, one that would catch hold and start growing, our job would be accomplished, they have felt. More often than not, this endless search for a single solution to a highly complex phenomenon has overlooked the most fundamental component—the learner.

Too often the learner in the teaching process has been either ignored, as though language existed outside of people, or taken for granted, as a captive audience. In more recent years, however, the spotlight has focused more and more on the learner. Today we are coming to realize that the student is central to the teaching process. Both WHAT, or subject content, and HOW, or technique, must be adapted to the needs of WHO, the learner. The key to facilitating language learning is to begin with the learner's needs. The quest is not to look for a single, elusive method but rather to help students discover ways to learn by themselves.

The nature of language affects the needs and potentialities of beginning learners in specific ways. Nor are all beginning learners the same. For that reason differentiation has been made in this chapter between children as beginning language learners and adult beginners. The first two sections of this chapter (pages 20-30) deal with the learner who is a young person, while the third one (pages 30-33) is devoted to adult beginners.

A. THE LEARNER IN THE CLASSROOM

The setting in which people are exposed to new languages is vitally significant. Therefore, our discussion of the beginning learner starts by viewing the actual location where language teaching takes place. Are all classrooms the same? Not at all. The most striking contrast lies between the modern classroom and the traditional classroom. The learner as an individual is affected by this difference.

1. The Traditional Classroom

A traditional classroom is one in which a number of pupils sit in rows facing the teacher. The teacher stands near a chalkboard and a desk. The desk is often an elevated podium to allow a better view of the whole class. From this position, the teacher is involved most of the time in the delivery of a "frontal" lesson. The pupils have very little opportunity of moving around in the room, and they remain seated in their places for most of the lesson. Some have the advantage of seeing and hearing the teacher simply because they are lucky enough to sit up front. Others find it much more difficult to concentrate or feel involved in any real sense since physically they feel more remote and removed from the teacher.

In the traditional classroom, a lot of teaching is carried out every minute of the lesson, but much less learning is possible. Discipline problems are quite apparent. The good and inventive teacher must resort to a variety of techniques to ensure the attention of the pupils. Suitable aids can be of tremendous help. It is, in fact, in this traditional classroom in which the physical conditions are constrained that the teacher will need a considerable amount of ingenuity in order to act as a facilitator of the learning process. Since in most communities of the world the modern classroom will be slow in arriving, it is of vital importance that teachers develop ways to cope with the more conventional setting. Interim solutions are desirable in order to encourage a shift towards facilitating language learning.

2. The Modern Classroom

If we are fortunate to live in a neighborhood where the modern classroom is already an accepted feature, we can probably visit one quite easily. The room is large and bright. It is filled with an atmosphere of warmth. The long rows of tables and chairs are gone. Instead, we notice groups of children in various parts of the classroom, all busy with special projects of their own. The furniture and its placement in the classroom are suited to group and to individual work. Some pupils seem to be interacting together while others are working by themselves. But where is the teacher? Is there actually a teacher in this classroom? Probably not, in the traditional meaning of this word. There is obviously no main desk and nobody is standing in front of rows of desks telling everybody what to do. Instead, we soon discover an individual walking around among the pupils, stopping to encourage one, praising another, and guiding a third. The whole classroom buzzes with the sounds of busy people working.

To the visitor it may seem that no teaching is taking place. In fact, this might be an accurate appraisal in a stereotyped way of looking at classrooms. In the modern classroom, although less teaching is going on, yet much more learning is taking place. The *teacher* (in the old sense of the word) has truly disappeared and has been replaced by a *facilitator* of the learning process. Instead of a chorus conductor leading a whole group, we now observe a room filled with actively engaged individuals, some working alone, others in pairs, or small groups.

The above is a rather idealized description of the modern classroom, one which is not yet commonplace anywhere in the world. It will require considerable funds, increased social awareness, and a period of time to make this the typical classroom. In most parts of the world, the traditional classroom still prevails.

3. The Individual Learner

The teacher in the traditional classroom has very little opportunity to consider the individual learners within the class. Obviously good and devoted teachers have always been aware of, and receptive to, the needs of individuals, but the size and the type of classroom within which they teach force them to make decisions that will be best for the majority of the pupils. The teacher in this situation must view the class as a whole rather than in terms of this or that individual pupil. The teacher must inevitably choose to teach at the expense of the very good as well as the very weak pupils. This approach, which advocates directing the lesson to the average, has been greatly attacked in recent years. Yet as long as the physical conditions do not change, there are only limited remedies available to us.

The modern classroom as described above has evolved out of a need to solve the problems of the traditional classroom. But since it requires more teachers per pupil, more space, more equipment, and more material, all of which require considerable time and budget, it is imperative to find short-range solutions. In other words, it will be our responsibility in the next decade to gradually turn our traditional classrooms into modern classrooms. Special teaching materials and additional time will have to be devoted to the weaker pupils in the large classroom. Different and more challenging materials will have to be provided for the better pupils who can do more work on their own. More attention will have to be given to interaction and group work within the regular classroom. Thus, the teacher can become a facilitator even within the regular classroom.

Many inexpensive and simple solutions are available to the creative teacher teaching in the traditional classroom. Thus even in a classroom where pupils sit in four rows facing the teacher, it is easy to create groups in a matter of seconds. Two desks or four tables are turned around and groups of four pupils are created. This allows work in small groups for at least part of the lesson. Each group is given an assignment and the teacher has time to walk around and facilitate the work in each group.

Another interim solution for the traditional classroom is to break away from the regular system at least periodically. Thus the facilitator may decide to have an individualized type of lesson at least once a week. If individual assignments and materials are carefully prepared, this can become a very useful activity even in the largest classroom. Ideas and ways of introducing the individualized lesson into the language course are discussed in greater detail in Part Two. Many of these ideas could be easily adapted to the needs of beginners.

In large overcrowded classrooms, it is vitally important to discover those small elements that can help each of the pupils feel that the lesson carries a personal message. There are many physical features of the classroom which can help make it a pleasant and warm place. The colors of the walls and the decorations can create either a gray and dreary feeling or a lively and inviting atmosphere. Even in a school where the financial possibilities are very limited, one can find simple ways of changing things. Posters, pictures, and postcards are vital. If the pupils are involved in collecting and preparing these decorations, so much the better. Perhaps the most valuable result of involving students in such effort is the fact that even the weakest one can contribute, and by doing so feel successful. Creating a hobby corner, a news corner, and other similar features can help individuals feel that they really belong.

A very common problem encountered by language teachers in many parts of the world is the fact that they are the ones who move from classroom to classroom. Since they have no permanent place, it is difficult for them to develop suitable classroom environments. Wherever possible the language teacher should strive to obtain a regular classroom which the pupils come to associate with their study of English. In this "English" room the language teacher is able to assemble an assortment of aids: pocket charts, felt-boards, posters, a tape recorder with a set of tapes, simplified materials, journals, books, etc. Thus the language classroom becomes an inviting meeting place which the pupils enjoy. When all the aids are at hand, teachers find that they utilize them more frequently and more effectively. With a little bit of ingenuity, the teacher can create a better classroom environment even in the traditional situation.

WORKSHOP ACTIVITIES

1. Imagine that you are teaching English in a non-English-speaking environment. You have just been assigned a room of the traditional type to use as a special English classroom. The school principal suggested that you use the basic furniture, forty desks and chairs, with a special desk

for the teacher. You have been told to ask for any additional furniture that you may need. Here is the plan of your classroom.

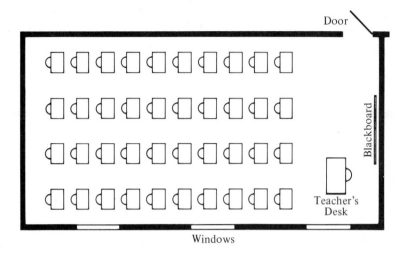

A Traditional Classroom

(a) How will you organize the seating arrangement for forty pupils? (You will be teaching three classes—first through third years.)
(b) What aids would you like to have in your classroom?
(c) What additional furniture do you need?
2. You are teaching two different classes in the same school—each class meets five hours per week on five different days. You always go to the classroom where the pupils have all their other lessons. What can you do to make the classroom environment more appealing to your pupils during the language lesson?

B. THE YOUNG BEGINNER

If the learning of the new language takes place in a non-English speaking environment, the young person usually learns the new language as a school subject. Adult beginners, however, often take foreign language courses because they are motivated to move to another country, to obtain a higher degree, or to improve their job opportunities. The adult beginner is typically motivated to acquire the new language quickly and effectively. The young beginner, on the other hand, needs to be motivated.

Both young and adult beginners face a different situation if the learning process takes place within an English-speaking environment. Here, both learners are highly motivated since they need the new language desperately in order to communicate with people in their immediate environment: the adult beginner needs to find a job, go shopping, rent an apartment, or succeed in school, while the young beginner wants to make friends, understand the jokes that others laugh at, join a game on the playground, and understand the teachers at school. But even in an English-speaking setting, there is a difference between the adult and the young beginner. The adult learner tends to rely more on the ESL class to acquire the new language than does the young person. The young beginner will become near-native in a relatively short period of time while the adult learner will have to work hard at it for a long time.

Language learning for young people is typically *not* a voluntary experience. For this reason, this section focuses on the motivational needs of young beginners. Young beginners are seriously affected, too, by pressures from the outside. These pressures can either stimulate or impede their success in the classroom. The pupil who works with a private tutor also comes with personal needs which must be taken into account within the program of instruction.

1. Within the School System

Most young beginners learn the new language in school. This essential fact profoundly affects the learner's attitudes toward the course, since all school systems possess certain limiting factors along with some advantages. Perhaps the most limiting factor that the school imposes upon the learner is the course itself. The average learner views most school subjects as something which "I am studying only because I have to. Someone else decided that I must study this subject." This factor can seriously interfere with the students' desire and interest in learning.

Another limiting factor is the environment itself, the classroom. Especially when we consider what language really is, the classroom is far from an ideal setting for learning. Further, there is only one language teacher in the classroom and so only one person to model the new language. The language course is far more effective if it extends beyond the classroom, if pupils can continue using the language in the outside world, at the supermarket, at the theatre, or on the playground. But this can only happen when the new language is learned in its own setting.

The school course, on the other hand, provides the learners with very important advantages. First, there is an expert on hand to guide them in the learning process. Moreover, this expert has numerous facilities available to make the learning more effective. Then, too, there are other learners, peers who are coping with the same tasks. The interaction that takes place between the learners during the course is of great importance. The element of competition also helps some learners overcome their natural inhibitions and take a more active part in the lesson. A supportive classroom atmosphere can help the reticent pupil feel less discouraged when the things he or she says sound funny or do not come out right, since that person is not the only one going through the process of language practice.

It is therefore the responsibility of the facilitator to find ways to counterbalance the limiting elements imposed by the school system, to turn the advantages into truly beneficial factors. Thus, ways must be found to motivate and interest the learner in the subject matter in spite of the fact that the course is required by the school. Ways must be found to extend the language experience beyond the classroom even in a non-native language environment. Further discussion and elaboration of such possibilities are taken up in Part One, Chapter Four, WHERE.

2. Peer, Parental, and Societal Pressures

The young learner's attitude toward the language course is often shaped by the pressures applied by peers, parents, or society. Negative and fearful experiences can affect the entire learning process. Only by understanding what pressures our learners are subjected to, can we develop suitable ways of dealing with their attitudes toward the language course. The learners' attitude should be of great concern to the facilitator since often it can provide the key to a successful course.

Here is an example of how peers can exert pressure on the learner. Little Jeana who was in fourth grade was starting a new school year. The new subject in the fourth grade class was English. Jeana liked to listen to English on television and to English-speaking tourists who visited her town. She was excited that she would finally learn English at school. She eagerly looked forward to this new school subject. Jeana was lucky that she was going to study English in the first open classroom that her school had established. All these factors seemed to promise Jeana a good start in the new language course.

At the end of the first school day, Jeana met her older sister who was in sixth grade. Jeana wanted to tell her sister how wonderful her first English lesson had been and how much she enjoyed her new subject, English. But one of the older boys was talking about his own experience with the English subject. Jeana was listening carefully: "Our English teacher is very tough. The lesson is boring. There is a lot of homework and too many tests. I just hate English."

After hearing what he had said and watching the other children agreeing with the speaker wholeheartedly, Jeana wasn't sure anymore that she wanted to tell her sister about her own experience with English. In fact, by the time she reached home she was ready to tell her mother how much she herself disliked English. Jeana's whole attitude to the language course had changed under the influence of peers, in spite of the promising start she had made.

Derek was another fourth grader in Jeana's class. He was also going to begin his new subject—English. Before the beginning of the school year, his father had a little talk with him. He tried to explain that English was a very important subject, that it was important to get good grades in the subject.

"Listen very carefully to your English teacher. Be sure to do exactly what you are told. I want you to bring home good grades in English. You'd better be good in English or you will certainly get it from me."

With this rather mixed blessing from his father, Derek walked into his English classroom with a weight on his shoulders. He was overanxious and worried. He had already developed fear of failure even before his first encounter with the new subject. He was sure the teacher was there to fail him and make his life miserable.

Don was another fourth grader in the same school. Since English is considered a very important tool of communication in his country, Don received the same admonition from his parents that Derek had. His reaction however was very different. While Derek tried very hard to live up to his father's expectations, Don looked for other ways of coping with his anxiety and fear of failure. Instead of taking the risk of "failing," he decided to play the role of the "uninterested pupil." He avoided getting involved in the new subject matter. He tried to attract the teacher's attention by being mischievous. Often he simply ignored the English lesson altogether.

Thus all three beginners, Jeana, Derek, and Don, although they had had every chance of developing a good attitude toward the language course, were negatively influenced by outside pressures. Their success in and enjoyment of the course had been jeopardized. Their teacher would have to be very aware of these pupils' attitudes in order to find suitable approaches to them. One would have to find individual ways to gain these pupils' confidence in the teacher, in the course, and, mostly, in themselves.

The types of pressures described above are often found in places where the foreign language has high prestige or is an indispensable tool for social advancement. When societal pressures are great, they often affect the language teacher. The teacher under such circumstances feels insecure and haunted by the need to cover certain specified amounts of material. (This type of tension is similar to the pressure of "accountability" associated with the teaching of beginning reading to native speakers in English-speaking countries.) The result of putting pressure on the teacher is often transferred to the learners in the classroom. The learning atmosphere, instead of being warm and wholesome, can become strained and unpleasant.

It is the responsibility of all those involved to work toward the relief of such pressures since they are known to affect the learning process negatively. First and foremost it is the duty of the planners of the course to find ways of relieving some of the tension by formulating realistic objectives. However, the most crucial factor in the system remains the teacher in the classroom. If we learn to regard each small section of the course, each single classroom session as an entire unit on its own, we may be able to find simple ways of coping with the pressures. If our limited, daily aim is to provide the learners with a pleasant, encouraging, learning experience, if we can relax and act naturally, we have already won half the battle.

Throughout the HOW section in this text we try to suggest ways of dealing with these problems.

3. Motivation

Learning anything as a school subject raises the question of motivation and interest. Once school systems change so as to allow more individual choices, the question of motivation in general may lose some of its significance. But in the conventional classroom it is a very crucial factor. Why should young learners be interested in learning a foreign language? Even if we can establish the importance of the communicative goals—to converse with outsiders, to read books, to understand television programs—young beginners are a number of years away from achieving such goals and therefore it is hard to hold them out as motivators. Also, the fact that people who know English may be able to get better jobs is still so remote from the immediate interests of young learners that this fact alone cannot be used as a goal in the first few years.

Young learners in foreign language courses, on the other hand, feel more grown-up and important once they start the new language. It is this feeling of self-worth that we can make use of. Setting short-term goals within each lesson, getting each learner involved in the activity, pacing the action to make the time spent in class seem to pass quickly—all these techniques make it possible to arouse interest in the young beginner.

It will certainly not do much good to walk into a class of beginners and start the first lesson by telling the pupils how important it is to speak a foreign language. Giving a long-winded speech about the importance of foreign language learning will actually turn young minds away from the lesson. If, however, the teacher walks into the classroom and begins with "I am ..." or "My name is ..." and immediately gets the pupils to tell the same thing about themselves, a degree of motivation is immediately established. The need for doing well in the new activity and the wish to participate in the communal game will be sufficient motivation for this first lesson, especially if each pupil feels a certain degree of success in meeting the specific goals of the lesson itself.

All too often in a foreign language course the pupil faces constant failure rather than success. Too often it is the teacher's objective to make the pupils feel that unless "they work hard" they are not going to make it. Teachers who regard their pupils' efforts in this negative manner usually receive discouraging results. The reason is probably because they themselves have subtly discouraged their pupils.

The consideration of motivation and interest should be closely linked with a consideration of the young beginner's span of attention. Since the attention span is normally quite short at this age, it is important to vary constantly the activities in the classroom. Personal involvement, positive tension during the lesson, and constant reinforcement of self-worth are indispensable. No lesson should ever end without allowing each pupil to be involved in some real instance of communication. Even if the communication is limited to "My name is …" or "I have a new …," it carries great importance because it provides personal involvement. A truthful statement about oneself, even if it is the most obvious bit of information, is always relevant, provided of course it has not been repeated too often.

In order to maintain and reinforce the learner's feeling of self-esteem, it is necessary to plan language practice so that it is both challenging and easy. If the practice contains small steps at a time and the learner can come up with both a successful and creative response, then a feeling of personal achievement is promoted. Praise and encouragement by the teacher are invaluable at this point. A good response which is ignored may discourage while one that is rewarded by the teacher's approving glance or smile may go a long way. But even the best of practice can become monotonous. Therefore it is important to maintain a quick tempo during the drill. There should be no time lag between model and response and between response and reinforcement or correction. The teacher must help the pupils move quickly from one item to the next, allowing no distractions to interfere. Thus a quick tempo throughout the practice will provide positive tension—the pupils will anticipate the next step. By utilizing these techniques effectively, it is possible to create a more motivating atmosphere for language learning.

Considerations of motivation and interest go beyond classroom work per se. Homework assignments are a very important part of language learning. But both mechanical, unmotivated homework and free, creative assignments which require a much higher level of proficiency than the students possess at this level, endanger pupil morale: the first bores the student, the second defeats him. Homework assignments must therefore be suited to the learner's level of knowledge. If, for instance, learners have just been introduced to five new vocabulary items, to ask them to make sentences with these items would be to force them into situations where they cannot help making mistakes and feeling defeated. If, on the other hand, we present them with gradual steps that help them understand the meaning of each item more fully, then gradually they will be able to use the new words by themselves. But even the first, most controlled steps should provide a challenge, a point of interest so as not to bore pupils. Matching the item with a definition, selecting the closest meaning from a number of choices, and filling a slot in a relevant sentence are some of the many ways which can be interesting and yet controlled activities for using new words.

Another important consideration in assigning activities to pupils is suitability to individual inclinations. By utilizing a variety of materials we might be able to cater to different types of pupils. The more precocious learners should be guided to work which will allow room for being creative and thus give them a sense of accomplishment. Less creative learners should work with materials that are more controlled in nature and therefore have built-in measures of guidance. Programmed materials are particularly suited for learners who seek quick rewards and reinforcement at the same time.

4. Outside the School System: Private Classes and Tutors

School courses are the formal settings within which most young people learn a new language. Only when the learner happens to move into the native environment where the language is spoken is there an informal setting for language learning since, then, learning goes on wherever the language is spoken, not only in the classroom. Learners in formal settings are captive users of the language while in informal settings they use and learn language more freely. Often, however, learners turn to a formal setting of language learning outside the school system, and of their own free choice. Such formal courses might take the form of lessons offered by private teachers or courses given by private companies. In either case, although the learners entered the course voluntarily, they remain captive learners since the situation is still a formal one.

The adult learner usually takes such a course out of basic interest or specific needs: travelling abroad, enrolling in higher education, and the like. The young learner who seeks a private class or tutor may either be a pupil who had been failing in the language class given within the school system and therefore in need of remedial help from the outside, or a talented person who wants to improve his or her knowledge of the language even further. In some cases young learners actually begin their first experience with the new language in such private classes prior to the school program.

Pupils who come to a remedial course need help. They have already experienced failure with the language and may have developed a strong antagonism or fear toward it. Such learners have also lost confidence in their ability to learn the language. Whether encountered in a private course or in a private lesson, they need to be encouraged and reassured. The most important element will be to free these learners from the fear of failure. These are people who must regain self confidence and develop the feeling of being good language learners. The tutor or teacher in this case must find the best way to help each individual overcome the barrier that has grown because of past failure.

In order to gradually build up the pupil's self confidence, the private tutor or the course organizer must review the material taught in the language classroom at school. This material will have to be clad in different attire since no one likes to feel that he or she is going back over the same material again and again. Sometimes programmed materials which present each topic in a series of small steps with built-in corrections are suitable for this type of learner. Further information on programmed material is given in Chapter Four, WHERE.

The second type of learner is the one who seeks a course that will provide possibilities for improving one's ability to use the new language. This type of learner is very different in nature from any of those discussed so far. This person is someone who has had success with language learning and is highly motivated to continue to do so. This type of learner will cope gladly with the material and will benefit from the broadest exposure to various facets of language which the regular classroom leaves untouched. Thus, the main objective of the course for such a learner is exposure to the culture, history, and literature of the new language.

The private tutor who usually teaches one pupil at a time has, in a sense, an ideal situation since he or she can do with each pupil what that particular individual needs most. In a classroom, on the other hand, both types of learners mentioned above might be placed together in the same group. In this case, it is imperative that the teacher use a large variety of materials covering the same basic topics. For example, the teacher can choose and adopt materials for the pupils who need review and reinforcement and choose other material for the pupils who want to further their knowledge. Thus, although the whole class may be working on the same topic, each pupil receives different exercises. The task is not always an easy one, but if the teacher is aware of the problem and of the need for adaptation and selection of suitable materials, it can certainly be done.

WORKSHOP ACTIVITIES

1. Select one of the two topics given below, according to their suitability to your own situation.
   (a) Have you ever experienced some type of peer or parental pressure which influenced your learning of a new language? Share your personal experiences with the others in the group.
   (b) If you live in a non-English speaking country, choose two different types of schools, e.g., vocational/academic, or state/private. Find out what objectives each of these schools has in teaching English.
2. Select a grammar lesson from a beginning textbook which you are familiar with. How would you motivate the pupils' interest in the lesson in *one* of these three situations:
   (a) a heterogeneous class of over forty pupils
   (b) one bright private pupil
   (c) a group of five pupils who require remedial work

C. THE ADULT BEGINNER

Adult learners are very different from younger learners in several ways. They come to the language course to meet specific basic needs and interests. They have had previous experience with learning in general and possibly with some foreign language learning. They have gained considerable knowledge in the real world and, perhaps most important, they have probably paid for the course. All of these factors give the adult learner certain advantages and certain disadvantages.

The adult learner's need for the foreign language might be the pressure to move to a different language-speaking community, temporarily or permanently. The adult learner may also seek a language course simply in order to get to know new people. In any of these cases, the adult learner studies language because he or she has decided to do so rather than to fulfill a school requirement.

1. Motivation and Goals Are Already Established

Adults who decide to master another language have a vital factor working in their favor even before opening the textbook on the first day. These adult learners have already decided to try to add another language to their repertoire of communication skills. Whether they live outside of an English speaking country where they must seek out people to practice speaking with, or if they hear the language all around them in an English environment, they have established their own goals in relation to their own lives. This fact alone contributes to the special rewards which a teacher can expect to receive from working with typical adult beginners—they are usually motivated to work at the task of language learning. Adult beginners are often much more ready than young beginners to repeat the same sentence again and again— if they think that this kind of practice will bring them to their final goal faster. Sometimes, because they have already paid for the course, they just want to get their money's worth.

At the same time, adult beginners have unique requirements which must be met by the teacher. Adults frequently want to be free to learn through the ways which they know are best for themselves. They want to be able to use their own previous experiences with language learning; they do not want the teacher to tie their hands behind their backs with prohibitions and admonitions such as "don't look at your book . . . just listen." How limiting that prescription is for the person who has been learning by means of the printed page for years. Yes, adults need practice in listening and understanding the new language. But if they can learn through visual as well as aural cues, why cut off one channel just because the target at the moment happens to be listening comprehension? Wise teachers encourage adult learners to "close the book" only when they feel ready and comfortable in doing so. Some adults are never ready to give up visual clues from the printed page. Others will move in that direction if they see it as a goal in itself.

The presentation of basic structures in the new language must be made in lively, interesting themes—just as it is done for the young learner. However, the themes are different for the adult. Children ask for milk or ice cream. Adults order coffee or beer. Children play with animals and toys. Adults work and travel. Children talk about their mother, father, sisters, and brothers. Adults talk about cars, movies, books, and friends. The topics used with adults must reflect their knowledge of the world, of people, of behavior . . . . Even the most basic language structures can embody lively ideas about people and events.

Frequently, adults need vocabulary in English which is appropriate for their vocational or occupational needs. A skillful teacher can adapt materials by embedding the vocabulary required by the adult learner in basic structures. "I want a monkey wrench/a jack/a screwdriver." In some specific fields, medicine and hotel administration for example, conscientious teachers have compiled lists of useful terms appropriate to their particular students' needs. The ingenious teacher finds as many instances as possible to utilize specialized vocabulary within the context of basic structures.

By facilitating learning for the adults at their intellectual level, the teacher soon sees that adult beginners make rapid progress. If the adult is a person who has had previous experience with new languages, so much the better. Adult students usually want to make use of those techniques which they used in previous courses. If the teacher has other strategies for them in mind, it may be tactful for the teacher to gently guide learners into new ways. Not to memorize vocabulary lists or not to rely too much on a bilingual dictionary are accepted practices in modern language pedagogy, but the adult beginner may not be aware of these facts. Experiences with new approaches to learning may be threatening. The wise facilitator works out compromise techniques which serve both worlds.

Adult learners usually benefit from being introduced to the form of language. They seek explanations about grammatical structures. The capable teacher always makes a point of talking about the whole forest, not just the trees. The adult learner will be most fascinated to discover that the same pronunciation rules apply to the -s ending on the plural of nouns, the third person singular on verbs, and the possessive ending on nouns in English. The capable language teacher provides information about language concisely and graphically. Sometimes a good chart is worth five thousand words. When possible, the teacher uses the student's own language to offer a brief explanation of a grammatical point. It is usually the most economical way to communicate. If the teacher does not know the student's first language, another student can be asked to translate the explanation.

The person who teaches adults in English-speaking countries frequently finds a potpourri of languages and backgrounds among the students. It requires considerable finesse to handle the typical range of educational backgrounds and the typical babble of languages which shows up on the night the course begins. A good facilitator tries to find out who is who as rapidly as possible. Who are the ones with limited literacy skills in their first language? These are the people for whom the written word in the textbook and the analytical explanation at the blackboard will have little or no impact. The wise facilitator considers whether any of these people might benefit from working with remedial reading aids prepared for native speakers of English. In most instances, a variety of materials concentrating on separate language skills are usually necessary among the enrollees in any one class at the adult level.

2. The Adult Beginner Needs Support, Too

Together with their special advantages, adult beginners have special problems as well. The insightful teacher recognizes these problems and plans accordingly. Some adults need a good deal of encouragement from the teacher; they have fears of not succeeding. Others place their goals for mastering a new language at too high a level. A good teacher is always honest with the students. A wise teacher makes it clear that language learning is a long-range undertaking; it does not happen overnight. The teacher helps students set meaningful, short-term goals for themselves so that they can experience success frequently during the course. If a beginning student can ask for a specific item in a market, or understand a recorded message over the telephone, realistic levels of language mastery have been met.

Adults, and there is little deviation here, never have enough time to devote to the business of language learning. Aside from competing interests, they have jobs, families, friends. They are apt to rationalize that after all it is possible to get along with just a few expressions in English. A useful class tries to give them the expressions and the structures they need for coping with a new culture, either as long-term immigrants or short-term travelers abroad.

Experienced teachers at the adult level try not to be dismayed by the turnover of population in their classes. This customary occurrence was described by one administrator in a large city as so dramatic that "we can have 60,000 people enrolled when ESL classes begin in September, and still have 60,000 when we end in June. But the rosters show that there has been an almost one hundred percent change in the names of the people enrolled!"

Rather than feel defeated, facilitators expect this situation to occur and will plan accordingly. Instead of thinking in terms of long-range objectives they set short ones. Activities are frequently viewed as no more than "one-night stands," perhaps to be repeated at a later date but probably with a different new audience.

Above all, the skillful teacher of adult beginners capitalizes on the fact that learners are people. They have individual needs and individual responsibilities. Since they come from other cultures, the teacher can learn a great deal from the adult students in an English language course. They can introduce the teacher to ways of behaving and to modes of life which are new and fascinating. The teacher who accepts adult beginners primarily as people, incidentally as students, has gone a long way toward establishing a congenial atmosphere for second language learning.

WORKSHOP ACTIVITIES

1. Select a language lesson in a textbook intended for young beginners. Point out why it is unsuitable for use with an adult audience.
2. Carry out the same activity with a lesson in a textbook for adults. Show why it is not suitable for young learners.

2

WHAT

The
Subject Matter
is
Language

OVERVIEW

A typical question at the beginning of a language teacher's methodology course is "What is language?" Many a lecture and many an article have been devoted to answering this question. But language is multifaceted. Even by professionals, it is not always viewed in the same way. For linguists, language is the object of inquiry; while for teachers, language is the subject matter which they present to students. Both the linguist and the language teacher are greatly interested in language but for different reasons and with different underlying motivations; consequently, they look at different aspects of a language.

The motivation behind the linguist's interest in language is the goal of explaining how human language operates. The result of a linguist's work is a scientific grammar. Teachers, on the other hand, are interested in pedagogical aspects; they are interested in finding the best way to facilitate the learning process. It is the object of this book to consider the needs of the language teacher rather than those of the linguist. However, the language teacher still utilizes some of the same concepts which guide the linguist's work.

All normal people *know* their native language. What kind of knowledge do they possess? Let's observe two people conversing with each other. They could be using any language. One of the two is at times the hearer, while the other is the speaker; every now and then they switch roles. How are they, in fact, carrying out this activity? The speaker starts out with a message or an idea which he or she wants to communicate to the hearer. In order to do that he or she must know how to produce sounds that will be meaningful to the hearer. The hearer, on the other hand, the receiver of the message, must be able to interpret the meaning of the sounds. Both the hearer and the speaker of the language must obviously know something about the sounds of the language. But is that all? It is clear that the sounds in the sequence in which they are used make up larger units of meaning. In order to be able to pair the actual physical sounds with meaning, both the speaker and the hearer must know the rules of arrangement. It is the knowledge of the sound system and these rules of arrangement that allow the pairing of meaning with sounds.

The possibilities for producing novel sentences in any language are infinite in number but since our human brain is finite in its capacity, it follows that the rules necessary to account for all the actual arrangements of sounds into meaningful units is finite. It is this finite mechanism that constitutes the basic elements of knowing a language. Thus, a human being who knows a language is able to communicate his or her ideas and opinions to others. Both the hearer and the speaker demonstrate the fact that they have such knowledge of a language, even though they never demonstrate that knowledge to its fullest extent.

The difference between the knowledge a person has and the extent to which this knowledge is actually demonstrated in the real world is referred to by the linguist as the difference between competence and performance. Performance is limited by physical factors or voluntary factors on the part of the speaker. Competence, on the other hand, is potential ability that the speaker has but which may never be fully turned into actual performance.

The dichotomy between competence and performance is related to the distinction between language SUBSTANCE and language SKILLS. Language substance includes the components dealing with sounds, meaning, and rules of arrangement. Language skills are the physical vehicles through which we turn competence into performance. In the act of oral communication we use the skills of listening and speaking to transform our knowledge of language substance into actual speech. A language course of study must concern itself with teaching both language substance and language skills. The careful correlation between language substance and language skills is particularly important in the early stages of learning a new language.

A. LANGUAGE SUBSTANCE

Language substance makes up the basic ingredient of the language course. But since the activity of teaching language is not a simple, do-it-yourself procedure, decisions regarding aims, scope, sequence, and application are made by three classifications of specialists: course planners, textbook writers, and teachers. We speak of these jobs in the plural because often they are carried out by teams or groups of specialists. The sketch of how these people interrelate their efforts is presented here in an idealized way. Although there is probably no place in the world where the system works so neatly, by looking at the interconnecting elements we can better appreciate the result—a successful second language classroom.

Each of the groups of specialists mentioned above—course planners, textbook writers, and teachers—make decisions concerning language substance. The task of teachers is perhaps the most difficult since they must understand the decisions made by the others and, on the basis of their understanding, make choices which are relevant to the needs of particular classroom situations.

Course planners have the job of deciding what the overall aims of the course are, taking into account societal needs and goals as well as resources. They must then present both the textbook writers and the teachers with the language framework for the course. The writers then break up the content of the whole framework into teachable units. The writers also decide on the scope and sequence in which these units are presented. Teachers, in turn, now have a threefold task: (1) to evaluate whether the materials are suitable for the students in terms of language substance; (2) to design ways and modes for presenting the materials effectively in the classroom; and (3) to adapt the materials to the interest level of the students.

The decisions made by course planners affect the decisions made by the textbook writers; the decisions made by textbook writers affect those made by teachers. Ideally, the cycle should be carried further and the classroom decisions should ultimately affect the revision of the textbook as well as other media utilized in the course. When this whole cycle works harmoniously, improvement and growth can be consistently nurtured.

There is considerable difference between designing an EFL course and designing an ESL course. The plan for the English as a Foreign Language course can and should be quite tight since language input is limited to the course itself. In the English as a Second Language course, however, the learner is constantly exposed to language outside the classroom. In the ESL case, therefore, the plan can only serve as an overall guide within which adaptation must be constantly carried out. The overall guide, however, is still of vital significance.

1. Goals

Language substance, as was mentioned at the beginning of this chapter, refers to the three components of grammar: the sound system, the system of meaning, and the rules of sentence formation, or syntax. It is syntax which provides the backbone of the course. The sound system (the elements of pronunciation) is of greater importance at the initial stage of the course although it is usually integrated throughout the course within the teaching of grammatical structures. The system of meaning deals with the lexical items taught within the course of study.

The major decision which the planner of the course has to make is concerned with the selection, the sequencing, and the grading of grammatical structures. Both linguistic and pedagogical considerations go into these decisions. A well thought out sequence of structures, with a suitable time allotment for each topic, is probably the most important step toward the facilitation of language learning.

2. Grammatical Structures

Sequencing the grammatical structures within the pedagogical grammar is probably the most important decision that the planner of a course of study has to make. The considerations that enter such a decision are of two kinds: linguistic and pedagogical.

When we look at the linguistic considerations, the first question should be to what extent does the nature of the new language help us break up the grammar into teachable portions? Does the structure of the new language help us decide which units precede other units? One of the best ways of trying to answer this question is to look at young children learning their native language. It is generally accepted today that in the normal acquisition of the mother tongue, children master simpler structures before complex structures; in fact, some of the complex structures are mastered rather late. Does it, however, follow that we should sequence the grammatical structures in the foreign language course of study from simpler to complex? Before we can answer this question we must examine the first language learner and the new language learner in order to see to what extent they are comparable.

Children learning their mother tongue have access to an enormous amount of linguistic data while they are acquiring the language. Parents, siblings, and all the people around them speak the language constantly. Moreover, children start out only with the human disposition and the ability to learn, but with no knowledge whatsoever; in fact, they have to learn what language is used for. So they must learn two things at the same time: how human language functions and how it is used to create contact with the world around them. Young children, in fact, learn language and formulate their first steps in perception and cognition almost at the same time.

Perhaps the most important aspect of learning one's mother tongue is the fact that it is a natural process. In spite of the fact that children are not limited by time and can take as long as they need to learn their native language, they learn it relatively fast and certainly without any kind of conscious effort.

Can we compare new or foreign language learners with children learning their mother tongue? A number of very important factors are different in foreign language learning. Firstly, foreign language students do not begin with a *tabula rasa*. They already know one language when they start out to learn another one (discussion of the bilingual situation is deliberately avoided here). This gives them certain advantages, as well as disadvantages over children learning their native language. The advantages lie in the fact that foreign language learners already know how a human language functions and will even know some of the grammatical rules of the new language—a basic part of the grammar of their language will be identical with the foreign language grammar since universal features of human language are part of all grammars. In this sense, foreign language learners are in a much better position than native or first language learners who start out with zero knowledge. And yet the disadvantages are quite considerable. It is actually the differences between the native and target language, the idiosyncratic features of the target language, that will create the greatest difficulties for foreign language learners. Most of their time and effort will be devoted to coping with these differences between the two languages.

Returning to the initial question of sequencing the grammatical structures in the foreign language course of study, can we conclude that the same sequence of simpler to complex that seems to work for native language learners should be adopted in total for foreign language learners? Or should we rather conclude that the differences between the language to be learned and the native language of the learners are decisive in the sequencing of grammatical structures? An additional question here will be, of course, the transfer of the knowledge of grammatical structures from one language to the other. But before we go deeper into these linguistic considerations, let us briefly consider some of the pedagogical considerations in foreign language learning.

The language data available to foreign language learners is, by and large, much more restricted than the linguistic data available to young children. In fact, the foreign language is often restricted to classroom use. Time, therefore, is also very limited in foreign language learning. From here it becomes obvious that the language structures cannot be presented at random, but must be very carefully ordered so as to make the foreign language course of study most effective and economical.

Another very important aspect of foreign language learning is the need of a conscious effort on the part of the learner. The learner does not feel an immediate need for the foreign language since his or her own language makes communication with others altogether possible. In other words, learning a foreign language is no longer a natural and unconscious matter, but rather the opposite—it requires effort and concentration and therefore the elements of motivation and interest play a very important role.

Taking into account all of the factors raised in the above discussion, what conclusions can we come to about the sequence of grammatical structures in a beginner's course of study for English as a new or foreign language?

In spite of various issues raised so far, it still seems that the scientific grammar of the target language is of greatest value in guiding us toward an effective sequence of structures. Since our overall aim in the course of study is to approximate native competence in the target language, we must try to build a proper sequence of structures so that each structure is well selected in its position in the sequence and so that the grading is an effective one—one that facilitates the learning process. In this sense the notion that structures are best learned by starting from the simple sentence and gradually proceeding to a more complex sentence structure seems most logical.

This approach is further reinforced by an examination of the elements of functional load and frequency of occurrence. By functional load we mean the productivity of a particular structure, its utility in constructing a large variety of sentences and its function as a basis for other structures. Thus, we can easily recognize the high functional load or productivity of sentences with "be" as the main verb ("The book is on the table, my sister is in the eighth grade," etc.). "Be" sentences are very useful and frequent in description, in conversations related to personal matters, and many other everyday situations. However, their productivity is further illustrated by the fact that "be" is a productive element in constructing sentences in the progressive aspect ("They are working.") and in the passive ("It was made by a good mechanic."). Thus, linguistic considerations lead us toward the decision to place "be" sentences very early in the course of study.

Up to this point we have considered only the target language and on the basis of its grammar decided to place "be" sentences at the very beginning of the course. Let us now consider the other areas as well. How does the native language affect our decision on sequence?

If we are dealing with languages such as Arabic, Russian, or Hebrew that do not have a comparable "be" construction, the equivalent to "He is a boy" is "He boy." Obviously, the same meaning is expressed by the two sentences. However, the surface structure is different, and the surface differences account for difficulties in foreign language learning. So we might arrive at the conclusion that since "be" structures are so very difficult for speakers of a language that does not have a similar surface form, we should postpone this structure for a while. In other words, we could say that we are progressing from easy structures to those which are more difficult for the speaker of a particular language.

Although this seems plausible at first glance, we must weigh the gains of such a decision against the loss of not placing such a productive structure at the initial steps of the course. With relatively little research, we will find that it would be quite disastrous to postpone the teaching of such a very productive structure: it would affect the ability to use language meaningfully from the very beginning, it would interfere with the learning of the progressive aspect ("I am doing my homework now") which is very useful in the classroom, and it would thus detract from the effectiveness of the course.

It seems, therefore, that the first and fundamental concern is with the nature of the target language. We should therefore try to design a sequence of grammatical structures which unfolds gradually, starting with simple and productive structures and moving towards more complex and less productive structures. In this manner the course can be viewed as made up of building blocks, one placed upon the other.

How then does the *native* or *first language* come into consideration? Let us for a moment return to the example of the "be" sentences. If our pupils are speakers of a language that does not have a surface representation of "be" they will find this a most difficult structure. It is, therefore, imperative that within a course designed for such speakers we should devote a considerable amount of time to the teaching of this structure. If, for instance, speakers of French can learn to use basic "be" sentences within a week—since French has a verb that operates very much like "be"—then speakers of Arabic will need several months to master this structure, simply due to the difference between Arabic and English. For speakers of a language that does not have "be," constant review of this structure is perhaps even more important than the time spent on teaching it initially.

Contrastive analysis of the two grammars can make an important contribution here by specifying the amount of review necessary within the course of study in order to ensure mastery of this very difficult structure.

To summarize the linguistic consideration involved in a decision regarding the ordering of grammatical structures in the foreign language course of study: we find that the nature of the target language together with the scientific description of its grammar jointly affect decisions about the sequence of structures to be taught. But it is contrastive analysis that tells us how much time, or in other words, how much practice, is necessary for any particular structure in that sequence, and more important, how much review will be needed throughout the course.

Once the sequence of structures has been basically worked out, the question arises: what is a teachable portion? In other words, how do we decide how much to teach of each structure at a particular point? Here contrastive analysis again plays a decisive role. The more difficult the structure for the particular group of learners, the more we have to break up the structure into smaller units. For instance, if we consider past progressive a difficult grammatical topic we might prefer to break it down in the following way: First, we present only past progressive positive, negative, and question sentences with a simple time expression in the past ("Yesterday at 5 o'clock I was reading"). Following this grammatical sequence, we can take the learner to a very different topic, for instance, possessive forms of nouns: "The baker's hat is tall." Then we may go back to past progressive and review what was taught with additional material to show simultaneity of occurrence ("While I was reading, she was drawing a picture"). Following this second portion of past progressive, we could have a section dealing with time clauses in the past, showing one verb in the past progressive while the verb in the clause is simple past ("When he came, I was reading"). Thus, the grammatical topic has been broken down in a number of small units and then the units have been placed in a sequence which will allow cyclic re-entry of the major topic. Such a cyclic sequence has been found useful for teaching grammatical topics, especially those that are difficult for the learners.

When we set out to teach a new grammatical structure, we must concern ourselves with two aspects of that structure: its formal features and its contextual features. It is not sufficient for learners to know how to construct the new structure; they must also know how to use it. Thus, for instance, beginners will learn to pluralize nouns in English and make the verb phrase agree with the subject of the sentence: "The book is new/the books are new." They have learned the formal feature of this structure. But they must also learn the contextual meaning which, in this case, will be the fact that the plural/singular feature does not apply to mass (noncountable) nouns. Thus a sentence like "The coffee is hot" cannot be pluralized in terms of the verb.

The contextual meaning of each grammatical structure poses different teaching problems. Take the example of "*can* + VERB." The native speaker of English uses this form to express physical ability or know-how, as in the following two sentences: "I can see well with my new glasses" (ability) and "She can play the piano very well" (know-how). In teaching this structure, it is important to distinguish the two contexts mentioned above so that the learner actually understands how to use "*can* + verb" with the above two meanings. At a later stage, other meanings of "can"—permission, probability—will be taught as well.

Another rather different example of formal and contextual meaning can be demonstrated by comparing the "simple present" with the "present progressive" aspects of the verb. The features of form of the two tenses will deal with some of the following: agreement between subject and verb, the use of the "be" paradigm, the *-ing* ending on the verb for present progressive, the question form which has inversion only in the present progressive aspect, the question form with *do/does* in the present simple and similar features of form.

Example:

agreement between subject and verb

| he | plays |
| they | play |

"be" paradigm and "verb-*ing*"

am	writing
is	writing
are	writing

the question forms

| Is he writing? | (inversion of "be" and subject) |
| Does she know us? | (use of "do"/"does") |

The contextual meaning of the two tenses on the other hand has to do with the fact that simple present is used for habitual activities and general facts while the present progressive is used to describe momentary actions. This contextual difference between the two tenses is vital in learning to use them. Thus contexts for teaching the present simple could be weather: "It rains in winter, but it doesn't rain in summer"; professions: "A baker bakes bread," daily activities: "I go to school by bus," etc. The present progressive, on the other hand, will always be used together with the demonstration of an action: "I am standing. You are sitting."

When the native language of the learner interferes with features of form of the new structure, practice and review will eventually overcome the difficulty. More attention must, however, be given to the differences in contextual meaning. Learners who make no distinction between two types of present, like the simple and progressive forms, in their native language, will have difficulty with the contextual meaning of the two tenses in English, even after they have mastered the formal differences. Constant reinforcement of the proper contextual meaning of a structure is therefore vital.

When the suitable context for teaching a certain structure has been established, our next requirement is to find a relevant theme. The theme must be close to the interests of each particular group of learners. Thus practicing a sentence like "He lives in New York," although it is contextually meaningful, may not be relevant to the learners unless we are talking about someone whom they know and who actually lives in New York.

The classroom teacher is the best judge of what is and what is not immediately relevant for the pupils. When the theme is relevant and related to the students' interests, the learning process is much more effective. If, for instance, the pupils in our class have just been involved in planning an outing or a sports day, it would be foolish not to use this as a topic for language work. If our pupils are interested in vocational training, it would be advisable to talk about the occupations that will result from such training rather than talk about other jobs that are of less interest. The textbook can often provide us with general themes of interest for a certain age group or for a certain expected, idealized kind of learner, but only the teacher in the classroom can then use that material so that it is immediately relevant to the particular group of learners in the class.

In teaching grammatical structures, proper sequencing, breaking topics into teachable units, contextualizing, and building thematic relevance must be kept in harmony. It is the responsibility of the textbook writer to: sequence, break down, and contextualize the structures presented. The area of relevance, however, is left entirely to the classroom teacher who really knows the pupils and their particular interests. The textbook writer can only select themes of general interest, not those of immediate individual interest. (Chapter Six, *Unfolding Broader Facets of Meaning,* p. 163.)

Although immediate relevance is a teacher's basic role, the teacher's task is not limited to that alone. Contextualizing and breaking down topics into teachable units is often within the realm of the teacher's work since not all textbooks take care of these problems. Adapting the textbook to the needs of the learner means also improving contextualization and organizing material into teaching units. Sometimes it might even mean a resequencing. Only the teacher who fully understands these elements in the teaching of grammatical structures can effectively adapt the materials to the use of a particular group of learners.

3. A Sample Grammar Sequence

A variety of considerations concerning the sequencing and grading of grammatical structures have been raised in this chapter. It ultimately seems a rather complex task, since at times we may have to cope with conflicting issues. Only by judging the problem in its entirety can we arrive at the best decisions. Let us look at an example of the kind of list of structures that might appear in a syllabus intended for the first two years of English as a new or foreign language:

1. "Be" sentences: (a) positive, (b) negative, (c) yes/no questions, (d) short answers.
   While teaching the "be" sentences, special attention must also be devoted to the following grammatical elements: (a) personal pronouns and agreement with the "be" paradigm, (b) singular and plural of nouns with non-definite and definite articles (examples: This is a book. The man is tall.)
   Review of "be" sentences.
2. "Have" as a main verb with the possessive meaning. Positive sentences only, with special attention to have/has.
3. Selected useful verbs in the progressive aspect: (a) positive, (b) negative, (c) questions, (d) short answers.
4. Simple Present, using chiefly the verbs used with Present Progressive. Positive sentences only, with special attention to the "s" ending in the third person singular.
5. Contrast between Simple Present and Present Progressive, positive sentences only.
6. Past form of "be" introducing past time expressions: (a) positive, (b) negative, (c) questions, (d) short answers.
   Review of "be" sentences in the Present.
7. Question and negative sentences in the Simple Present (examples: I don't have breakfast at 8 o'clock. He doesn't wear glasses.). Additional contrast between Simple Present and Present Progressive.
8. Simple Past with selected irregular verbs, positive sentences only, following a review of "be" in the past.
9. Simple Past with regular verbs.
10. "Be" + "going to" + verb to express future.
11. Questions and negative sentences with Simple Past.
12. Comparison of adjectives.
13. Review of contrast between Simple Present and Present Progressive.

The above sequence of grammatical structures is an example of decisions made on the basis of all the considerations presented in this chapter. Let us now review this sequence step by step.

The grammatical structure selected to begin this course of study is "be" sentences. This selection was obviously made on the grounds of productivity of the structure, frequency of occurrence, and, last but not least, the fact that "be" sentences are so useful in talking about the immediate environment and about oneself. From the smaller topics mentioned as part of the first work unit, we can easily deduce that considerable time is devoted to "be" sentences. However, the exact amount of time will depend greatly on the native language of the learners.

The second structure was selected mainly because of its utility in the classroom. The verb "have" with the meaning of possession is very useful in talking about the immediate environment and together with "be" it therefore provides many motivating activities for the learner. However, since the dummy element of "do/does" in questions and negative sentences often causes difficulties for learners, the teaching of these more complex sentence structures was postponed for a while. It is quite possible to use "have" sentences in a natural way without negative and question sentences.

Utility in the classroom was again the reason for the selection of the third structure. The Present Progressive is easy to demonstrate and activate in the classroom. Its second virtue is the fact that it reinforces the "be" paradigm which was learned not long before. This provides helpful continuity and a feeling of building blocks placed one on top of the other. If we consider the form of Present Progressive—"be-ing"—it is rather complex, but the meaning is quite easy to demonstrate. In view of all these factors, Present Progressive was placed in position three.

The fourth grammatical structure in the sample syllabus is Simple Present, in positive sentences only. The Simple Present, as has already been mentioned, poses problems of meaning. It is very difficult to explain the use of the Simple Present. At this stage we would probably limit the Simple Present to everyday activities, although there are many more contexts within which the Simple Present is used.

The next topic, the contrast between Simple Present and Present Progressive, allows us to reinforce the form and meaning of both aspects and emphasize the distinction between the two, which we know will cause difficulties. At this point, however, we would avoid complications of these structures, for instance, stative verbs like "love," "understand," "believe," which do not take the -ing form, would not yet be introduced. Nor would preverbal frequency expressions like "generally," "usually," "often," since, although they reinforce the meaning nicely, their position in the sentences is often confusing for the learner.

The next structure, "be" in the past, is relatively easy at this point and allows reinforcement of "be" sentences in the present.

Only now are question and negative sentences in the Simple Present taught. This allows a return to a structure that was taught not long ago but which needs further reinforcement. The syllabus works spirally at this point.

The eighth grammatical structure suggested here is the Simple Past of selected verbs. Many readers will probably raise their eyebrows at this point, since it is much more common to teach the regular before the irregular verbs. First, we should stop and weigh the arguments for putting the irregular verbs first.

The irregular verbs number about 140 verbs in English. It might be considered that this relatively small number should not worry us in the initial stages of the course of study. However, most of these verbs are extremely useful and are of very high frequency of occurrence. It is, in fact, almost impossible to present a natural context describing an event in the past without using some irregular verbs. It makes, therefore, more sense to select a few useful verbs and teach them in very small groups, but in a contextualized manner. Thus, although the pupils meet strange forms in the Past, they can easily learn them since they meet them only in groups of three or four at a time. Just before the pupils begin to feel discouraged by the fact that every verb looks different, we show them the regular verbs. Now it is easy to apply the regular rule, always checking first whether the verb is not an irregular one before over-generalizing and applying the regular rule to irregular verbs. This sequence of introducing a selected number of irregular verbs first and then giving the regular rule also allows the preparation of materials that are more natural and realistic than if they were limited in a stilted manner to regular verbs. If, however, regular verbs are introduced first, pupils tend to overgeneralize and produce forms like "teached," "standed," etc. It is also psychologically more difficult for pupils to accept so many irregular forms when they have been led to think that the past formation of verbs is regular.

The first form of future time suggested in the sample syllabus is "be" + *going to* + verb. The form of this structure, although it results in long sentences, is easy to handle since it looks very much like some kind of extension of the Present Progressive. It again allows a review of the "be" forms and a reinforcement of the Present Progressive form in a spiral fashion.

From the sample syllabus we learn that at each point all the considerations of sequence and time must be taken into account, but that in each case a different factor may be the decisive one. We have also seen that at the very early stages of the course, the pedagogical issue often has priority over the linguistic one.

The sample sequence presented above is by no means the best or the only sequence; in fact, one could argue against every decision in its preparation. The essential fact, however, is that all issues were considered before decisions were reached, and the function of this chapter is to emphasize the importance of this decision-making process.

4. Sounds and Pronunciation

When we listen to the flow of speech in an unfamiliar language, we cannot understand what the sounds mean. Even if we can recognize some of the sounds, we still hear the foreign language as an unintelligible stream of human noises. What is missing for us to be able to understand the noises is the system of arrangement which occurs in that particular language. Without knowing the system, we do not know how to break up the flow of speech into sounds.

The field of phonetics deals with the physical aspect of human speech sounds, while phonology deals with the system of arrangement of sounds in particular languages. In teaching a foreign language, both aspects of human sounds are relevant. For example, from phonetics we get information regarding the articulation of sounds. An explanation of the position of the tongue can help a learner of English to pronounce the "th" sound. If we ask the learner simply to imitate the teacher, he or she may never get it right.

The sound system, or the phonemic system, on the other hand, is very important for the foreign language learner. Only a few of the speech sounds will be completely different in the target language, but the sound system may be totally unfamiliar. We are therefore most concerned with it in the course of study. The sound system of a language contains a number of elements which are all vital in the teaching of English as a new language: intonation, word stress, sentence rhythm, and the consonant and the vowel systems. Each of these elements will contain important differences between the native and the new language.

Intonation in the foreign language is important since it carries meaning. What is usually very difficult in English is the intonation of WH-questions. Although they are questions in every other sense of the word, yet they carry statement, or falling, intonation in English. Thus, the intonation patterns of "What's the time?" and "It's late" are almost the same. The pupil cannot rely on intonation in distinguishing between questions and statements although he or she probably does so in the native language.

Word stress is another area where languages differ considerably. In some languages the position of the word stress is easily predictable, in others it is more variable. In most cases when there is mispronunciation of the word stress due to foreign accent, it will not interfere with communication. However, it seems wrong to settle for this level of performance since without proper word stress the learner will be very far from any kind of an approximation of a native speaker's speech.

In English, word stress in polysyllabic words often accompanies reduction of the vowel quality in the weak syllable. This area is particularly confusing to foreign language learners. Words like "interesting" or "comfortable" are notorious for causing difficulties to learners of English as a foreign language. The problem, of course, is twofold—learners must know where the main stress should be, and then they must know which vowels to reduce.

Sentence rhythm is formed by the amount of time devoted to each syllable in the sentence and the intervals occurring between syllables. In some languages this is not a problem, since all syllables get equal time and appear at equal intervals. In English, however, a sentence like "Cats drink milk" is not much shorter in the actual time it takes to say it than the sentence "Some cats will drink some milk." Words like "cat," "drink," and "milk" receive more time than words like "some" and "will" in English. The result is that the latter are almost stuck on to the former. This feature of English makes life very difficult for the learner of English as a foreign language. For a long time he or she will miss the words that are short in duration and will find it hard to follow the meaning of the sentence. Sentence rhythm should therefore be given considerable attention in both planning the course of study and in presenting material in the classroom.

So far we have discussed the elements which have to do with the larger units of speech, i.e., the sentence and the word. Let us now go on to the segmental sounds utilized by a language. As was mentioned above, the most efficient way of looking at the segmentals of a language is by considering the consonant and the vowel systems separately.

The consonant systems of different languages can easily be compared by using the basic features of consonantal sounds. Let us begin with a very basic feature—voicing. All languages contain voiced and voiceless consonants. The question is: what representations of voiced and voiceless consonants does each sound system allow? For instance, when inflections like the plural or possessive "s" or the past tense inflection "ed" in English are added to a voiced consonant, they become voiced as well. When these same inflections are added to a voiceless consonant they become voiceless. Compare "books" with "pens," for instance. Voiced consonants also affect the vowel sounds that precede them by lengthening their duration. Thus the word "bag" is longer than the word "back" since the vowel before /g/ is longer than the vowel before /k/. The distinction between voiced and voiceless consonants in English plays, therefore, a very important role in the sound system of this language. As a result, it is not enough to teach all the consonants that appear in the chart of any particular language. It is essential to emphasize and explain the features which affect the rules of the sound system.

If a high degree of approximation of the native speaker pronunciation is to be attained, then attention must be given to more subtle details of the consonant system. When pronouncing the following consonants in English, /t/, /d/, /l/, the tip of the tongue is placed behind the tooth ridge (just behind the upper teeth). A speaker of French, for instance, would place his or her tongue in a much more frontal position while pronouncing these sounds. It must be the decision of the planner of the course of study and of the individual teacher whether under certain circumstances attention to such subtleties will be worthwhile.

The vowel system is probably the most vital area of pronunciation since the essential element in every English syllable is the vowel sound. Languages differ considerably in their vowel systems. Many languages have five vowels, while some utilize meaningfully no more than three or four different vowel units or sounds. English, on the other hand, has between eleven and thirteen different vowel sounds, all of which contribute to changes in meaning (the exact number of vowels depends on the particular English dialect). The vowel system, therefore, requires considerable attention when planning the course of study. Perhaps the most important consideration here is whether we want to achieve a certain degree of approximation of the native pronunciation of the vowels or whether our emphasis will be placed on the receptive skill of listening only. This distinction must be clearly specified in the syllabus and in the teaching materials.

If we accept the underlying principle that grammatical structures are the backbone of the new language course of study, then it seems that pronunciation would be best taught by being integrated into the teaching of the grammatical structures. Thus, while teaching *"can + verb"* we will pay attention to rhythm and word stress. Pupils will then learn from the first encounter with this structure that "can" is less stressed and takes less time within the sentence than the verb which follows it. This seems to be a plausible conclusion and one that can be implemented at all stages. However, as regards the pronunciation of individual segmental sounds, it is best to devote more attention to their pronunciation in the first and second years. At this early stage, learners have not acquired bad pronunciation habits and have enough time within the course to practice pronunciation.

5. Words, Words, Words . . . .

To the average person knowing a foreign language well means knowing a large number of words in that language. From the whole discussion developed in this chapter we must conclude, however, that words by themselves are probably not the most important element. This may be an oversimplification of the problem, but vocabulary items can and will constantly be added to the overall knowledge of the learner. The learning of new words will eventually take place outside the organized course of study. It is, however, the function of the course of study to provide the learner with a good sequence of grammatical structures, with ample practice of the sound system and with a basic list of vocabulary items.

In discussing words and elements of meaning as parts of our syllabus, we must first distinguish between what are called function or structure words (prepositions, articles, pronouns which carry structural meaning only) and content words which represent things in the real world. In the section on the sound system, we saw that stress is placed only on content words in English, while the structure words are not stressed and are very short in duration. The structure words should obviously be taught as an integral part of relevant grammatical structures. The content words, on the other hand, greatly depend on the contextualization of the grammatical structures or on the situations within which these structures are taught. A useful principle for teaching of content words in the first year of the foreign language course is to limit content vocabulary to concrete words that can easily be depicted or demonstrated. The teacher thus does not need to give complicated explanations or equivalents in the native language.

It is helpful to view words as related not to written forms, but rather to units of meaning. It is therefore preferable to refer to lexical items rather than words. A lexical item is a unit of meaning made up of one or more words (for example, *book, give up, as soon as,* are obviously single lexical items).

Once we accept the principle of teaching lexical items that are simple and concrete as far as demonstration is concerned, our next criterion for selection of lexical items concerns the interests of the learner. It is best initially to teach words that relate to the learner's immediate environment and areas of interest. At a later stage the selection of lexical items may be dictated by the content of a story read or a film viewed.

Contrastive analysis between the native and the target language is again important in evaluating the problems that may occur when teaching certain lexical items. For instance, when we teach the lexical item "pick up," the question will arise of the distinction between "pick up" and "raise," which may not exist in the native language. Secondly, the fact that "pick up" has a number of different meanings has to be considered carefully: do we teach all the meanings at the same time, or do we use a spiral approach as we did with grammatical structures? It seems that the latter is a safer approach but the course planner, textbook writer, or teacher must ultimately make this decision. This ultimate decision will also depend on whether it is an ESL or EFL course. Although the cycling approach will work very well for the EFL situation, more flexibility is necessary in the ESL one. Thus, with the lexical item "pick up," ESL pupils are very likely to bring in various additional meanings of this item. The facilitator should be prepared to explain the full range of meanings and to take full advantage of them.

WORKSHOP ACTIVITIES

A Sample Grammar Sequence

1. Take any of the structures appearing in the sample grammar sequence above. Consider the following questions in relation to some course of study that you are familiar with: (a) Is the form of the structure difficult for the pupils that you have in mind? (b) Is the meaning difficult? (c) Are there any other considerations that would support the suggestion to teach this structure later or earlier in the course?
2. Look at the following passive sentences:
   (a) America was discovered by Columbus in 1492.
   (b) Their house was robbed.

(c) This hall is used for meetings.

(d) A new building is being built in the center of town.

How would you divide this large grammatical topic into teachable units? How would you sequence these units? Present all the relevant considerations.

3. Choose some course of study that you are familiar with or a language textbook for beginners. Analyze the sequence of grammatical structures presented there.

Sounds and Pronunciation

1. Drills which are designed to practice the English vowels are usually prepared in minimal pairs:

bed   bad
set   sat

Prepare three minimal pairs for each pair of vowel sounds in these words:

(a) live   leave
(b) bat   bought
(c) cup   car

2. Find five more pairs like

récord(N)   recórd(V)
pérmit(N)   permít(V)

Words, Words, Words   Select any ten English lexical items that happen to appear in a reading passage. Look each one up in the dictionary to find its complete range of meaning. Then compare each lexical item with its equivalents in some other language you know.

B. LANGUAGE SKILLS

Using language as a tool of communication involves the use of four language skills: listening and speaking in oral communication and reading and writing in written communication. The sender of a message uses the spoken or written form in order to communicate ideas and the receiver of the message utilizes the listening or reading skills in order to interpret the message. The skills used by the sender are PRODUCTIVE and the skills used by the receiver are RECEPTIVE or INTERPRETIVE.

When we use language we utilize substance—sounds, meaning, and rules of arrangement—and the four language skills. In turn, the use of each skill draws upon the various components of language substance. Each skill involves the use of a specific vehicle: the listening skill requires sound discrimination, speaking requires the techniques of sound production, reading requires the mechanics of reading and writing the mechanics of writing. *Diagram No. 1* shows this interrelationship.

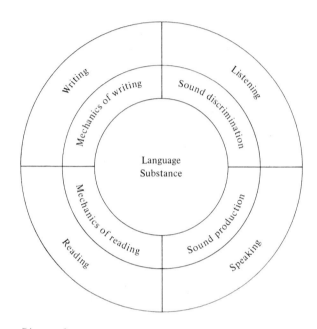

Diagram 1

1. Goals

In the language course it is often necessary to group the language skills in a variety of ways depending on the specific objectives or of the particular activity. *Diagram No. 2* shows a more inclusive representation of the relationship between language substance and language skills.

The most idealistic goal in learning a new language calls for an approximation of the native speaker's knowledge of both language substance and language skills. Thus the highest level of proficiency within the speaking skill is an approximation of the native speaker's ability to produce meaningful sounds. Within the listening skill the highest level of proficiency is the ability to understand the natural flow of native speech. In the reading skill, the goal is to read with full comprehension any material written in the language (provided the content does not present any problems of understanding). The usual expectation is the ability to communicate through writ-

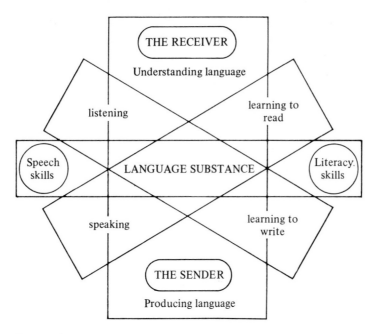

THE RECEIVER

Understanding language

listening

learning to read

Speech skills

LANGUAGE SUBSTANCE

Literacy. skills

speaking

learning to write

THE SENDER

Producing language

Diagram 2

ing as well. From Diagram No. 2 we can see that the listening and reading skills are the receptive skills, while speaking and writing are the productive skills. Many language courses aim at an integrative use of all skills. Yet a learner usually attains a much higher level of proficiency in the receptive skills than in the productive skills. This occurs in one's native language as well.

In spite of the lofty overall goals specified above, realistically we cannot expect the foreign learner ever to achieve the same level of proficiency as the native speaker. Therefore it is necessary to specify more exact intermediate goals. Mastering the language skills, like mastering any kind of skill, requires a considerable amount of practice. With every new stage in the developmental process, the learner becomes more proficient.

The initial period of most modern language courses is referred to as the aural-oral stage. During this stage the listening and speaking skills are paired up and utilized within a very limited amount of language substance. Thus, if we look back at the diagram of the skills, only the part specified in Diagram No. 3 below is activated in the aural-oral stage of a beginner's course of study. The aural-oral part of a language course of study enables real communication between sender and receiver but only in the form of spoken language.

Often the objective of a language course is to develop the receptive skills only. In such courses prominence is given to both the listening and

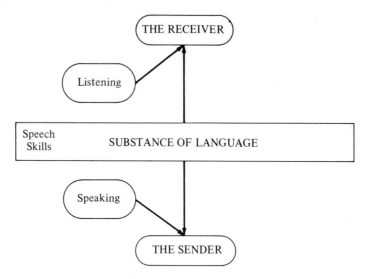

Diagram 3

the reading skills (reading is probably silent reading). In such courses considerable development of language substance is required. For such a course the diagram will look like Diagram No. 4.

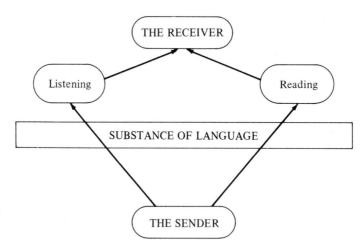

Diagram 4

Sometimes the participants of a language course of study start with a relatively high level of proficiency in the receptive skills and therefore need to devote special time and effort to the productive skills of Diagram No. 5.

In an integrative course, or one in which *all* skills are taught, the initial aural-oral stage is usually followed by the teaching of the mechanics of

```
                    ┌─────────────────┐
                    │  THE RECEIVER   │
                    └─────────────────┘


┌────────────────────────────────────────────────────────┐
│              SUBSTANCE OF LANGUAGE                       │
└────────────────────────────────────────────────────────┘

        ┌───────────┐              ┌───────────┐
        │ speaking  │              │  writing  │
        └───────────┘              └───────────┘
              ↖                    ↗
              ┌─────────────────────┐
              │    THE SENDER       │
              └─────────────────────┘
```

Diagram 5

reading. The overall goals of the language course will affect the teaching of the mechanics of reading. When the emphasis is only on reading for comprehension, it is possible to entirely ignore the connection between orthography and pronunciation and deal exclusively with the connection between orthography and meaning. In an intergrative course which aims to teach all four language skills, the mutual reinforcement which takes place between speaking and reading skills is important. This kind of reinforcement is typically overlooked in the grammar-translation method. It is commonplace to hear a person who is a product of such an approach say, "Why didn't they ever tell me that there is a rule which helps me to know that *cap* and *cape* are not pronounced the same way?" Unlike the grammar translation approach, in the integrative course such information must be presented.

In the aural-oral stage of the course, when the learner's knowledge of language is still very limited, mechanics of reading help the learner acquire fundamentals of graphic/sound correspondences, along with a small number of individual items that do not abide by these correspondences, but which represent vocabulary items which the learner masters orally. For the non-native learner of English as a new language, the mechanics of reading present a number of problems. For example, since English orthography is not based on a system of a letter-sound correspondence (except in a small number of consonants, for instance *m* and *t*), other more complex rules of correspondence must be used to explain letter combinations such as: *mb* (never pronounce the *b* following an *m*), *kn* (never pronounce the *k*), *ch, th.*

Vowel letter-sound correspondences present a more complex situation since they depend on the graphic environment in which the vowel letter occurs. Many rules for such correspondences work quite consistently. Thus *pat, pet, pit* are quite predictable since the shape of the syllable is

C-V-C (consonant, vowel, consonant). There are other rules for English spelling which connect the graphic shape of the word to its meaning, so for example the distinction between *bear* (the animal) and *bare* (without clothing) is kept separate by the different spellings, which is an example of a homophone. There are, of course, cases of homonyms as well, for instance: "bear" (to carry) versus "bear" (animal), where spelling does not help us make a distinction.

It is during the early stage of the teaching of the mechanics of reading that we want to take full advantage of the correspondence between orthography and sounds. In this way the speaking and reading skills at this early stage reinforce each other. It will be easier for the pupil who has learned at least to recognize the differences in sound between cap/cape or pen/pan to learn the graphic distinctions pertaining to such pairs.

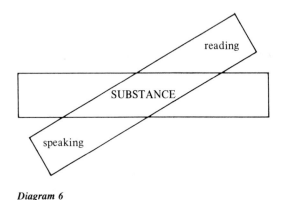

Diagram 6

The sequence of Diagrams 3-6 shows how the four language skills can be paired up according to the needs of the particular course. The specific goals must be specified in terms of each language skill. The teacher must, however, take advantage of the mutual reinforcement that one skill provides for learning the other.

2. The Listening and Speaking Skills

During the early aural-oral period, emphasis is placed on the speech skills—listening and speaking. Communication at this stage takes place by means of the spoken language only. The sender utilizes the speaking skill in order to send the message while the receiver utilizes the listening skill in order to receive that message, as shown in Diagram No. 2 on page 53. The listening and speaking skills are reciprocal: one reinforces the other. The learner starts at the receiver's end but needs to experience being the speaker as well. Diagram No. 7 shows the mutual reinforcement that takes place during this early stage of mastering the listening and speaking skills. To summarize this relationship between the listening and the speaking

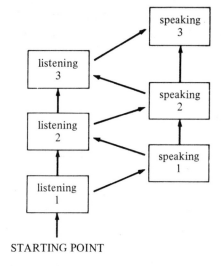

STARTING POINT

Diagram 7

skills, "You begin to hear it better after you have tried to say it; you say it better after you have learned to hear it."

What technical features are involved in learning to use the listening skill in the new language? We can analyze the listening skill as being made up of abilities in sound discrimination, recognition of new intonation patterns, familiarity with new sentence rhythm, and auditory memory.

When beginning learners listen to the new language for the first time, they are confronted with some new sounds that they have never heard before. If they are not taught to discriminate these new sounds from other sounds, they will often not be able to hear them at all—they will continue to hear only the sounds of their own language and replace familiar sounds for the sounds of the new language. The example of the two sounds of /th/ in *think* and *this* pronounced by many foreigners as *sink* and *zis* is quite well known. In this case learners who are unfamiliar with the voiced and voiceless /th/ sounds substitute the closest sounds in their own language for the two unfamiliar sounds. It is, therefore, obvious that sound discrimination in the new language is an important task to be learned by the beginner.

Many non-native speakers of English find it very hard to recognize that "where is your book?" or "where have you been?" or "how are you today?" are questions, when they listen to the intonation pattern typical of such questions. Only when they learn to recognize the question words and the question inversion do they understand that these sentences are really questions. Beginners must therefore learn to hear and interpret different intonation patterns from those that they are used to in their native language.

One of the favorite statements that foreigners like to make about speakers of English is: "They swallow their words so much that I can't understand them." The foreigner is probably bothered by English sentence rhythm, as well as by discrimination abilities. The uneven rhythm of English allows two sentences like the following to be almost identical in the length of time needed for their oral production:"Children play games" and "Some children will have played some games." This is possible since in English only words like "children, play, and games" get prominence in terms of time, while the other function or grammatical words are pronounced at a very rapid rate. Any foreign language sounds very "fast" to our ears because of all the things mentioned so far, but the characteristic rhythm of English sentences contributes an added difficulty.

We all remember instances from our childhood in which older children confronted us with a long slur of nonsense syllables which we were supposed to repeat but found it difficult to remember. Only after considerable practice did we finally manage to do so. This is exactly what the beginner is faced with in the foreign language. In order to really make Diagram No. 7 indicating the speaking and listening skills work, we must help the learner develop auditory memorization ability. Therefore, ample examples of the same sentence must be provided both in each listening step and in each speaking step.

It is a common layman's opinion that speaking the foreign language is the most difficult task of all. Experience shows there is much truth in that statement. For most people, the ability to *speak* a foreign language is, unfortunately, not acquired very easily. Therefore, one of the most important elements in the process of acquiring the speaking skill is constant motivation and opportunity for the learner to develop a feeling of achievement. Graded and sequential practice is of great value in developing the speaking skill.

The goal of sounding like a native speaker is unrealistic in any course of study (there are always individual exceptions!) The crucial element is the degree of approximation which is aimed at in the course. Continually, the teacher must play the role of a realistic evaluator. If the learners have a great amount of difficulty producing an English sounding *r*, it is not necessary to attach attention to the issue. Real communication can still take place if the *r* sound is non-native. At every stage it is desirable for learners to use what they know and to have practice talking with native speakers, even if they do not sound like native speakers themselves.

3. The Reading and Writing Skills

Reading and writing are often called the literacy skills. The term "literacy" indicates that these skills are not acquired as part of the natural process of learning one's first language, but at a later stage. The young child learns the substance of language and the speech skills first. A person in fact knows his or her language before knowing how to read and write. The fact that literacy skills are learned after the speech skills in the native language is often used to justify the generally accepted sequence in foreign language courses: listening, speaking, reading, writing. In the new or foreign language situation, however, the fact that the individual has already become literate in a first language or the native tongue, allows us to shorten or sometimes even skip altogether the aural-oral period—especially if the course centers around literacy skills.

In written communication, as opposed to oral communication, there is usually no contact between sender and receiver beyond the written page. There is no feedback going back from the receiver to the sender. The sender is often miles or years removed from the receiver. It is therefore possible to view the reading and the writing skills as operating independently. A good reader is not necessarily a good writer. Thus, there are many courses that place the reading skill as their priority objective and the writing skill is given very little attention, if any.

At the initial stage of mastering the reading and writing skills, there is a certain amount of mutual reinforcement between the two in spite of the independence that they manifest otherwise. When the beginner learns to differentiate letter shapes and to recognize graphic environments, the writing skill helps reinforce the reading skill. After shaping a letter in writing, it becomes easier to recognize it in reading. Gradually, however, the two skills grow apart, and in most EFL courses importance shifts towards reading. In ESL courses, on the other hand, the writing skill is of greater importance although probably never as vital as the reading skill. The ability to write is particularly important, however, for people who need to use English as a medium through which to learn other school subjects.

4. Planning a Reading Program

A "good reader" is someone who is quick and effective in decoding written messages. The preliminary requirement for becoming a good reader is the mastery of the mechanics of reading: letter/sound correspondences, spelling/sound correspondences, spelling/meaning correspondences and effective letter discrimination. But a good reader must also possess reading habits which go beyond the mastery of the mechanics: being able to quickly grasp whole ideas in their written form, to separate the main topic from the details, to scan pages, along with other such techniques. It is mastery of the mechanics of reading paired with effective reading techniques that should be the objectives of any reading program.

In EFL courses it is useful to view the language and the reading program as separate but parallel units within the language course. At times, these two programs will interlock, but a quite clear separation is necessary. With young learners, for instance, it is necessary to devote the whole of the first year to promoting mastery of the mechanics of reading. During that period language substance is learned and developed through the speech skills alone. Gradually, as the learner's mastery of the mechanics increases, the reading skill is utilized for language practice as well.

In order to indicate the internal elements, the following pages set out the details of a hypothetical reading program. Such a program can be viewed as having three major stages each with its specific objectives and two transition stages which connect the major stages to one another. (See

Diagram No. 8 on page 61.) The aim of the first stage is mastery of the mechanics of reading. This is the shortest stage of the three, but its actual length will vary according to the learners' age, environment (native or non-native setting), and language background. With younger learners the first stage needs to be considerably longer than with adult learners. If the new language has a writing system which is similar to the one used in the native language of the learners, the time necessary for stage one will be shorter. In ESL courses where reinforcement of the written language is available in the setting, stage one will be shorter than in an EFL course. Although the *objectives* of each stage in the program for ESL and EFL courses are basically the same, the time and mode of instruction will vary considerably.

When a satisfactory level of mastery of the mechanics of reading has been achieved, we move from stage one into a transition stage. It is during the transition stage that the four language skills will have to be combined. All the skills can be employed here in the acquistiion of new language material. One may view this stage as one which typically presents the pupil with a cycle of listening, speaking, reading, and writing with every new language topic. The major objective of the transition stage is the founding of a basic knowledge in all four language skills: a knowledge upon which the rest of the program will be based.

In an ESL course, as opposed to EFL, the first stage can be merged with the transition stage. In the ESL program, it is both possible and necessary to expand the use of the reading skill to include activities outside the classroom even before mastery of the mechanics of reading has taken place. Learners can be encouraged to read street signs, advertisements on cereal boxes, instructions for playing games, and other such things all during stage one. This will increase the rate of progress in reading as long as the mastery of the basic elements of the mechanics of reading is kept as the objective of stage one.

The second stage of the reading program aims at developing better reading habits and at increasing the learner's vocabulary stock. Learners in the EFL or ESL course may already possess good reading habits in their first language. We should not, however, assume a direct transfer of such habits from the first to the second language. Special attention must be devoted to the promotion of such habits in the new language as well.

The duration of stage two of the reading program is much longer than the duration of stage one. In fact, it is at least three to four times as long. Here again, the actual time depends on the particular learners and the circumstances under which the language course is taken. Younger learners in an EFL course need more time with this stage than adult learners. Young learners in the ESL course, on the other hand, might receive some of this training not only in their ESL class, but also in subject matter classes such as social studies. Collaboration between the teachers of other classes and the ESL teacher can be extremely important in these cases.

The overall objective of stage two in the reading program can be viewed as the end point in an ESL course which is given within a school system which utilizes English as the means of instruction. Beyond stage two, the learner should be able to join a regular class. Thus, stage three of the reading program can be considered outside the scope of the ESL course given either at the university or school level. This stage does, however, play an important role in EFL.

The third and last stage of the reading program is one in which the learner makes full use of the mastery of the mechanics of reading, of effective reading techniques, and of a rather well developed stock of vocabulary items. At this stage the learner reads materials that were originally written in the new language rather than those which were adapted or simplified. The transition period between stage two and stage three helps the learner move from simplified to original reading matter.

Stage three of the reading program actually belongs in Part Two of this book, but the teacher of a beginner's course should be aware of the aims of stage three. Many of the early activities in the classroom can help to lead towards the final goals. Activities in silent reading, working with whole sentences, bringing in a variety of previously unseen reading selections which learners can cope with on their own are but a few examples of the things which, when done carefully at the early stage, ease considerably the

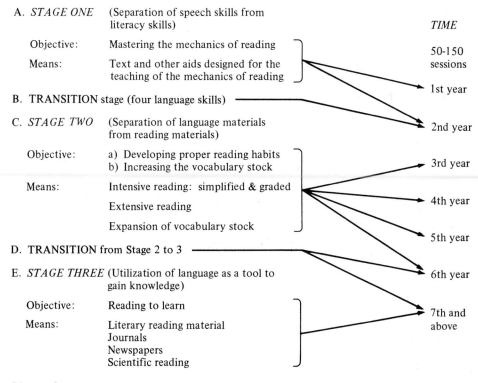

Diagram 8

progress into the later stages. Constant awareness of the final aims serves to guide the teacher in many didactic decisions in the classroom.

This suggested program, although it appears to be very tight, contains considerable flexibility and thus allows for adaptation to special needs. Larger classes of the conventional type may require more time for completing the stages than small classes. Ideally, individual pupils should be able to progress at their own rate. The above suggested program would work compatibly with an individualized approach provided all the necessary types of material are available for each stage. Each learner could then be guided to move at his or her own rate of progress from one stage to the next. Thus all pupils will, at different times and through different ways, reach the same final goals. In an ESL course such an individualized approach would be highly suitable since previous experience with reading may vary greatly among students. (Further discussion of the individualized approach is given in Part Two, Chapter Five, WHO.)

What are the specific learning tasks which the beginner tackles in the first part of the program? Stage one involves learning to recognize and distinguish between the English letters, learning to pair graphic shapes with sounds, learning to recognize words as smaller units of meaning and learning to recognize whole sentences as larger units of meaning. Learners whose native language has a writing system different from that used in English and who are in an EFL course, will need a prereading stage during which they will develop reading readiness. This pre-reading period is concerned mainly with familiarizing the learner with the shapes of the new alphabet and with whole words that are part of the pupil's classroom life or everyday life. Most teachers prepare special cards to paste on different objects in the classroom: blackboard, door, wall, etc. They use posters, charts, and other elements to create a reading environment. The pupils do not necessarily learn to read these words in the full sense of the word, but they begin to feel more at home with an unfamiliar type of writing.

Returning to the learning tasks specified above for stage one of the reading course, the first decision which faces the planner of the reading course is whether to combine the teaching of all the above-mentioned tasks in an integrated manner or whether to present each task in its own right. In order to make such a decision, one must take a very careful look at English orthography. English orthography, as has been mentioned before, is a system made up primarily of spelling patterns or sound-spelling correspondence rather than a system based on letter-sound correspondences. This fact becomes clearer if we consider the different sounds that correspond to the letter "a" in words like: hat, hate, star, ball, bay, sofa. It therefore seems futile to try to teach reading by using letter-sound correspondence. What then should be the basic unit of work for teaching the mechanics of reading and writing in English?

It seems that this basic unit should contain the combination of a letter within the graphic environment within which it occurs. Thus the letter "a" in the environment of *Consonant-a-Consonant* CaC, corresponds to a different sound than the same letter "a" in the environment *Consonant-a-Consonant* +silent *e*. An example is the difference between *hat* and *hate*. Furthermore, we get yet a different correspondence when the letter "a" is followed by the letter "r" or by the letter "l," as in *car* or *ball*. A similar type of complexity exists for all vowel letters in English—something which is quite evident from the fact that there are only five vowel letters in English with at least 11-13 vowel sounds in most English dialects and an additional number of vowel diphthongs. All these sounds are represented by the five vowel letters but within different graphic environments. A very confusing situation for the learner.

The situation with consonants is obviously much simpler. Most English consonants do have a sound-letter correspondence. There are, however, a number of complexities with consonants, too. For instance, the letter "c" has two sound correspondences in *city* and *call*. Or, letter clusters result in other consonant sounds like "th" or "sh." It is, therefore, imperative that, when teaching English, our basic unit of work within the mechanics of reading be based on sound-spelling correspondences.

One of the major decisions in planning the reading program of a course involves decisions over units to teach and in what sequence to organize them. Since the vowel is the nucleus of the English syllable, it makes most sense to organize the course according to correspondence of a *vowel letter + graphic environment with a vowel sound*. Thus one unit of work will be C-i-C like *pin, rip* and another unit will be C-i-Ce like *pine, ripe*. The consonants that are selected for the initial lessons in the reading course are usually those that have letter-sound correspondence and therefore pose no difficulties. Another consideration, of course, may be sounds which are the same in the native and new language.

The reading course, therefore, may start with the environment C - V - C when the consonants are: *p, n, t, m* and the vowel is *a*. Thus the combinations possible in this lesson might be: man/pat/nat/mat/map/etc. Let us assume, for the sake of the discussion, that this is how our young beginners start their reading program and let us, therefore, return to the question of which learning tasks they will have to cope with and in which sequence. The first task is one of recognizing the shape of the letters: m, n, p, t, a. The second task is to learn to recognize and generalize the notion that our basic unit is one of the CVC shape. The third task is to recognize units made up of these letters as meaningful words.

Keeping our final objective in mind, during the early lessons of the first stage we also want to show the learner what an English sentence looks like. Should we now separate these tasks or should we integrate them? The answer to this question is linked with the principle of stressing contexts which have meaning for the learner. The above mentioned tasks when separated will not allow any meaningful treatment of the problem, but will result in technical, unmotivated, boring drills of letter recognition or syllable recognition. By integrating these tasks, we can bring in more meaningful learning situations. The case will again be different in the EFL and ESL course. In the ESL course it is relatively easy to use, for instance, the vowel letter *a* in the environment C-V-C with meaningful words only. In the EFL course, however, if we limit ourselves to the words that the pupils know at this early stage, we would never get enough practice of this particular sound/spelling pattern. It is therefore necessary in the EFL course to combine a number of key words which are meaningful to the learners at this stage like *map, cat, hat* and then go beyond these items and practice sound/spelling correspondences with words that are not yet meaningful for the learner.

The recognition of letters is often one of the more difficult tasks involved in reading. Writing practice can greatly facilitate the recognition of letters. While writing the letters, learners become more efficient in recognizing their shapes. While writing words they become more efficient in recognizing the shape of basic spelling patterns. Thus the reading and writing skills are closely related at this stage and mutually reinforce each other. Yet our aim is to develop a good reader rather than a good writer, and so we use the writing skill mainly to reinforce reading and not as an end in itself. Furthermore, speech, and specifically pronunciation can help reinforce the consistent sound/spelling correspondences. Diagram No. 9 shows the three skills in action.

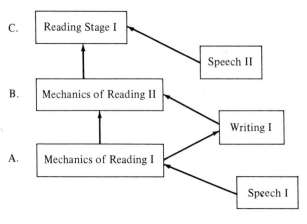

Diagram 9

5. Combining the Language Skills

The integration of language skills starts as soon as the learners have mastered the mechanics of reading. Now we are at a point where we must foster the use of all language skills. It is best to view this stage in the EFL course as a transition stage, very much like the transition stage between stage one and stage two. In the ESL course, however, it could last for a much longer period of time and carry much more importance. (See Diagram No. 8 on page 61.)

During the period when the four language skills are combined, the course syllabus should present the learner with the basic elements in language substance that are outlined in Section A: Language Substance. Thus the learners get the opportunity to establish a solid grounding in both language skills and language substance. This part of the course may very well follow a sequence of listening, speaking, reading, writing, or any other order which seems to be suited to the learners' needs.

During the next stage of the course, we face an interesting contradiction of aims—on one hand all efforts are still placed at integrating the use of all language skills, and on the other hand, it is now necessary to shift emphasis towards receptive competence rather than productive competence. This can be the case in both ESL and EFL courses at this stage, but is especially true in a course in a non-English speaking environment since it is difficult to stress the goal of productive competence.

While the teaching of language structures will continue to promote the integrative use of all four language skills, special attention might be given to aural comprehension as a skill in its own right, and to reading comprehension as the most attainable aim of the course. Thus, while integrating the skills in the language lesson, the emphasis will have to be shifted towards reading in the reading lesson, and perhaps towards listening during a lab session. What about the writing skill, however? In most cases the writing skill from now on is viewed only as a tool in the learning process. If, however, the learner is to become a student or an official in an English speaking community, writing might become important in itself.

Stage two of the reading course starts only after the transition stage described above. During stage two, it is usually important to separate the language text from the reading text in order to allow both integration and separation of the skills. It becomes evident at this stage that we must define the competence and performance aims more clearly. As far as the speech skills are concerned, pupils will most probably be able to understand much more than they actually produce at any time. The speech skills will continue to play an important role in the language lesson but gradually more time within the course will be devoted to the literacy skills and mainly to the reading skill. The writing skill is realistically limited to the function of a tool in the process of learning, but reading for comprehension becomes a very important aim of the course—often the most important one from this point on.

The objective of the second stage in the reading program is developing proper reading habits. In order to do this effectively, the reading material used for teaching should be divided into intensive reading matter, to be handled very carefully in class, and extensive reading matter, to be dealt with by the individual pupil at his or her own pace. The relation between these two types of reading matter is crucial: the extensive reading should be much easier and geared to the interest of the pupils. The intensive reading matter, on the other hand, should be constructed so as to foster and develop a good vocabulary stock and at the same time develop proper comprehension and reading abilities.

The intensive reading material should also incorporate all the language structures taught up to that point. Sometimes intensive material can introduce a limited number of structures which the learner has not learned actively in the language lesson but which can be comprehended when given in context. Thus, we develop in the learner a higher receptive competence in reading than in speech. This is a very important aim in itself, since an effective reader knows how to guess from context and interpret the meaning of a whole paragraph or passage even when he or she does not understand every single word. By slowly and gradually exposing learners to a wider use of language in the written material with which they cope intensively in class, we prepare them better for the extensive reading that they do on their own outside the classroom. The careful combination and coordination between these two types of reading matter during the second stage of the reading course will help prepare the learner for stage three of the course, the period where he or she will read for information, enrichment, and enjoyment. The major objective of the extensive reading matter is to develop in the learner a feeling of enjoyment and pleasure in reading in the foreign language. Only when the fear of the written page is truly overcome can a person become an effective reader in the foreign language. The process towards this goal must be slow, carefully graded, and divided into small but effective steps.

When a learner reaches stage three, the point at which he or she reads freely in the foreign language, one must again become aware of the mutual relation between skills. Total competence in language will continue to develop and increase even if the only practical skill used is reading, since the learner will be exposed to a constantly widening range of both structures and lexical expressions.

WORKSHOP ACTIVITIES

1. Visit two or three schools in your neighborhood or two or three different foreign language courses (not necessarily English). Try to find out how the teaching of the language skills is sequenced and integrated.
2. Visit the textbook section of a well equipped library (a USIS center or the British Council, if either is available to you). Try to make a list of some

language texts, some intensive readers which contain vocabulary and comprehension work, and some extensive readers. Imagine that you are about to teach a fourth year of English. Could you select textbooks for your class?

3

HOW

Making
It Work
in the
Classroom

OVERVIEW

This chapter deals with a fundamental question which language teachers ask themselves every day: HOW do I make the learning process work in the classroom? The basic formula which provides the answer to this question is: select the appropriate WHAT (as discussed in Chapter Two), pair it with information about WHO (Chapter One), then add the right selection of HOW. In carrying out this formula, the facilitator must be a constant decision maker. It is the objective of this chapter to present principles which will guide people to make effective choices in their own teaching-learning situations.

In selecting HOW, we are concerned with the needs of pupils and with the features of the subject matter. But we must also consider overall approaches in education which affect the teaching-learning process. The first section in this chapter deals with the choice of a suitable didactic approach—the inductive and deductive ways of presenting new material, and a comparison of the aural-oral and the cognitive-code theories of language learning. The starting point for actualizing HOW is to select an overall didactic approach.

This chapter on HOW also deals with practical matters in the classroom. Such matters can be explained best through exemplification. The second section is, therefore, devoted to the presentation of a basic framework, a series of activities which can be applied to the integrated substance and skills of WHAT. While working through this section, the reader will become involved in decision making which is typical of the language teaching-learning process. Although the framework for planning activities appears to be tightly structured, it actually contains ample room for flexibility and adaptation. In its tight format it is more suitable for the EFL situation, but by allowing constant adaption we make it work for ESL. Both ESL and EFL courses operate within the same basic framework. In both, the language facilitator makes responsible decisions guided by the same underlying principles.

A. SELECTING THE APPROACH

One of the first decisions the language facilitator is faced with is the selection of a suitable overall approach. This section discusses how to find the approach which best fits our learners, our subject matter, our own personality, and our particular situation.

Although the selection of an inductive or deductive approach is often made by the planner of the language course or by the textbook writer, the language facilitator can actually make the final adaptation in the classroom. Similarly, both aural-oral and cognitive code approaches can be combined by the teacher into effective, eclectic procedures. In fact, the strong tendency today is not to pit one approach against another, but instead to utilize all of them.

1. The Inductive and the Deductive Approaches

New material can be presented to learners in an inductive or a deductive way. When the inductive approach is employed, the learners encounter examples of the new topic first. They work with the examples without being told what the rule of organization or the generalization that applies to the examples is. The examples, however, have been carefully selected by the teacher to lead the learner to the proper generalization. Thus the learner is led to arrive at the rule inductively.

When the deductive approach is utilized in the presentation of new material, the learners are first presented with the rule or generalization. Only when they understand this rule are they asked to try to apply it to instances provided in the material. This approach is based on the fact that the learner is "told" or "given" the rule which is to be learned. The learner then practices the application of the rule.

In modern education there has been an increasing tendency to mix the two strategies. Thus for certain topics the inductive approach may be preferred to the deductive approach and for others the reverse may be true. In some cases the decision may depend on the learners and their learning habits. Moreover, it is possible to employ both strategies within the same presentation. Thus, for instance, one may start with the inductive approach, but when the learners prove incapable of arriving at the generalization on their own they are given the rule and then they start applying it. On the other hand, when material is first presented deductively but the learners do not seem to grasp the rule, it is possible to reverse the process and instead of letting them apply the rule, they are guided to arrive at it inductively by using examples.

When new language material is first presented inductively, the learner is exposed to a particularly selected and controlled set of examples of the new language topic. These examples must be so selected that they demonstrate effectively both elements of form and elements of meaning. The learner is then given an opportunity to experience the new material by carving out some kind of controlled activity involving it. It is hoped that on the basis of this exposure to instances of the new topic and some individual experience with it, the learner will arrive at a generalization applying to all the examples presented, concerning both form and meaning.

An example of the inductive presentation of the present perfect as a new topic might take the following form: the teacher presents the learners with a dialogue that contains a considerable number of sentences with the present perfect aspect. The learners are helped to understand the dialogue. Then they may be guided to memorize it or use it actively in a variety of controlled activities. Only following such activities will the present perfect be singled out and the learners will be guided to state a simple rule concerning the form of the new structure: *have + verb-en*, and the meaning or usage of the tense, for which they will undoubtedly need the teacher's help. The rule, however, has been arrived at on the basis of the examples practiced in and after the dialogue.

In contrast, when new language material is presented deductively, the learners are first presented with the rule. The rule is explained and discussed, and then the learners are encouraged to test examples and see how the rule works. When an error is made during such activities, the rule is cited as an explanation of what is wrong. Thus taking the example of present perfect again, the deductive approach would guide the teacher to start by telling the pupils about the present perfect (by using an example, of course) giving an explanation of the form and the meaning. Then the teacher would let pupils use that rule concerning present perfect in exercises.

Many modern methods of language teaching have demonstrated a preference for the inductive method since it allows for a certain amount of discovery procedure on the part of the learner. By providing the learner with examples first, the learner will soon tend to guess what the teacher is aiming at in the new lesson. It will therefore encourage the learner to discover the generalization by himself or herself. This type of activity can be viewed as a certain type of discovery. But such processes can take place only if the material is carefully selected so as to induce generalization. Many modern courses have therefore adopted such an approach.

In spite of these tendencies in modern language methodology, it is often the case that the deductive procedure is still favored in the classroom. Very often this preference is simply based on teaching and learning habits. Many teachers and learners feel more comfortable if things are stated clearly at the very start of the lesson. Thus, it is often the case in an adult course that the deductive approach proves more effective. Adults have developed learning strategies, they look for short cuts and analytical explanations as early as possible, they need to logically compare what they know about other languages with the new language and therefore the deductive approach might be the only one that will work with a particular group of adults. On the other hand, a group of ten-year-olds may lose all interest as soon as the teacher comes in with a lengthy explanation of grammar. They will be much happier starting with the actual language, imitating, practicing, using it, and while doing so many will discover the organizational elements by themselves. Very often, therefore, the choice of approach depends more upon the learners than upon the material. (See WORKSHOP ACTIVITIES, page 75.)

2. The Aural-Oral and Cognitive Approaches

The aural-oral approach to teaching language maintains that the speech skills must precede the literacy skills in the learning process. Thus the golden rule of the aural-oral approach says: learners should not say anything that they have not listened to first; they should not read anything that they have not practiced saying first; they should write only material that they have listened to, that they have used in speaking and in reading. This sequence of speech skills followed by literacy skills affects the planning of each lesson as well as the planning of the whole course of study when the aural-oral approach is favored.

A course of study based on the aural-oral approach will begin with a period during which only the speech skills are used. The length of this period may vary from several weeks to more than a year. The rationale for this approach is the belief that the learner will cope with reading and writing much better after he or she has had some experience with the speech skills and acquired a basic amount of language substance. According to this belief, starting with all four language skills at once will result in considerable confusion. The reading skill may interfere with speech if there are differences between spelling and pronunciation. Reading comprehension on the other hand, may be affected by limitations in the speech skill with the result that comprehension would be greatly impaired.

A typical lesson based on the aural-oral approach always begins with some listening activity. From the listening activity it goes on to oral practice in varied drills and exercises. Only after considerable drilling do pupils continue with reading and writing of the topics they have just encountered orally.

The aural-oral approach to language teaching developed on one hand as a reaction to the previously dominant grammar-translation method, and on the other hand as a result of developments in the area of linguistics and psychology. How can we explain the aural-oral reaction to the grammar-translation method? The primary purpose of the grammar-translation method is to prepare the learner to be able to explore the literature of the new language and in doing so to develop an overall ability to learn. In order to achieve these goals, the grammar-translation method places great emphasis on the learning of grammar and vocabulary. The grammatical rule is presented deductively and is followed by exercises practicing the application of the rule. The vocabulary items are usually given in long lists and are to be memorized by the learners. As the name of the method implies, much of the learning time is devoted to translation. The literacy skills in the grammar translation method are primary and very little or no attention is given to the speech skills. Although this method has lost considerably in popularity, it is still effective wherever the course aims at the objectives stated above.

The need for more emphasis on speech skills—on an aural-oral approach as opposed to the literacy approach of the grammar-translation method—was pointed out as early as the end of the nineteenth century. The real boost, however, to the aural-oral approach came from the development of descriptive structural linguistics and the school of behaviorism in psychology, both of which gained considerable ground in the 'thirties and 'forties of the twentieth century.

A number of important features of the descriptive structural school of linguistics and a few features of behavioral psychology deserve to be given special mention since they contributed to the development of a number of widely used teaching methods incorporated in the aural-oral approach. Among these methods, the audio-lingual method stands out as the most known and possibly the best representative of the aural-oral approach. The audio-lingual method, therefore, combines the key features of both structural linguistics and behavioral psychology and uses them in the aural-oral approach.

The important contribution of descriptive structural linguistics to the audio-lingual method lies in the following principles: speech is considered primary; each language must be viewed within its own context as a unique system; the speaker of a language may know nothing "about the language" although he is perfectly capable of using it; learning a new language should be viewed as a sequence of activities leading to habit formation. All of these linguistic principles combined well with the trend toward behaviorism in psychology. Behavioristic psychology developed a mechanistic approach to learning. This mechanistic approach led to viewing learning as a series of stimuli and responses, the connection between which was created by the reinforcement of correct responses.

The audio-lingual method and with it the aural-oral approach flourished for a considerable number of years. In fact, the audio-lingual method was eventually viewed by many teachers as an over-all approach. But just as the roots of the aural-oral approach grew from a reaction to the earlier grammar-translation method, so the more modern cognitive-code approach to teaching developed to a certain extent as a reaction to the audio-lingual method. Today it seems that both approaches are quite common throughout the world, with a general tendency towards synthesis. The modern language teacher must therefore be familiar with the various approaches and methods in order to be able to work out an approach of his or her own which ideally might be eclectic in nature.

The cognitive approach to language teaching is also influenced by both linguistics and psychology. The mentalistic trends which have developed in these disciplines have guided the development of the cognitive approach in language teaching. Learning is thus viewed as an active mental process and therefore only by means of meaningful learning can the learner acquire significant knowledge. Both generative-transformational grammar and the cognitive view in psychology emphasize the function of the mind in learning.

In reaction to the audio-lingual method, the cognitive approach establishes a number of principles which may remind us of the grammar-translation method. The overall goals, however, differ from the grammar-translation method and in fact are similar to the audio-lingual goals of fostering near-native ability in the new language. The attitude towards the learning process is, however, very different. While the audio-lingual method views learning basically as a habit-formation process, the cognitive approach views language learning as the learner's acquisition of competence. It is from competence that the learner should proceed to performance. The learner must therefore know the system first. He or she must know the rules and then apply them. The foundation is therefore made up of the grammar of the language. In this sense there is great similarity with the grammar-translation method, but the important difference is that since language is viewed in terms of its creative characteristics, the learner must be guided towards creative activities in all language skills.

When comparing the audio-lingual method with the cognitive approach, it is important to look at the methodological procedures that result from each of them. Perhaps the most important difference lies in the fact that since learning is viewed more as understanding rather than habit formation, the task of the teacher in the cognitive classroom changes too. Thus, the teacher in the cognitive course must facilitate learners' acquisition, organization, and storage of knowledge rather than help them develop automatic responses. The learners share in the responsibility for learning and must be always made aware of what they are learning. The emphasis on speech skills is greatly minimized by the cognitive approach. There is, however, no necessary contradiction between the aural-oral approach and the cognitive approach. The contradiction exists only between the audio-lingual method and the cognitive approach. It is, however, possible to develop other methods that would be based on an adaptation of both the aural-oral and the cognitive approaches.

The audio-lingual method inherently requires an inductive way of presentation since the learner must first have real experience with the language by practicing it in a controlled manner. The cognitive approach, on the other hand, encourages a deductive presentation of the grammatical rule followed by its application. However, by combining the aural-oral approach with the cognitive approach, we bring about a mixture of the inductive and deductive ways of presenting new teaching material. In order to arrive at such decisions, one must be very well acquainted with the features of each approach and adapt them to the specific goals of specific learners.

Various research projects have been devoted to the comparison of the efficacy of the audio-lingual versus the cognitive approach. In most cases it was found that the audio-lingual approach worked better with very young children or with adults in an ESL course. It worked, however, less effectively with teenagers. The audio-lingual method was also found more useful with beginners in general, while the cognitive approach is usually much more effective with advanced students. In many cases, adults interested in higher education prefer the cognitive approach, especially in the EFL course. In some instances it was found that the audio-lingual method works better with less talented pupils while the cognitive approach is preferred by the talented as well as the highly intelligent students. These various results seem to further reinforce what was said earlier: the approach must be suited to the learners and their needs. The decision as to which approach is to be selected for any particular course remains therefore basically within the responsibility of the teacher.

WORKSHOP ACTIVITIES

1. Use the past simple tense with regular verbs as the grammatical structure that you want to teach:
   (a) Design a presentation which is *inductive* in approach.
   (b) Design a presentation which is *deductive* in approach.
   Which do you personally prefer? Why?
2. Select a textbook that you are familiar with and that is intended for teaching English as a new language. If you wanted to use it in a classroom and adhere to the aural-oral approach at the same time, how would you have to adapt or supplement the textbook?

B. A FRAMEWORK FOR PLANNING ACTIVITIES

In designing instructional materials at the beginning levels, we work with a basic framework which can be applied to grammatical structures, pronunciation, lexical items, reading passages, or writing assignments. The framework consists of methodological steps which are pertinent to the teaching-learning of any language element. Actually, it provides the bare skeleton; the flesh and blood is supplied by the teacher whose role is to fit the framework to the needs of particular learners. It is, therefore, this basic framework which makes it possible to fuse WHAT and WHO in order to create HOW.

An important principle in planning activities is to proceed from strict control to a gradual lessening of control. The framework sets up a series of steps through which lessening of control can take place. Although the exact steps are not parallel for each language substance or skill area, the order of firm control to less control remains the same. Gradually we want to foster the learner's creative use of language. In the early periods controls are quite strict. The recurrent theme in each area is a series of steps which points the learner towards eventual autonomy.

The framework assumes as its objective the acquisition of an integrative knowledge of language. It begins with the aural-oral approach at the early stage of the course, then slowly shifts emphasis to literacy skills. But even at the early stage, some elements of cognitive theory are incorporated so that attention is also directed to the learner's overall competence in the new language. At each step, considerable attention is given to practicing the skills on the one hand and understanding the whole system on the other. Furthermore, by combining inductive and deductive approaches, the framework allows for maximum flexibility.

1. Grammatical Structures

To utilize the framework of activities most effectively, it is necessary to state the exact objectives for each step and to provide a number of ways to reach these objectives. The ways can be selected most appropriately when the actual learning situation is understood by the teacher and when the learner's goals are taken into account. Although an individual teacher will reuse the basic steps every time a new grammatical structure is taught, the ways selected to do so will differ greatly according to the specific grammatical topic and the specific learners.

Step I Presentation of the new grammatical structure.

Objectives: (a) Motivate the learner's interest in the new topic by presenting something relevant;
(b) provide simple and clear examples of the new structure indicating both form and meaning;
(c) contextualize the structure so that it presents a real-life (language) situation.

Ways: (a) A brief story or anecdote particularly written to fulfill the above objectives;
(b) a dialogue;
(c) a set of example sentences;
(d) a song;
(e) a picture which is described;
(f) demonstration through role-playing by the teacher.

Techniques: (a) It is best for the teacher to prepare the presentation. This is the only way to make sure that the presentation is relevant to the particular group of pupils.

(b) If we follow the aural-oral approach, the material will be presented orally to the pupils who listen but also attempt to understand. This will ensure the presentation of both syntactic and phonetic properties of the structure.

Step II   Controlled practice

Objectives: (a) Activate the pupils' skill of speaking, using proper intonation, rhythm, and stress.
(b) Pinpoint the structure by lifting the key examples out of the presentation. Both the syntactic and the phonetic properties can be emphasized.
(c) Provide practice of the form.
(d) Prepare pupils for the generalization by isolating the structure.

Ways: (a) Repetition: choral, individual, or combined.
(b) Simple substitution drills:
(i) Pupil fills slot with a given section of the structure.
(ii) Pupil fills slot with another element not essential to the structure.
(iii) Pupil fills slot of teaching point.

Techniques: Since the objective of controlled drilling is to drill form, it is not vital to make the sentences connected. However, the fact that they were taken from the presentation already ensures meaning. The following techniques are important:
(a) fast tempo and natural intonation;
(b) moving back and forth from choral to individual responses so that an element of tension and surprise is always kept up;
(c) correct modeling of response whenever the response was not clear or was not heard by all;
(d) the drill should be of short duration and must be stopped before pupils get bored.

Step III   Generalization

Objectives: (a) Help the pupils arrive at the grammatical rules in terms which are understandable to them based on the examples that were used so far (inductive guidance).
(b) Help the pupils retain the rule so that they can then apply the rule to more creative activities.

Ways: (a) Teacher writes key examples on the board and asks pupils to explain form as well as meaning. This can be done:
(i) in the native language;
(ii) in simple new language;
(iii) graphically.

(b) Teacher presents the generalization graphically on the board if pupils seem to have trouble generalizing themselves.

Techniques: (a) Use blackboard with colored chalk.
(b) Prepare chart at home.
(c) Use flashcards in pocket chart.
(d) Lead useful oral discussion of rules.

The question arises here of whether the teacher should compare the grammatical rule in the new language with similar rules in the native language. Here the teacher must certainly use his or her discretion, since the answer depends considerably on the two languages. The criterion is always: "Will the comparison with the native language help the learner retain the new rule or will it interfere?" Thus, when speakers of German are taught the present perfect in English, they might as well be told right away that although the form of this tense resembles the past in German, it does not function in the same way. If, however, one is teaching the distinction between present simple and present progressive to a speaker of Arabic or Hebrew, there is no productive comparison in the native language.

Step IV   Less controlled practice
In this stage we gradually release controls, guiding learners slowly to more productive types of drills. This step is longer in duration than the previous three, and contains oral drills, as well as written exercises. During this step learners will gradually improve their performance on the basis of the competence which they have already reached in Step III. The only way to a high level of performance is by drilling the application of the grammatical rule until it becomes almost automatic.

Objectives: Provide learners with the opportunity of gradually supplying more elements of structure by themselves and within a suitable context.
Ways: Oral drills: (a) multiple substitution drills;
(b) conversion drills of various kinds;
(c) completion drills.
Written exercises: (a) fill–in exercises;
(b) answers to questions and vice versa;
(c) matching two halves of a sentence;
(d) supplying sentences with the structure given in the form of clues only.
Techniques: (a) Individual rather than choral drills in class.
(b) More drills with written cues and aids.
(c) Written exercises to be done in class or as homework.

In Step IV of the sequence it is important to ensure meaningfulness of the sentence and all the language material utilized. It is a common feature in many textbooks to find exercises that require the learner to "change a positive sentence to a yes/no question." For example, change "The book is new" to a yes/no question. This is a meaningless type of activity since we are never faced with such a situation in real communication. Instead, by making a slight adaptation of the instructions to the drill we might suggest to the learner the following: "There is a book on the table. You want to know whether the book is new. Ask the question!" Or, in a written drill one might simply instruct the learner to write the questions for given answers: "Yes, the book is new."—Form the question that will fit this answer.

Step V   Productive activities (oral)

Objective:	Provide opportunity for using the structure creatively.
Ways:	(a) Guided conversation;
	(b) simulated situations;
	(c) role-playing;
	(d) games.
Techniques:	(a) Teacher initiates activity and lets pupils continue freely.
	(b) Teacher provides cues from which pupils can develop free activity (pictures, objects).
	(c) Role-playing—teacher establishes a situation and certain characters and pupils volunteer to act out the characters. At first this may be lightly guided, but the controls may slowly be completely released.
	(d) Language games are a particularly useful technique in aiding the learner to utilize the language material that has just been learned. When the learner is involved in the game he uses language naturally without "stopping to think" about the structure. Such games should be adapted to the special needs of each language structure, in order to become an effective part of the learning process.

In order to test and analyze the steps presented above, they are shown below incorporated in a sample lesson. We will assume that we are to teach the past progressive in the third or fourth year of English as a foreign language.

Sample Lesson

Step I   Presentation

The topic lends itself readily to presentation in a brief narrative. Remember—it has to be motivating and relevant, and it should provide good context for the structure of past progressive.

Sample Story:

"Yesterday at three o'clock, I came home from school. I walked into the house. It was very quiet. I looked into the kitchen. There was some soup cooking on the stove. I looked into the living room. The cat was sleeping on the couch. My baby sister was playing in the playpen. The TV was on and the announcer was giving the news. Where was everybody? I looked out of the window and there they were. My mother was standing in the back yard. My brothers were standing next to her. They were all looking at something."

The end of the story can be easily adapted to the particular country or environment in which the course is taught—it might be a pet, an unusual flower, or anything suitable and interesting to the pupils. Thus the presentation of the structure can be made relevant to the particular group of learners. The presentation of this story should be done orally by the teacher, while the pupils listen to it once. Then the teacher can return to pinpoint orally the sentences that contain the structure.

Step II Controlled practice

The sentences which contain the structure now provide the content of the repetition drill:

What was happening when I came home?
—In the kitchen—the soup was cooking.
—The cat was sleeping.
—The baby was playing.
—My mother was standing in the yard.
—My brothers were standing next to her.
—They were all looking at something.

The repetition drill will be closely connected with the presentation. Thus the story used for presentation provides a link with the activities to follow. Step I is the source from which Step II gets its content. Following the repetition drill there will probably be at least another controlled drill in Step II—a substitution drill. Since the major objective of the activities in Step II is to practice *form,* a mechanical substitution drill would be a suitable activity.

a. Teacher:	The baby was sleeping.	
Class:	The baby was sleeping.	
Teacher:	playing.	
Class:	The baby was playing.	
Teacher:	eating	
Class:	The baby was eating.	
Teacher:	drinking	
Class:	The baby was drinking.	
b. Teacher:	I was reading.	
Class:	I was reading.	

Teacher: He
Class: He was reading.
Teacher: We
Class: We were reading.
Teacher: They
Class: They were reading.

There should be usually at least two different substitution drills in order to practice the elements of *form* in the structure. In the above example, we want to emphasize two things: the fact that the verb is in the -ing form and that "be" in the past agrees with the subject.

When all responses in the substitution drill are given by the whole class, then the teacher need not reinforce the correct response every time, only when it is not clear or to change the tempo of the whole drill. If, however, individuals respond at times, the teacher must reinforce the correct response so that everybody in the class continues to hear the proper model. From the point of view of interest and motivation, it is best to conduct the substitution drill so that we switch from responses given by the whole class to responses given by individuals and then back to the whole class. This keeps all pupils on their toes and there is an element of surprise which is very useful for this type of mechanical drill.

Some teachers like to make the substitution drills more meaningful by using pictures as clues instead of individual words (wherever possible). Since the objective of this drill is really *form* and not meaning, it may, however, not be worth slowing down the drill.

Step III   Generalization

Following the substitution drills, we can move to Step III in order to arrive at a generalization. The generalization has to refer both to *form* and *meaning*. It is therefore important to go back to the initial presentation which provided good examples of both form and meaning. Thus the teacher may now start with:

What was happening at home when you came back yesterday?
–The soup *was* cook*ing*. (Write on board and use colored chalk to emphasize "be" and -ing)
–The cat *was* sleep*ing*.
–My brothers *were* stand*ing* in the yard.

If the pupils are now guided carefully they can probably come up with the generalization concerning *form*—namely the fact that "be" is in the past form and the verb is in the -ing form.

It may be more difficult for pupils to generalize the meaning of this tense. However, if they have really understood the "progressive" aspect of the present progressive, they might be able to generalize by themselves. If, however, they are not able to arrive at the generalization by themselves, the teacher may now help them and thus provide them with the correct grammatical rule. It is often necessary to allow pupils to generalize about meaning in their native language since their English may be too limited to come out with a clear generalization.

Some teachers like to have pupils write all generalizations in a special notebook or on cards. In other cases the textbook contains grammatical rules which can later be used by pupils for reference.

Step IV Less controlled practice

Following the generalization concerning the grammatical topic, we begin a long series of gradually less controlled drills and exercises and a variety of other activities which aim at practicing both the form and the meaning of the new structure. In fact, this application of the grammatical rule to various instances provides learners with practice in moving from competence to performance and improving their competence, hopefully reaching a stage where they will concentrate only on the message which they want to communicate rather than the manner in which they have to carry out communication.

Step IV is therefore much longer in duration than any of the previous steps. It may start with additional oral drills—aiming more towards individual than choral response:

Multiple substitution drill:

The baby was	sleeping.
The cat	
The cat	was	sleeping.
		playing
The cat	was	playing.

After oral drilling which seems sufficient for the particular group of learners, we move on to written exercises. The first and most controlled written exercises are much freer in nature than the oral drills up to this point. They are, however, still rather controlled. Thus, there will be fill-in exercises and completion exercises.

A very quick but effective substitution drill could be used for reinforcing the form in the later classroom sessions:

Teacher:	The boy	was	sleeping.
			read
Class:	The boy	was	reading.

Step IV should be as long as is necessary for the particular group of pupils to learn to cope with both form and meaning of the grammatical structure in question.

Step V Productive Activities

Step V is probably the most important step towards making the new grammatical structure part of the learner's active use of the language.

Here are just a few examples of the type of activities which will allow somewhat natural, although simulated, use of the grammatical structure:

a. Two pupils are asked to leave the classroom for a few minutes. The teacher asks some pupils to carry out certain activities: one is writing on the board, another one is reading, a third pupil is dancing. While they are doing these actions, the two pupils are called back in and asked to watch all the pupils carefully. Then the acting pupils are asked to go back to their places. The teacher asks the two pupils to try to remember what was happening in the classroom when they walked in.

b. The teacher brings a picture in which many different things are happening. She asks all the pupils to look at the picture very carefully and try to remember the things that are happening. Then she puts the picture away and asks pupils to remember what was happening in the picture when they saw it. This activity can be easily turned into a game by dividing the pupils into two or more groups. The teacher should have several sets of pictures each depicting a different activity. First the pupils just describe the activity in each picture using the "present progressive" tense. Then the teacher puts all the pictures away. The first group is asked to enumerate all the activities that they can remember using now the "past progressive". For every activity remembered they get a point.

c. When the pupils are ready to write a little paragraph or even a number of paragraphs, they can be given an assignment like the following: "When you go home today, walk into your home quietly and for a few minutes try to see what is happening at the moment of your entrance. Then write an essay describing what was happening when you came home."

d. When the pupils have mastered both questions and answers in past progressive, they can start role playing. For instance, one pupil can be given the role of an investigator who comes to investigate an accident, a robbery, or any other event. Or a pupil takes the role of a reporter collecting information for a newspaper or television program. He will have to ask a lot of questions concerning "what was happening at a certain time"... Other pupils will, of course, have other roles which will require that they provide suitable answers to these questions. (See WORKSHOP ACTIVITY (1), page 103.)

2. Pronunciation

In the initial stage of the course where pronunciation is given special treatment, it is necessary to break down the content of pronunciation into segmental sounds, word stress, sentence intonation, and sentence rhythm. (These elements were discussed in Chapter Two, *What: The Subject Matter is Language*.) Each of these elements will receive special attention and yet they will all be practiced together in an integrative manner. Thus the lesson plan is basically the same for the initial stage of the course and the more advanced stage—it is always centered around a basic grammatical structure. Within the drilling of that structure, both sentence intonation and sentence rhythm are practiced. The selection of the vocabulary items to be used while practicing the structure will depend upon the learning environment, the learner's interests, and most important, the ability to demonstrate or use the item meaningfully. At the initial stage, however, as opposed to the more advanced stage, the selection of the vocabulary items will also be affected by the sounds to be practiced.

For example, take this typical lesson for beginners. The lesson is centered around "be" sentences. The vocabulary items are all selected from the immediate environment of the learner. Thus, we may decide on items like: "pen," "book," "map." All of these may be suitable items from the point of vocabulary selection but how about the segmental sounds that deserve special treatment at the beginning stage? For many speakers of other languages, the vowel sound in "pen" is not new. However, the vowel sounds in "book" and "map" are. Attention must be paid to these sounds so that the learner begins by hearing and possibly also imitating them correctly. Such special attention to the segmental sounds can be given only at the initial stage while sentence intonation and sentence rhythm are practiced constantly throughout the whole course of study, as part of regular oral language drills.

The segmental sounds of a language must be divided into two systems: the vowel system and the consonant system. In English, however, the vowel system takes precedence over the consonant system because in English, the vowel is the nucleus of the syllable. Many English consonants will pose no difficulty for the learners because the sounds will resemble consonants that they know in their own language. There will, however, also be quite a number of sounds that differ considerably. For example, the English "th" and "r" sounds will probably be new and strange; the "w" and "y" sounds might be unfamiliar. In all of these cases, using articulatory explanations when the new sound is first encountered is helpful. In fact, showing and telling pupils to put their tongue between their teeth when pronouncing "th" could solve this problem. The problem of the "r" might, however, be much more difficult to solve. If so, the teacher will have to make a decision as to the importance of a proper "r" pronunciation, since a "foreign" "r" is not very likely to interfere with intelligibility.

It should also be remembered that the arrangement of consonants in English is often more important than the pronunciation of individual segments. The English language is quite rich in consonant clusters in both initial and final position and this feature often creates difficulties for many learners. For example, foreigners often mispronounce the word "film"—they say "fil-em" instead. This mistake occurs because the speaker has difficulty with the consonant cluster and inserts a vowel within the cluster to resolve this difficulty.

The consonant clusters are particularly useful in English and therefore deserve special attention at the early stage. Similar problems of pronunciation will appear as morphological inflections are learned, which result in final consonant clusters like the "-ed" of verbs in the past.

Returning now to the vowel system in English, it was mentioned above that the vowel system is more important than the consonant system in English in the sense that vowels act as nuclei of syllables. It is the vowel sound that will play a vital role in the selection of vocabulary items for the initial stages of the course. In the example given above: if we decide to introduce the words: "book," "map," and "pen" and the learners have difficulty with the vowels in both "book" and "map" we may want to postpone one of these two sounds for a while. We will decide now, for the sake of the presentation, that "map" and "pen" are kept for this lesson while "book" is postponed. Obviously then we need to add more words with the same sound: *hat, cat, mat* versus *hen, net, bed.* Thus we will give the learner a chance to practice the two sounds in meaningful contexts—hearing and imitating them after the pronunciation model. However, in order to really foster recognition in hearing the sounds properly and perhaps eventually also imitating them correctly, we will need many more examples than just those that can be made meaningful at this stage. It will be necessary to select suitable minimal pairs to drill the sounds, even if these minimal pairs are not always meaningful to the pupils: *bed/bad; head/had; ten/tan.* This deliberate practice of the sounds will be a vital part of the lesson in the initial stage of the course and will be added to the activities for teaching language structure. Thus, the series of activities in the total frame of the lesson might take the following form.

1. PRESENTATION of the new language structure in a context. For example, "be" sentences for object identification. "This is a hat." "That is a cat." (with pictures and real objects). The words which are selected for practicing the structure will fit the vowel sound to be practiced, in this case /æ/.
2. ORAL DRILLING of the structure with emphasis on natural sentence intonation and sentence rhythm.
3. Special PRONUNCIATION drills to practice the vowel sound /æ/, first with the meaningful items which were introduced in the presentation above: "cat," "hat"; and then with more items that fit this sound pattern.
4. MINIMAL PAIR practice in order to help the learner develop at least auditory discrimination between /æ/ and /e/. These drills concerned with minimal pairs will be sequenced so that we allow for maximum facilitation between the listening and speaking skills, as discussed in Chapter Two, *What:*SKILLS. Listening and speaking activities will therefore be alternated throughout, so as to improve gradually the learner's ability to discriminate auditorily, as well as approximate the production of the new sounds.

In the above steps, (1) and (2) provide the basis within which pronunciation is practiced throughout the whole course of study, while steps (3) and (4) are typical of the special attention devoted to pronunciation only in the initial stage. In the first steps of the above series, the learner is coping simultaneously with the syntactic, semantic, and phonetic features of the language structure, while in steps (3) and (4) pronunciation is singled out.

Sentence intonation and rhythm are practiced best as parts of the grammatical structures taught at each point and throughout the course. Care must be taken, however, to present and practice new grammatical structures with a natural intonation and rhythm and without slowing down or overenunciating elements in the structure. In order for pupils to achieve any kind of approximation of the native speaker's ability to use the language, they must be exposed to the natural flow of speech as early as the first classroom session. Obviously, this must be done within the boundaries of their knowledge.

The importance of pronunciation at the initial stage of a course can hardly be overemphasized. There are two basic requirements, however, that must be fulfilled at this early stage if the course is to achieve integration of the four language skills:

1. If pronunciation work does not start at the beginning of a course, wrong pronunciation habits might develop. Such habits because they are acquired at the very beginning, are very hard to correct at a later stage.
2. Fostering some auditory recognition ability before reading and writing are begun will greatly help to prepare the learner for the teaching of the literacy skills. If learners cannot hear the difference between /e/ and /æ/ as in "bed" and "bad," it will be very hard for them to learn the relevant sound-spelling correspondences. It is imperative, therefore, that the learners receive considerable practice concerned with vowel pronunciation prior to the initiation of the literacy skills.

Very often we might add a third requirement to reinforce the need for special treatment of pronunciation at the early stage of the course: beginners are usually young learners and can therefore imitate a good pronunciation model more easily.

The only area that has not been discussed so far is word stress. The learning of word stress cannot be separated from learning the meaning of the word. Word stress is therefore most effectively taught if the teacher pays special attention to stress whenever a new word is introduced. When learning a new word, the learner should practice both its meaning and its phonetic features. These phonetic features will involve the main stress as well as the weak vowels which require special attention in English. In other words, the problem arises with polysyllabic words, and as such is often relevant only in the more advanced stages of a beginner's course for young learners, or right from the start in a course for adults (due to more sophisticated topics handled in adult courses). In addition to practicing proper stress as part of the presentation of a new word, it will prove useful to present the learner with special drills for word stress.

Here are some examples:

tícket	tomórrow
cústom	expénsive
lésson	contrástive

(See WORKSHOP ACTIVITY (2), page 103.)

3. Lexical Items

When learning a new lexical item, pupils must become familiar with its semantic, syntactic, and phonetic properties. In teaching lexical items, the same basic series of steps that has been introduced for teaching a new grammatical structure is followed. The teaching-learning process begins with high control and there is a gradual release of controls. This release of controls enables learners first to learn to recognize the properties of the new lexical item and then gradually to start using the item productively.

The first step is to introduce the new lexical item. During this introduction, three types of properties must be made clear: the exact meaning of the item, how it is used syntactically, and its features of pronunciation. Therefore, new words are best introduced orally first in order to illustrate the sound features. They must then be introduced within a suitable context (a sentence or sometimes more than one sentence) so that both their semantic and syntactic features can be shown. If the item is polysyllabic, it is very important to explicitly indicate proper word stress.

Consider, for example, the word "integrity." When this lexical item is first introduced, a number of examples like the following can be given:

1. A person who has *integrity* is very honest.
2. Her *integrity* will prevent her from doing anything dishonest.
3. People trust him because they know he has *integrity*.
4. People who have *integrity* would not take advantage of a situation like
   . . . .

Sentence (1) above is suitable for introducing the new item if the pupils know the meaning of "honest." One sentence, however, is never sufficient and at least two additional sentences will be necessary to ensure the learner's grasp of all the properties of the item. The basic syntactic property—namely the fact that this lexical item functions as a noun that takes no articles—was clearly illustrated when a number of different examples were given. It was also made clear that a person "has" or "possesses" integrity.

In addition to having the learners repeat the sentences containing the new lexical item, the item must now also be isolated for pronunciation purposes and repeated by all of the learners in the group, both in choral fashion and individually. Following this oral presentation of the new lexical item, the pupils must be shown the written equivalent with stress indicated clearly. In most cases it is enough to show the main stress. Sometimes, however, it may also be advantageous to point out the weak syllables and to use a special mark for them.

Following the presentation of a new lexical item, the learners must encounter the item in various contexts. This can be done orally or through reading materials. Finally, learners must be required to start to use the word by themselves.

The activities now have to be carefully graded. In order to avoid mistakes, learners are first given the context and required only to pair the new lexical item with that context. The common type of exercise for this step is the "fill-in" exercise. Such exercises contain sentences with empty slots that are left for the learners to fill in. These exercises exist and can be designed in a number of different ways. Two types are described below:

1. A number of lexical items is practiced at the same time. For example, the learners are given ten fillers (new items) and only seven sentences with slots. They must choose the seven suitable fillers among the ten provided and put them into the right slots. While doing this they have a good chance to again check the context within which each item must appear. They also have a chance to check syntactic and morphological features as well as spelling and/or pronunciation features, depending, of course, on whether the practice is done only in writing or in writing and orally as well.
2. Only one sentence with one slot is provided together with three or four different choices. For example:
   Our mayor is known for his _____ . Since he began to run the city, people have developed trust in the adminstration.
   a. efficiency
   b. integrity
   c. good looks

Each choice could fit the blank syntactically. However, the meaning restricts the choice to (b) only. Choice (a) is close enough to the correct choice, while choice (c) is quite remote. Learners are thereby forced into a situation where they must define the accurate meanings of the lexical items. This will help them develop competence in using the item.

Only after the learners have worked with the above types of exercises can one expect productive knowledge. Only then can one encourage them to use the lexical items to communicate ideas of their own. And only after the pupils are able to use the lexical items correctly both in speech and in writing have they learned the item productively.

The above steps in teaching lexical items are necessary only when the learners expect to use the word as senders of messages. One may, however, rightly decide that there are many words which people need only to recognize. If this is the case, it will not be necessary to handle the item as carefully as has been described above. In fact, all that the learners then need is exposure to the lexical item in a number of contexts. The facilitator only aims, in other words, at helping the learners "comprehend." Usually such items are aids in reading comprehension and will be again mentioned as part of the teaching of reading. (See WORKSHOP ACTIVITY (3), page 103.)

4. Reading

Activities for the teaching of reading are developed in three phases: (a) *mechanics of reading,* (b) *intensive reading,* and (c) *extensive reading.* These phases are closely coordinated with the reading program presented in Chapter Two, *What.* Each of these three types of reading follow the basic progression from a controlled stage to a step-by-step release of controls.

Stage One of the reading program is devoted to the acquisition of the mechanics of reading. The major elements that must be included in the mechanics of reading are: letter recognition, pairing letters with sounds and spelling patterns with sounds, developing the learner's recognition of words and whole sentences, training the learner in silent reading, and using the mechanics of writing in order to improve reading. It is only after mastering the mechanics of reading that the learner can move on to intensive and extensive reading.

Once mastery of the mechanics of reading is achieved, usually at the beginning of Stage Two (see Diagram No. 8, page 61), emphasis must be placed on the development of proper reading habits and acquisition of a good stock of lexical items. To ensure the achievement of these two goals, it is necessary to separate language work from the reading program. This separation allows thorough treatment of intensive and extensive reading.

Once Stage Two of the reading program is initiated, we must distinguish between the intensive reading part of the course which is handled in class under the guidance of a facilitator, and the extensive reading part which is carried out by the pupils on their own, usually outside the classroom. Both the intensive and the extensive reading programs play a very crucial role in the achievement of a good level of reading comprehension. Since reading comprehension is often the ultimate aim of a language course, even if it is an integrative course of study, special attention and therefore a special series of activities is presented for each type of reading.

(a) The Mechanics of Reading The mechanics of reading play a major role in the new language course during the period that follows the aural-oral part or Stage One of the reading program. During this period, most of the lesson time is still devoted to work on language structure by utilizing the

speech skills, while about a third of the classroom time is devoted to the mechanics of reading. Activities for the teaching of the mechanics of reading in English are very important, particularly for speakers of languages which do not utilize the Roman alphabet. They would, of course, be highly abbreviated for the adult learner. There would not be a serious difference between the EFL and ESL course except for the fact that more advantage can be taken of the availability of English writing in the ESL pupil's everyday life.

Step I   Presentation of a teaching unit

An example of a teaching unit is a sound spelling pattern like the letter /e/ within the syllable *C V C*, a number of consonants that have a one-to-one letter sound correspondence like *m, t, n, d,* or a letter cluster like *ch* or *sh*. Whatever is chosen, the presentation of this new element in the code must be carried out in a meaningful context. The new spelling pattern might, for example, be introduced first orally by showing the pupils a picture of a "pen" and a "net." The selection of the items will be guided by which words the pupils already know and which additional words might be needed in order to present the spelling pattern clearly.

The sentences used to practice these items are usually "be" sentences.

Examples:

This is a pen (holding up a picture or real object).
This is a net (picture).

The pupils must repeat both the sentences and the individual items. When they are familiar with the words, they must be shown the printed word on a flashcard. The picture and the flashcard are then paired together.

At this stage the learner is thus introduced to the fact that a syllable like "pen" or "net" represents real words in English and in this way also learns to recognize, when written, all of the words that he or she knows.

It is necessary to continue to practice the recognition of the spelling pattern as a whole, as well as the recognition of the letters that make up the pattern. Work must now start, therefore, with words that may not be meaningful to the learners but which follow the spelling pattern closely. Words like *men, ten, den, hen,* etc., must be practiced. Also, constant change of the initial and final consonant letters is most important at this stage if the learners are to become skilled in the recognition of the patterns.

There are various aids available for such practice: e.g., a simple nail board on which it is possible to change individual letters within the pattern; pocket charts, sliding cards, flannel boards, etc. One can also find various sets of letters and cards in order to practice such spelling patterns with individual pupils and/or small groups of pupils.

Step II   Silent recognition work

Here learners should be trained to work by themselves with the

printed page in front of them. Thus, this step will accomplish two objectives: it will help the learners improve letter recognition; it will also train them to read silently. Such drills can take the following form:
1. "Underline all of the words that begin with the same letter."

Example:

pin
tap
pen
bat

2. "Place a line between the words in Column A and the words in Column B that end in the same letter or letters."

Example:

A	B
tip	cat
tin	bin
tap	lip
bat	lap

Step III The writing skill

By learning to write the letters, the pupils will also learn to recognize their shapes more accurately. It should be remembered that there is a difference between those learners who are familiar with the Roman alphabet and those who are not. The former will not require a great deal of work with the individual letters; they will be able to focus their attention on the whole spelling pattern at an early stage. The latter will, however, need to practice the individual letters more diligently because they are completely unfamiliar with them.

Step IV Recognizing the spelling pattern within the structure of a whole sentence

There are two types of drills here. The first utilizes only the language structures familiar to pupils and trains them to recognize whole sentences. For example, "This is a pen" written on a chart next to a picture of a "pen." The second drill also trains pupils to recognize whole sentences. However, it also pays attention to details within the sentence at the same time. In this type of drill, pupils will distinguish between sentences like "This is a pen" and "This is a den" when the emphasis is on the shape of the letters.

Example:

"Underline the two sentences which are the same."

This is a pen.
This is a den.

This is a ben.
This is a pen.

Step V   A productive step with learners reading out loud as well as in-dicating understanding of the meaning of the spelling pattern

This will be the step which tests how well the learners have coped with the whole entity of the sound-spelling correspondence.

The type of drill suitable for this activity might take the form of the teacher reading one word in each of the following pairs. The pupils are asked to mark the word which they hear.

pin   tin
pen   ten

Here the pupils are expected to distinguish between the vowel *i* and the vowel *e* in the same environment. This could also be done for consonants:

den   din
pen   pin

Another example would be to ask pupils to match pictures and objects ac-cording to spelling and meaning.

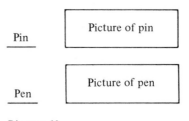

Pin | Picture of pin |

Pen | Picture of pen |

Diagram 10

Step VI   A combination of language structures and reading

Wherever possible, we should combine the performative and compe-tence aspects of the reading skill by guiding the pupils to read for mean-ing. Step six also provides the link from Stage One of the reading program to the transition stage which follows it.

The transition stage that follows the first stage of the reading program combines all four language skills. This stage also further fosters each of the four language skills. It is during this transition stage, therefore, that the learner is first provided with opportunities to use equally all four language skills within the boundaries of his or her knowledge. All of the activities are centered around the language structure and are designed to help the pupils master that structure.

The choice of activities in this transition stage depends on the basic approach of the course of study. If the aural-oral approach is used, the framework of activities will be: (1) oral presentation of the grammatical topic while the pupils engage in listening activities; (2) oral practice aiming to develop spoken fluency; (3) reading material centered around the same language structure; (4) guiding the student in writing the structure first in controlled and eventually in less controlled activities. Thus, all four language skills are utilized and practiced while a new grammatical structure is learned.

If, however, the cognitive code learning theory is the basis for the course, the sequence of skills could be very different. For example, the order could then be: reading, speaking, and listening. No matter which approach is selected for the transition period, however, it is the intensive reading phase which minimizes the differences between the two approaches by shifting the emphasis towards literacy skills.

(b) Intensive Reading   The intensive reading text aims at fostering good reading habits. It should contain stories that are simplified but that also provide interesting material which pupils will like to read and discuss. If the reading material is good, the facilitator will be able to select key lexical items and teach them actively.

The aim of the language text, as opposed to the intensive reading text, is clearly different from this point on. Whereas the language material must be graded carefully so as to facilitate mastery of language structures, the reading text may allow more freedom in order to present more natural language and thus promote the receptive skill of reading comprehension.

The aims of the intensive reading text coincide with the aims of the second stage of the reading program. (See Chapter Two, Section B.) The ways to implement these aims in the actual intensive reading text are:

Aim 1. Gradually increase the lexical stock by introducing a limited number of lexical items in each reading passage. These items must also be carefully reviewed throughout the text. The selection and grading of lexical items are, in other words, the important features of a good intensive reading text.

Aim 2. Develop good reading habits through material which lends itself to the following activities:
(a) pointing out the main idea of reading selections
(b) grasping details which support the main idea
(c) providing material that can be scanned quickly
(d) improving the learner's speed of reading
(e) promoting techniques for "guessing from context"

Aim 3. Expose the learners to a natural use of the language substance they have learned so far. In other words, all the language structures known should be used in an accumulative fashion.

Aim 4. Expose the learners to structures that have not been learned as yet and which need careful preparation before the actual teaching. For example, it may be advantageous to introduce some form of passive sentences before the actual passive construction is taught in the language text. Such passive structures will be understood by the learners and will help them prepare for the eventual learning of the structure. For example, a sentence like: "America was discovered by Columbus in 1492." will be understood by pupils who have not yet learned how to convert "Columbus discovered America." to "America was discovered by Columbus." It seems valuable to introduce learners to such passive sentences even before they learn to produce the structure since this early exposure might help the learning process considerably. An intensive reading text can serve this purpose quite effectively.

Aim 5. Promote a feeling of enjoyment from reading through the selection of good stories. Though this has been mentioned above, the suggestion cannot be stressed enough. If the pupils are interested in the material and if the reading process is pleasant and encouraging, the learners will enjoy both.

An intensive reading text that tries to fulfill all of the above-mentioned requirements should contain two types of reading selections: (1) those that present both new vocabulary items and, at the same time, a substantial content which can be discussed and worked on so that the pupils are trained in both the general and supporting ideas of the passage; (2) those that are much simpler, shorter, and easier and which are read silently and individually by the pupils under the supervision of the teacher.

Each reading selection of type (1) above, which introduces new lexical items, must be followed by vocabulary exercises. These vocabulary exercises will follow the grading mentioned in Section 3, Lexical Items, above. They will help the learner acquire an active knowledge of these items and thus fulfill the first aim of the intensive reading text, namely increasing the learner's lexical stock. In addition to vocabulary exercises, such reading selections must be followed by carefully designed comprehension exercises. These should help the pupil develop good reading habits by guiding him or her to grasp the main ideas as well as details contained explicitly and implicitly in the reading selection. Finally, the type (2) "silent reading selection" should put the learner's knowledge of the lexical items, as well as his or her comprehension habits, to immediate use.

(c) The Intensive Reading Lesson The intensive reading lesson is a unit composed of two consecutive classroom sessions. The first session contains the following methodological steps:

Step I: Introduction to the intensive reading selection. A short presentation is made of the key lexical items vital for a general understanding of the story or reading passage during the first reading. The number of items handled at this point should never exceed six to eight. These items must be introduced in meaningful contexts as mentioned in Section 3, Lexical Items, p. 87. Only a presentation of the items should, however, be given at this point. The introduction of the intensive reading passage may also include some background information and cultural elements that are connected to the passage since the objectives of the introduction are to acquaint learners with everything they need to know in order to grasp the main idea of the passage during the first reading. The amount of time and information needed to introduce a passage will depend on both the passage, and the knowledge and experience of the learners. Another important aim here is to motivate the pupils' interest in the passage.

Step II: First reading of passage. At this stage of the overall course of study (third or fourth year of English), the intensive reading passage should always be read out loud by the teacher while the pupils listen. This step is a combination of listening and reading for comprehension. The objective of this first reading is to train pupils to look for the main idea of a passage. This is a very important skill that any effective reader has, but which often seems to be difficult in foreign language learning. It is important to guide learners to free themselves from the need to understand every single word. The goal is to grasp the idea even if some of the words are not understood.

Should books be open or closed during the teacher's first reading? Although there are diverse opinions on this point, it should be remembered that the atmosphere must be relaxed and the teacher's reading meaningful if comprehension is to take place. In order to have a truly relaxed atmosphere, it may therefore be necessary to allow pupils who greatly depend on visual cues to keep their books open. It is a source of confidence for some learners to have the text available, even though they might never glance at it during the reading of the teacher.

It is also important to guide pupils to not ask questions or stop the teacher in the middle of reading. Only by listening to an uninterrupted reading will the students be able to grasp the main idea.

Step III: The teacher asks general comprehension questions immediately after the first reading of the passage. These questions should require simple answers: yes/no, or some other one-word answer which will tell the teacher that the pupils got the main point of the passage. Thus, this step also has a twofold aim: First, it helps pupils summarize the content of the passage for themselves in very general terms; second, it helps the teacher to assess the level of difficulty of the passage and the comprehension of the pupils. The facilitator, therefore, uses these comprehension questions in a diagnostic fashion in order to decide how to continue the series of activities from this point on.

It is advisable to direct most of these "easy" questions to the weaker pupils in the class. If the weaker pupils have no trouble with the passage, the teacher can go on to a freer stage. If, however, the passage is difficult for the weaker pupils, then special attention is directed to comprehension. The next step depends on Step Three, the diagnosis, and presents two alternatives.

Step IV: There are two possible choices here.

1. If pupils of different levels had no trouble understanding the passage, it can now be divided into smaller sections. The pupils will read each of these smaller sections silently and then answer more involved questions on each section. The objective of this step is to train pupils to understand the passage in greater detail. The questions asked at this step require answers that are not available verbatim in the text. Rather, they have to be inferred by the skilled reader.

2. If the passage is difficult, the teacher reads it a second time, but instead of going straight through to the end, breaks it down into smaller sections. After each section the teacher explains and paraphrases necessary sentences and then asks questions of inference.

Step V: At this point the focus is on lexical items intended for productive knowledge. The exercises mentioned in the section dealing with lexical items can be utilized here. In addition to vocabulary work, the assignment includes written exercises on the content of the passage in order to deepen the pupils' understanding of it.

This step brings the teacher to the end of the first classroom session of the intensive reading passage. The next classroom session should also be devoted to the passage. It should, however, be shorter in duration and bring the class to the next step.

Step VI: This step concentrates on fuller understanding of the passage and the ability to relate its content to one's own experience. It can take the form of a discussion or of more detailed questions about the passage. The questions should require expression of personal opinions. They should also elicit personal reactions to the passage and the way it is written.

Step VII: The last step tests achievement in the skill of reading comprehension. A way to do this is to give learners a silent reading passage that contains most of the words of the first passage but which is much easier and shorter. The pupils read the passage on their own and then answer questions of a multiple-choice type that tests their general comprehension. This way both the teacher and the learners are able to assess overall improvement in reading competence. The above series of activities was suggested as a basic framework within which most reading selections can be handled. This framework is, however, intended as a flexible one. The sequence might be changed so as to fit a certain reading passage. Thus, step I might be skipped altogether if the passage is an easy one. Even silent reading might become the first step for certain passages. The whole sequence of activities is given here as a basic sample which can guide the facilitator and yet allow considerable changes within the sequence. It is generally advisable not to use the same sequence constantly but to vary the steps every now and then, especially when the particular passage allows or even requires such variation.

Throughout the series of activities dealing with intensive reading, reading aloud has never been suggested as one of the techniques—although it is probably widely used throughout the world. It is usually *not* advisable to encourage reading out loud in a traditional classroom situation. By so doing, an imperfect model is presented. Also, the pupils who must sit and listen often become bored. Reading aloud can, however, be utilized in a laboratory situation. For example, each pupil can practice reading aloud while imitating a model on a tape or while comparing his or her own reading with that of the model.

All of the objectives and activities described in the intensive reading program prepare pupils for extensive reading on their own. This goal is the major objective of an overall reading program. (See WORKSHOP ACTIVITIES (4), page 103.)

(d) Extensive reading   Learners who participate in an effective intensive reading program gradually develop good reading habits. To capitalize on these newly acquired habits, however, they must begin to read on their own. The objectives of extensive reading are multifold:

1. Learners should develop the ability to gain satisfaction from reading on their own in the new language.
2. They should be exposed to language used in a more natural and less structured way.
3. They should develop a feeling for the language—a feeling which can never develop while using more structured materials.
4. Extensive reading should have a beneficial effect on other language skills, namely, writing and speaking.
5. Extensive reading, or reading for pleasure, will ultimately help the learner maintain and continue to use the language long beyond the end of the course of study.

All of these objectives carry considerable importance, but the last one deserves to be singled out, namely, "reading for pleasure." If extensive reading material is to fulfill the objective of encouraging reading for pleasure, it must have two basic qualities: it must be interesting, and it must be easy. Only material that is easily understood can be fully enjoyed; only material that is interesting can be called pleasurable reading.

Learners should never be placed in a situation where they are confronted with something that they simply cannot do. Extensive reading can only take place after ample experience coping with unfamiliar passages in the classroom and after considerable success in understanding the pages in the intensive reading lesson.

When the extensive reading program is initiated, the facilitator faces two major problems: first, how to make a wide enough variety of simplified texts available to the learner, and, second, how to guide the learner into reading activities which are pleasurable, without turning them into "school" activities. Each of these problems deserves special consideration.

Various texts suitable for extensive reading at the lower and more advanced levels are available today in simplified versions. And, it is quite easy to find interesting reading materials for all levels above the first year of English as a foreign language. Because these materials are both graded and simplified, the learner can be encouraged to increase his or her proficiency in reading while enjoying the content.

Guidance in reading for pleasure requires a very tactful approach. The activity should never be just another type of homework assignment. Learners must feel that they can choose what they like and that they can read it at their own pace. They must also feel that they are reading for pleasure and not for a grade or a test. On the other hand, pupils need considerable encouragement during the first stages of extensive reading. It is a time when they either gain confidence or become completely discouraged. We often come across a text in the library in which the first page is covered with penciled-in translations of every other word. The rest of the book, however, is very clean. The penciled translations were probably made by readers who started with high hopes and ambitions, but soon became tired of looking up every word in the dictionary.

In order to facilitate the first steps of extensive reading (in the second or third year of English), the teacher will have to begin with some semi-extensive reading activities. The first extensive reading text should be selected with the whole class in mind. However, it should also allow the teacher to guide and encourage individual pupils. Also, first experiences should include a visit to the school library, a public library, or even a book store. The purpose is to involve the pupils in the acquisition of the text even though it is not their own choice at this point.

The pupils then come back to the classroom with the book selection. It is advisable to first spend a few minutes talking about the title, the author, the cover, and any other features or facts that might arouse interest. Then, to start the semi-extensive technique, the first few pages should be discussed in class, while the teacher continues to arouse the pupils' interest. The pupils then take the book home and read it at their leisure. Although some kind of deadline must be set so that they know there is a time limit, ample time should be allowed.

Some pupils will go home and finish the book the same evening. Some will put it on a shelf and ignore it completely. Others will decide with good intentions to read it the following day but will forget about it nevertheless. And a few will methodically read a few pages every day. It is therefore important that the teacher motivate the pupils in order to involve as many as possible in the reading activity.

Since the main goal here is reading for enjoyment, it is most important to continue to emphasize the element of interest. Self-motivated pupils can help generate enthusiasm among the less motivated ones. Thus, a week or two after the book has been taken out, the teacher can ask the pupils to bring their books to class. Because the emphasis must be on interest, the teacher prepares some questions on the story, the characters, or some incidents that take place in the story in order to get a discussion started in class. Thus, those pupils who read the story will feel a sense of achievement while those who didn't will possibly want to begin reading it. Also, if another week is then assigned for further reading or rereading of the story, there is a good chance that a number of pupils among those who have not read the book will decide to try to read it.

But at the end of two weeks, discovering that no one has read even one page of the text, one could feel a sense of frustration. Instead, the teacher in this predicament should really stop and consider if the book selection was appropriate to the students in terms of both language complexity and subject matter.

Assigning the same text to the whole class enables the teacher to: (1) discuss certain elements of the story; (2) point out characters and events of particular interest; and (3) help the pupils develop a taste for reading in general. Although this type of guidance is valuable for beginning readers in a foreign language course, it must be remembered that different pupils like different types of stories. The teacher should, therefore, suggest a variety of stories after the pupils have read the first extensive reading text, so that groups of several pupils will read the same book.

When a number of pupils read the same book, special types of activities suitable for group work can be designed. For example, pupils can be asked to dramatize scenes from the story. They may prepare a poster or other types of art work which involve drawing and not necessarily language. In a more advanced class, those pupils reading the same story can be given questions that lead to discussions. They can also tell the story to the rest of the class after such discussions. Thus, by working in small groups, one can get the better readers both to assist the weaker ones and arouse interest in wanting to read.

Finally, pupils are encouraged to go to the school library to pick any book they like on a level which seems comfortable. When they do this, there is, of course, little guidance that the teacher can give. However, if the pupils have received previous help in extensive reading at the time the whole class read the same book and/or when they worked in groups, most of them will now be ready to try to read something completely on their own. Since grading or testing extensive reading should be prohibited, reading cards are helpful. Pupils can be encouraged to prepare cards with basic information about the story they read at a very early stage. As they increase their knowledge of the language, they can write more information on their cards and even explain why they would recommend their story selection to a friend.

In order to check up on individual reading, the teacher may assign oral composition based on reading. Once again, the teacher starts with considerable control over the situation. Gradually and persistently, the teacher introduces a situation in which the learner becomes the initiator of the activity and in which the learner makes use of his or her own creative abilities within the boundaries of the language lesson. The techniques for extensive reading described in this section are derived from the same basic principles that have served as guidelines for the development of the entire course: one first helps the learner develop competence. Then the facilitator creates a situation in which the learner can both apply this knowledge and test his or her own ability to do so at the same time. (See WORKSHOP ACTIVITY (5), page 103.)

5. Writing

Writing, like the other language skills, needs to be considered from both its mechanical point of view (the code) and from its productive/creative point of view (writing ability). When considering the writing code, there are two aspects: shaping the letters properly and spelling correctly. Writing ability, on the other hand, depends on one's total knowledge of the language.

During the period devoted to the mechanics of reading, emphasis is also placed on the mechanics of writing. While practicing writing the letters correctly, the pupils also practice recognizing the letters. Thus, because the learner is acquiring both skills at the same time, a direct reinforcement takes place between the mechanics of reading and the mechanics of writing. The learner can, in other words, recognize letters when he or she reads and can copy those letters in his or her own handwriting.

The mechanics of reading also deal with the various arrangements of letters into sound-spelling correspondences. Again, there is a definite connection between reading and writing. During the first part of the course, spelling is closely connected to reading. If aided, the learner can grasp the regularities in English orthography while reading. It should be remembered, however, that words that do not fit the regular sound-spelling correspondences must be learned as individual items from the very beginning, words like *live, have, give,* for example, which are very common in everyday speech and do not fit a regular pattern.

During this initial period of the course, very little attention is given to what might be called writing ability. Writing activities at this initial stage should be restricted to sentences which the pupils write in answer to given questions. However, as the mechanics of writing are acquired, more emphasis can gradually be given to developing the learners' ability to express themselves in writing.

Like reading, writing must also be designed and planned on a continuum. The ability to express oneself in writing must be acquired by moving gradually from one step to the next. Of utmost importance are decisions about where to include writing activities. Should they be part of the language lesson or in the intensive reading lesson?

Based on the connection between reading and writing, it might be decided that the intensive reading lesson should contain writing activities. However, a more careful consideration makes it evident that the material presented in the intensive reading lesson is by nature slightly more difficult than the language material which is intended for active production on the part of the pupils. It is in the grammar part of the course rather than the reading segment that the pupil is expected to produce language of his or her own. For this reason, it is wiser to relate writing activities to the acquisition of language structures.

In planning a series of writing activities, we again follow the method that begins with controlled initial activities, then gradually releases controls to the point where the learner is free to write his or her own ideas. The earliest writing activity should take place at the sub-sentence level. The task here is to fill in blank spaces in sentences which are part of the language material which the pupil is working on. Thus, the writing activity fulfills a very important function at this level in that it helps the learner practice the new language structures while providing him or her with writing experience at the same time.

Gradually we move up to the sentence level, remaining for quite a long time since the sentence is a useful unit for practicing new language structures. The sentence level might, in fact, suffice for the first three years of the course. The types of exercises typical of this stage are answering questions, describing pictures and events, using elements introduced as grammatical structures, and making up new sentences.

Eventually the learner will move on to paragraph writing. This stage will also require considerable time since the learner must reach a certain degree of competence before he or she can actually begin to write paragraphs. It is important to include writing activities at the paragraph level also within the language material. For example, pupils acquiring active knowledge of the past tense should also be required to write a whole paragraph of connected sentences using the simple past.

The same basic principle of designing activities which proceed from strict control to a lessening of control applies to writing. The following graded activities are given as an example:

1. Substitution tables are used to make up a set of sentences which then become a paragraph.

2. A set of questions is given. The pupils write the answers which will then result in a well structured paragraph.
3. The pupils are required to complete sentences that are a part of a paragraph.
4. Pupils write summaries of paragraphs appearing in the text.
5. Pupils are asked to write a paragraph that was guided only in content.

Example:

    1. A substitution table:

My friend		in tenth grade
He	is	a basketball player
		tall

    2. Answers to guiding questions:
       a, Where did you go last night? (a concert)
       b. What was the name of the orchestra and what did they play? (Philharmonic/Carnival of the Animals)
       c. Did you enjoy it?
       d. Are you going to go to another concert soon?
The pupil might write something like the following:
I went to a concert last night. The philharmonic orchestra of this city played Carnival of the Animals. I enjoyed it very much. I am going to go to another concert next week.

    3. Completion of sentences in a paragraph:
       Every summer we go to . . . . . .
       There are many . . . .at . . . .
       I like . . . . . .
       My friends . . . . . .
       We enjoy the summer vacation because . . . . .

    4. A summary of any text read in class:

    5. A paragraph guided only in content might be something like the following:
       a. Tell about a visit to a friend's house.
          Tell what you saw, what you ate, and what you did there.
       b. Invite a friend to your house and tell him what you are going to do together.

    If these kinds of activities are carefully carried out throughout the language work in the second stage of the reading program, learners will be ready for more advanced composition writing at a later stage in their development. (Further writing activities are discussed in Part Two.)

WORKSHOP ACTIVITIES

1. Use the "simple past" of regular verbs as the structure with which you are working.

Examples:

> We walked home yesterday.
> He studied at Pinewood College last year.

Prepare examples for each of the steps in the series of activities for teaching grammatical structures as illustrated in Section 1.

2. Select two minimal pairs that would be relevant for the language background of your real or imaginary pupils.

Examples:

telling/tearing	for speakers of Japanese
pen/ben	for speakers of Arabic
live/leave	for speakers of Hebrew

Prepare a few drills for the minimal pairs that you selected.

3. Select five lexical items and prepare the following:
   (a) suitable example sentences to introduce the items to your pupils.
   (b) one exercise to make the pupil use all five lexical items.

4. Select an intensive reading text. Design an intensive reading lesson for one of the reading selections in the text. Work according to the steps described in Section 4 (c) above (page 94.)

5. Make a list of five extensive reading texts for English as a foreign or second language available at your local library. For what age level is each appropriate? Explain what motivational techniques you would use to introduce the books to students.

6. Prepare a writing exercise to be used while learning the past progressive.

Example:

> When the doorbell rang, they were watching television.

4

WHERE

Going
Beyond
the
Textbook

OVERVIEW

Although many teachers bring in a variety of aids and materials from the outside into the classroom, it is still true that most teachers rely on the textbook as the basic, unifying element in the course. Since this happens so often, it is important to emphasize how to make the best possible use of the available textbook, even before thinking about bringing in other elements.

We recognize that the textbook is written for an imaginary average learner. It can do relatively little to ignite enthusiasm. Any textbook requires a facilitator to add the elements of motivation and interest for the pupils. The best textbook, even though it provides a large variety of activities, cannot cater to individual needs. The facilitators' job is first, to choose the items relevant for their particular pupils and second, to supplement the textbook. Supplementing the textbook begins by making each lesson directly relevant to the students' own lives. Through the use of local place names, current happenings, and the students' own names, the alert facilitator brings each textbook drill to life.

But there are further ways to explore. This chapter presents various possibilities for enriching the language classroom with materials that go beyond the textbook: teacher-made aids, programmed instruction, instructional television, the language laboratory, and multi-media equipment. Finally we are also concerned with assessing achievement.

A. TEACHER-MADE AIDS

The most prominent aid that teachers have at their disposal is the traditional blackboard or chalkboard. Those who learn to use the blackboard effectively find it to be a much more versatile aid than it might at first appear to be. Its greatest advantage is the fact that it can be used spontaneously as problems or points of interest come up during the lesson. However, it is also possible to plan the use of the blackboard beforehand. For example, one can prepare written items on the blackboard before the lesson but only uncover them during it, thus introducing an element of surprise. By using colored chalks, the visual effect can also be made much stronger.

If the blackboard happens to be made of metal, it becomes a magnetic board as well. Such a board can also be used spontaneously. Instead of writing on it with chalk, one can attach pictures and cards to it with the aid of small magnets. Thus, the use of the blackboard is extended by varying the technique. And, if a teacher finds such a technique helpful in a classroom where the blackboard is not made of metal, it is very easy to use a small metal sheet as a magnetic board.

A rather similar aid, although different in appearance, is the flannel or felt board. Like the magnetic board, this is an excellent device for changing words, cards, or scenes. The difference between the flannel and magnetic boards lies mainly in the technical application of the flashcard. The flannelboard works on the principle that certain rough surfaces adhere to other rough surfaces when pressed together firmly. Flannel or felt is usually used to cover the board while another rough material is attached to the back of the cards. When the card is then pressed against the flannel board, it easily adheres to it. Figures and cut-outs made from flannel can also be easily attached to the board in this way.

The pocket chart is another excellent device for showing cards. This aid (about 8 × 12 inches) is particularly useful in demonstrating grammatical elements and their arrangement in sentences. The three easy ways that any teacher can make a pocket chart are shown below.

1. Cut slits in a piece of cardboard and insert cards in the slits (Diagram 11):

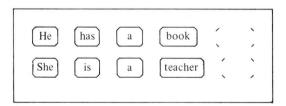

Diagram 11

2. Attach paper clips to a piece of cardboard (Diagram 12):

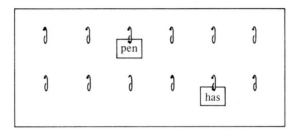

Diagram 12

3. Fold a large piece of paper so that it creases to form pockets and then glue the paper to cardboard (Diagram 13):

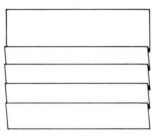

Diagram 13

In each pocket place cards to form sentences (Diagram 14):

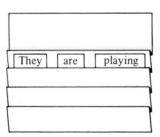

Diagram 14

The plastigraph is an aid that can easily be made by any teacher. Identical in function to the magnetic and flannel boards, the plastigraph simply consists of cutouts and a board that are both made from plastic. This aid works effectively since plastic sticks to plastic very easily. The storage of the cutouts can, however, be a problem since they too stick to each other very easily.

The overhead projector is another aid which is becoming very much a part of the modern classroom. It is a very simple machine that projects transparencies onto a wall or screen. Although one can write on transparencies that are being projected in much the same way one writes on a blackboard, they are usually prepared in advance. The advantage of the overhead projector is that one can use it without having to darken the room or turn his or her back to the class. The teacher can, in other words, face the class and point to a transparency while the learners watch it on the wall. Transparencies are particularly efficient and helpful when a teacher has to illustrate something that would take a long time to draw on a blackboard.

All of the above aids should be found in the classroom. Also needed in every classroom, however, are those versatile elements that make those aids work. For example, on the blackboard one uses colored chalks; on the magnetic board one places word and picture flashcards; one also places specially prepared word and picture flashcards on the feltboard and pocket chart; on the plastigraph, one uses plastic cutouts.

Effective teachers start using word flashcards at the very beginning of the course. A teacher can attach flashcards to various objects in the room—door, window, wall, etc.—even during the reading-readiness period, so that the pupils will learn to recognize whole words in a global fashion. In fact, it might even be desirable to go a step further and use cards that contain the whole noun phrase—a door, a window, a wall, etc.—especially when the teacher is dealing with pupils whose native language does not have an indefinite article.

The flashcards themselves should simply be rectangular pieces of cardboard on which the words have been written with a felt marker. The letters must be clear and large enough to be seen by all of the pupils in the classroom and the cards should be of a size that makes it possible to use them in the pocket or slot chart as well. Word flashcards can also be used in structural drills, in pronunciation sessions, and in vocabulary reviews. They can also be used for reading practice.

Picture flashcards are similar in size and shape to word flashcards. They make it possible to build sentences that are made up of words and pictures at the same time. For example, to teach a sentence like: "The apple is big" one can use a picture of an apple instead of the word. One can put the emphasis on "be" and its complement "big:" "This _____ is big." Of course picture flashcards are also useful for introducing and reviewing lexical items.

The alert facilitator constantly collects pictures, even when designed picture flashcards are available. Cut out of magazines, borrowed from other teachers, or drawn by the teacher or some talented pupil, pictures can depict both a situation and individual objects. They might also be used for individual work. For example, the teacher could paste a picture and a short paragraph that relates to it onto a piece of cardboard. Individual pupils could then be given these reading cards for individual reading. For more productive activities, the teacher can ask the pupils themselves to compose short paragraphs about the picture, either orally or in writing.

Use charts, posters, and large maps for various types of language practice. For example, a chart with pictures of objects, some of which belong to count nouns and others to non-count nouns, can be used effectively for drilling the grammatical features of these two types of nouns. A chart with pictures depicting actions can be used for practicing the present progressive tense. A city map can be used for oral compositions, for writing activities, for vocabulary study, and for many other similar types of activities.

The various aids described above can all be used in a variety of language activities. There are also three simple teacher-made aids, however, that are particularly useful in the teaching of the mechanics of reading:

(1) The ABC chart. Indispensable during the early period of preparation for the mechanics of reading and writing, this chart contains all of the letters printed in both lower and upper-case. Sometimes the vowels are in a different color. It is used to play games or sing the various ABC songs in order to help the pupils learn to recognize the names and shapes of the English letters.

(2) Letter cards. These are also useful during the early reading stages. Although each pupil should ideally have a set, letter cards can often work wonders when just the teacher has them. For example, a teacher can use letter cards effectively on a simple nail board if it is designed so that one can create a sound-spelling correspondence on it and then easily change each of the letters within that pattern.

(3) Sentence strips. These are longer pieces of cardboard on which individual whole sentences are written in clear letters. An example is shown in Diagram 15 below.

Our teacher is in the classroom.

It is nice outside.

The books are in the library.

Diagram 15

Sentence strips are used to practice the reading of whole sentences. The teacher flashes the sentence strips at the pupils. The speed is gradually increased and thus the learners get good practice in sentence reading. Since the sentences written on the strips represent the grammatical structures learned at any particular time (in the example above: "be" sentences), this activity provides additional reinforcement of the grammatical structures.

The above-mentioned aids are all visual in nature. The facilitator can, however, also prepare self-made audio-aids. The easiest way to do this is simply to bring records and pre-recorded tapes to the classroom. However, because cassette taperecorders are so readily available today, many teachers record dialogues, stories, and descriptions of pictures on their own cassettes. If the teacher is not a native speaker, it is valuable to find native speakers to record the material.

All of the above aids are inexpensive and easily prepared. If used effectively, they add a very important dimension to classroom activities. The modern language classroom must contain a large variety of such aids if it is to provide the learner with an active teaching-learning situation.

B. PROGRAMMED INSTRUCTION

Programmed instruction refers to materials and/or procedures that involve self-instructional programs. Such programs usually attempt to provide the learner with conditions which enable him or her to learn effectively with little or no outside help.

Programmed exercises present small steps that can be easily followed by the individual student and answers are given so that the student can correct his or her own work.

Example:

> Play
> > I am playing.
> > You are playing.
> > He is playing.
> > They are playing.
>
> *Fill in*:
> > am   is   are
>
> > 1. He _____ playing.
> > 2. You _____ playing.
> > 3. They _____ playing.
> > 4. I _____ playing.

answers
1. is
2. are
3. are
4. am

Modern methodologists often treat programmed materials with caution since these materials are associated with the behaviorist theory of learning. In fact, many educators say it is a mechanistic approach that cannot handle internal and mental processes. Although this might be true, the modern language facilitator should be familiar with the characteristics of programmed instruction. Without such familiarization, one will not be able to make use of the capability which the method possesses.

Although the self-instructional aspect of programmed instruction is probably its most important feature, there are a few additional ones that are also inherent in it. For example, programmed materials typically employ a carefully prearranged and sequenced series of small steps through which the material is presented to the learner. Thus, in the above example, pupils are guided to read the sentences after presentation of the material. Then, they fill in the blanks in the same sentences. Gradually, they will fill in the blanks in sentences new to them. Each such step requires an active response which is then promptly confirmed or corrected. By providing such small steps that require immediate responses, programmed materials can help considerably in strengthening the learner's power of concentration. It may therefore prove to be a useful technique for learners who suffer from a short concentration span.

Programmed materials also have the advantage of being highly individualized since each learner works independently. An able learner can use programmed materials at an accelerated rate and therefore advance more quickly, while the slow person can take as much time as needed in order to achieve the required proficiency. If the programs are carefully constructed, they may also help the slower learner reach a much higher level of mastery than would be the case otherwise.

The inherent features of programmed instruction that make it advantageous under some circumstances also make it unfavorable under others. For example, the fact that the material is broken down into many small units is obviously helpful for the slower learner. For the fast learner, however, the steps might be too small. Because bright pupils may be capable of gaining much more information through fewer steps, they sometimes find programmed materials repetitive and therefore lose interest in them.

Most programmed materials are linear. They present the teaching elements in a sequence of small steps. All learners using the materials will be activated through the same number of steps in order to learn the same material. The problem, however, lies in the fact that not all learners need the same number of steps—some can learn the material more quickly than others and therefore could do with fewer steps. Linear programmed materials do not work well with learners who possess a variety of abilities.

Material that takes the form of branching programming does make it possible for different learners to simultaneously cover a different number of steps that are more closely geared to individual needs. The core of the branching approach is the fact that even the selection of an incorrect answer offers a diagnostic clue to an individual's particular needs. Thus, the programmer builds the materials so that the distractors contain predicted mistakes. If pupils select one of the distractors instead of the correct answer, they will be directed to a specific series of steps—a separate branch line which will help them master the item with which they have difficulty. Faster pupils, on the other hand, go straight to the next step. Thus, one may vary both the element of time and the type of activity needed for different people.

The following is an example of a simple branching programmed unit. Let us assume that the pupil is learning to distinguish between the simple present and present progressive aspects of the English verb. Because the programmer wants to make sure that the learners have also mastered the *be* paradigm as an integral part of the present progressive form, the following step is included:

Look at the boy in the picture. (The picture shows a boy walking.) Then choose the best filler from (a), (b), (c) below.

> *He is a pupil. He* _____ *to school.*
> (a) is walking (continue to next item)
> (b) are walking (turn to items. . .)
> (c) walks (turn to page. . .)

Learners who select the right answer go on to the next item. Those who make a mistake in the agreement between the subject and the *be* form are directed to a branch-line where they practice the *be* paradigm. Those who make a mistake in tense selection are directed to an explanation that differentiates between the two tenses. In both cases they return to the regular sequence of steps only after the branching section has been completed.

For programmed materials to be advantageous in individualized learning, the pupil must be interested in learning: the learner must be a conscientious, hard worker as well. Since each person works alone, each must be responsible for correcting one's own work. To use programmed texts, it is frequently necessary to train the pupils since learners with shorter concentration spans often lack good work habits as well. By working with programmed materials, however, slower learners might very well improve both their work habits and concentration powers.

Programmed materials usually take the form of either a teaching machine or a specially designed text. The latter is the more common type and is usually used for language learning. Such a programmed text will present various questions or problems for which multiple choice answers are given. The learner selects one of the given answers and checks his other choice by using a key given within a text.

For example:

Choose the best filler from (a), (b), (c), or (d) below.

The cat _____ *cheese every day.*

    a. is eating
    b. eats
    c. eating
    d. eat

a. If this answer was chosen, this student obviously does not distinguish between the use of simple present and present progressive and needs to do some work on this. The text will therefore direct the learner to suitable exercises.
b. If this answer was chosen (correct), he or she can go right on to the next exercise.
c. If this answer was chosen, he or she probably needs to practice the "be" paradigm. The text will direct the learner to suitable exercises.
d. This student needs to practice the "s" ending with third person singular. The text will direct the learner to suitable exercises.

This type of programmed material is suitable for reading and writing, but if spoken language is to be stressed, recorded material of an audio nature must be added.

C. INSTRUCTIONAL TELEVISION

Instructional television is becoming more and more a part of modern education throughout the world. The shape it takes, however, depends on the educational system operating in any given country and on the particular type of instructional television initiated there. Although educators throughout the world have come to recognize the great potential of instructional television, many are still unsure about how to best use it. Often their uncertainty is due to a conflict between producers and educators. It is also due to a basic fear of letting the "tube" or "box" take over and control the classroom. Though there is controversy over the use of instructional television, it is important for the language facilitator to become familiar with the inherent features of the medium and the various ways in which it has been used so far.

Before one can discuss the efficacy of television for educational purposes, however, it is necessary to distinguish between two different approaches that result in two basically different types of programs. The two types of utilization are: (a) the learner views the program alone at home; (b) the learner views the program within the classroom as part of the regular school activities.

Home viewing is very different from classroom viewing since it entails voluntary participation on the part of the learner. In addition, there is practically no control over the learning situation, and the feedback, indeed if there is any at all, has very low reliability. A television series that is designed for this kind of viewing must therefore take all of the above factors into account. One of its requirements is to motivate the viewers' interest as they watch the program. In order to ensure proper learning, such a series will also have to have a considerable amount of review built into the programs. The selection of topics and content should be such that the programs cater to as wide a range of learners as possible.

Viewing at home is divided into two types: those programs that present the whole course of study, and those that use television as one element in a whole course which may also include textbooks, tests, correspondence, and sometimes even scheduled meetings of the viewers. When home viewing is of the latter type, it resembles classroom viewing in many ways.

The most effective programs for home viewing are those that include: a textbook for the learner coordinated with a series of telecasts as well as scheduled meetings with other viewers under the guidance of a tutor. Such programs enable the learner to work individually in the textbook, view the telecast by himself at home, and then periodically clarify his questions with the tutor. At these scheduled meetings the individual learner also has a chance to share his experience with other learners. Achievement tests are given at these meetings and so the learner is able to evaluate his or her own progress. Although this type of program provides an entire course of study, the learning responsibility lies with the learner alone.

Classroom viewing is, however, different from home viewing since there is a teacher who guides and prepares the pupils for the telecast and who later makes use of the content of the telecast on the basis of the pupils' reactions. But even programs intended for classroom viewing can take two different forms within the overall course of study: they can be used for the purpose of enrichment only, or they can be an integral part of the entire language course. Of particular interest here is the latter type of program, since it suits the overall approach that has been presented so far.

Instructional television as an integral part of a program of study is generally viewed as being only one of many media utilized in creating the best learning conditions within the classroom. The question therefore that immediately arises is: what can television do best for both the language learner and the language facilitator?

Various media are needed in order to open up the classroom to the world outside, to bring, in other words, experiences that are not usually available to the learner within the school. Television is the *par excellence* choice for the job. The object, however, should never be simply to rely on television as an inside-the-classroom baby-sitter. The situations that are brought into the classroom should also be put to good use. To do this, one must answer the question: "Where in the learning process can the telecast play its best role?"

In order to answer this question, we must consider the teaching of language substance, as well as the teaching of language skills. It is quite obvious that television as a medium is most suited to promoting the speech skills. It is in its very nature to expose the learner to a considerable amount of spoken language. On the other hand, the use of television to promote the literacy skills is much more difficult to recognize. Experiments have shown, however, that television can be used effectively for teaching literacy skills as well.

Television can be used in the teaching of lexical items, especially if they are of a concrete type. All three aspects of a lexical item can be shown at the same time: its meaning, pronunciation, and spelling. But although the role of television can be easily explained in these areas, it probably contributes most to the teaching of grammatical structures.

The classroom teacher and the textbook writer are constantly searching for meaningful situations in which to present and practice grammatical structures. When used in the classroom or in the textbook, such situations often become contrived and artificial. Television, on the other hand, can easily bring into the classroom, natural, real situations from the outside world. Such situations make the use of the grammatical structure more natural and therefore attack the basic need for utilizing relevant materials.

An important element in teaching grammatical structures is the rule or generalization about the meaning and the form of the structure. In the regular classroom, the teacher looks for a variety of graphic ways in order to insure that the rule is remembered. Here, again, television can be of great value in helping emphasize the specific features of the grammatical structures. For example, when we teach the formation of questions in English, we sometimes try to show the process by moving the syntactic elements around in a rather awkward way on the blackboard. But this can be an awkward and confusing demonstration. By using animation and other exciting techniques, television easily shows the same movement of elements in a sentence in a much more lively way.

Some grammatical structures are particularly suitable for the medium of television. Thus "be" sentences which in the classroom are limited to the immediate environment can be easily experienced via television in almost any situation. Similarly, "present progressive" can be easily demonstrated on the screen in any conceivable situation. In this case the televised situation provides a very welcome expansion of the classroom environment. There are, however, other structures for which a good television program might provide the key to the learner's understanding. Structures referring to future or past time need considerable verbal explanations in the regular classroom situation while the screen provides ample techniques for a visualization of the meaning. Let us imagine two blobs of clay talking to each other on the screen and having the following conversation:

A: What are you going to be?
B: I am going to be a cat. What are you going to be?
C: I am going to be a dog.

As soon as the conversation is ended the two blobs turn into a cat and a dog respectively. Two or three such examples will make the meaning of this rather difficult structure very clear. This little televised fragment provides the learner with a key to understanding the meaning of the structure.

By providing the teacher with both a meaningful and natural situation in which a structure is used and a clear graphic representation of the rule concerning that structure, the television lesson also provides an excellent presentation of the speech skills. If the actors are native speakers, pronunciation per se will be favorably affected because more models of the language will be brought into the classroom. When the teacher is not a native speaker, other models are of the utmost importance. Even when the teacher is a native speaker, however, it is always very useful to expose the learners to other native speakers. If the telecasts use native speakers as models of pronunciation and thus constantly expose the learners to the natural flow of English, aural comprehension will be favorably affected even if no special effort is made.

Pupils who are accustomed to watching an instructional program once a week usually show marked improvement in aural comprehension—if the program is interesting and appeals to them. Because of the link between the skills, their speech will also be favorably affected. Although it is possible to design special drills to affect pronunciation in a more direct way, this technique can easily become mechanical and therefore boring. Because of this danger, many programs have stayed away from explicit pronunciation drills. It is an area, however, that deserves more exploration and experimentation.

Another language component that can be handled well by television is the learning of new lexical items of a concrete type. Because television is a powerful medium, it can help the learners associate meanings and sounds by simultaneously showing objects with their names. In fact, learning new words within the context of a situation may become a useful aim in itself. Here again, it is important to emphasize the need for a synthesis of skills and substance similar to the one that exists in the classroom. It might be that the need for such a synthesis is even greater on television because of the screen's intrinsic power to attract attention. Television can play an important role in the blending of substance and skills within a meaningful situation because it can single out formal features and show them graphically in a lively and engaging manner.

Some typical "problems of form" in English are: the addition of "s" to the verb with a third person singular subject, the use of the base form of the verb with questions and negative sentences in the past; the use of VERB-*ing* following verbs like "enjoy". These features of form require considerable explanation and practice in the classroom. Animation on the screen may present an invaluable reinforcement of the specific feature. For example, in sentences like:

He speaks French
She rides her bicycle to work.
Did you finish your work?
I finish*ed* my work.

the italicized parts are flashed on and off several times. This blinking, or flashing, draws attention to the features of form which may cause the learner difficulty.

Television also has the potential to teach literacy skills. One must first distinguish between the mechanics of those skills and their actual use for comprehension. Television can obviously play an important role in reinforcing the mechanics of reading. It can present the letters in various ways by animating their shapes and features, thus greatly assisting the learner in letter recognition and discrimination. Since sight and sound are simultaneous, television can also help the learner to master the correspondence between sound and spelling patterns. All of these possible uses of television seem to make it a very useful tool for improving the mechanics of reading.

The mechanics of reading is often an area that producers are least excited about, however. Many feel that it is nothing more than a boring, mechanical "process" that reduces the medium to an animated blackboard. And although teachers and educators have argued again and again that the mechanics of reading is the area where television can help most, few producers have as yet been convinced that it is true.

On the other hand, the use of television for reading comprehension presents definite limitations. Only a small number of words can be effectively placed on the screen. Thus, if one tries to use the screen for reading comprehension one of the most important features of effective reading is destroyed—namely, the ability to grasp a whole sequence of words that make up an idea or a whole thought pattern. The effects of television on the aspect of reading for comprehension must still be determined. If it is used to teach this skill, a whole group of pupils would read together from the screen. Will this affect their individual performance when they go to the library and select a book that they are interested in reading on their own? Will there be a transfer of learning from the screen to the individual page? Although these questions remain unanswered at this stage of the development of the medium, the problems presented must be thoroughly investigated.

Although the topic of motivation has been avoided until now, it is probably the area in which television can play the most decisive role. Because of sociological and personal attitudes, the learning of a new language is often viewed negatively by learners in many parts of the world.

The task is typically considered to be difficult and even menacing. Television can help conquer such fears simply by making the learning of languages much more pleasurable. For example, it is known that foreign language became a favorite subject in many countries where instructional television was an inseparable part of the teaching program. In these places the programs were well constructed and took the learners' interests and background into consideration. If properly used, therefore, television can definitely play a strong motivating role in the overall program.

Although it is now clear that television has a positive role in the learning-teaching process, the very vital question of utilization still remains unanswered. How can one make the best use of television within the classroom situation? A television series can become an effective element within the learning process at either the beginning or slightly advanced stages, if it is constructed as an integral part of the course. However, the teacher must consider it as only one of the media available in the classroom. Although it may prove to be very powerful, it should never become more than one of the elements in an integrated course. Close coordination between textbooks and television programs is of the utmost importance. Close coordination between the production teams and the planners of the course of study is indispensable. Only through close collaboration between educators and production people, both keeping constant touch with the real teaching-learning situation, can instructional television contribute positively to the new language course.

D. THE LANGUAGE LABORATORY

The language laboratory has become a commonplace in many schools and colleges all over the world in the last fifteen years or so. As is often the case with new tools and instruments, it was first received with great enthusiasm. However, it seems that in those places where enthusiasm was greatest, the disappointment and disillusionment are now most bitter.

When one considers the language laboratory, one often envisages complex and sophisticated hardware that appears to be able to solve many of the problems of foreign language teaching. In fact, the most modern hardware can contribute very little to learning without suitable "software." "Software" is the content of the course presented by means of the language laboratory equipment. Many schools and colleges become discouraged with their modern language laboratories because, although they spent huge sums of money on the hardware, they spent little time and money on the preparation of suitable software.

The language laboratory, like any other tool or medium of instruction, must be put to effective use. This means that it should be part of an integrated course of study and used where it can inherently contribute the most. In fact, only when the language laboratory is planned as an integral part of a course can it begin to be utilized most efficiently.

A language laboratory can take several forms:

A very sophisticated lab has individual booths in which there are taperecorders which the pupils can operate to listen or record themselves. All the booths are controlled from a central control board. And, the teacher can listen to the individual pupils and guide them during their practice.

A less sophisticated type of lab is known as an "audio-active" language lab. The individual learner can only listen to the recorded lesson since there are no facilities for self-recording. Many new labs are of this type because teachers are often skeptical about the practical value of having pupils record—mainly because they listen to their own mistakes at least part of the time. This type of lab is also popular because it is both less expensive and easier to maintain.

A much simpler language laboratory consists of one taperecorder with a number of earphones for a small group of pupils. Although this type of lab could easily seem to be vastly inferior to the more sophisticated types, it has proven to be very effective. It is also much less problematical than a full-fledged laboratory which requires a special room, acoustical construction, installation of booths and complicated equipment. What is more, software intended only for listening activities can be prepared more easily.

What makes the language laboratory so useful that it is worth going to all the trouble of installing such expensive equipment? Suitable software is the answer. If it is available, the language lab provides both good models of pronunciation and a highly individualized type of activity—two very important elements in language learning. Courses that aim at a high level of proficiency in the speech skills will profit considerably from using a language lab. The language lab helps the learner develop fluency in speech and proficiency in aural comprehension. When used effectively, the language lab can therefore contribute considerably to the teaching-learning situation.

There are a number of different ways in which language laboratories are utilized within the regular course of study. In some courses the lab is viewed as one of the aids that assist both the teacher and the learner in the teaching-learning process. In such cases, the lab is made use of in certain sections of the course, in order to fulfill a specific function. For example, let us assume that we are dealing with a language course that centers around grammatical structures. It would seem wise to plan such a course so that the introduction to a new grammatical topic is always done by the facilitator in order to insure that motivation and interest are kept at a high level. However, after this introduction, the more controlled part of the lesson, the language lab becomes a very useful aid. The activities then continue from the oral presentation by the teacher to the listening and production activities that take place in the language laboratory. Thus, the language lab is specifically used for the aural-oral part of teaching grammatical structures, and at the same time provides more opportunity for language practice than the regular classroom does.

Another way of utilizing the language lab is to view it as a special aid that can be used for a specific purpose such as fluency in speech or developing aural proficiency. In such cases, courses that use only the language lab must be designed. And, although the learners would attend laboratory sessions regularly, there would be no real connection between their meetings in the basic course of study and the lab sessions. Even in such cases, however, the language lab lesson still consists of a short presentation at the beginning of each session followed by the learners' individual work in the lab. Thus, the facilitator has an opportunity to give some theoretical guidance before the pupils start to work on their own.

A somewhat different way of utilizing the language laboratory is to make it a voluntary part of the course. In such a case, the pupils come to the language laboratory individually and at their own convenience. At the lab there is a technician (instead of a professional instructor) who helps them select the right kind of tape or lesson based on guidance received from the language teacher, or according to the learner's own preference. Although the learner can get any technical assistance needed in such a situation, the actual utilization of the recorded lesson is his or her own responsibility. In order for a lab of this type to be effective, it must be well supplied with a variety of tapes and recorded materials. There should be tapes for general listening, tapes that practice pronunciation and structure as well as other types of tapes, so that the learner can choose the kind of tape needed most.

Finding the right way of utilizing a language lab is not enough, however. It is also necessary to define the specific objectives of the laboratory course and then design the software accordingly so that both the software and the hardware are used effectively. It is quite obvious that the language laboratory can be made to play an important role in the new language course of study. Research, however, has shown that while some learners benefit tremendously from a language lab course, others are affected only in a very superficial way. One must therefore be cautious when deciding how much prominence the language lab should have within the total course of study.

E. THE MULTI-MEDIA CLASSROOM

The dream of almost every language teacher today is to be able to work in what is known as the multi-media classroom. Although this is gradually becoming a reality for some teachers, it is still only a dream for most. The major problem is that large budgets are needed to equip such classrooms. If, however, the superiority of the multi-media classroom is constantly and energetically stressed to authorities, the dream will perhaps turn into reality in the not too distant future.

The multi-media classroom contains most of the aids and media that have been discussed so far. It has a television set with a videotape machine attached to it in one corner, a film projector and a collection of films and film strips in another corner, a taperecorder with a number of earphones and a wide variety of tapes in a third corner, and an overhead projector with ready-made transparencies in a fourth corner.

The multi-media classroom also contains teacher-made aids mentioned in the previous section. Thus, there will be a pocket chart corner, a magnetic board corner (or area), a flannel board corner, etc. Individual pupils and smaller groups can work with all of these aids. The multi-media classroom should also contain a variety of reading corners. One such corner should contain pictures and story cards, another should contain short extensive readers and a third should contain reading charts.

A multi-media language classroom which contains all of the above-mentioned tools can be an ideal place for learning if the software necessary for the best utilization of all of the media is available as well. Without the software, however, even the most sophisticated equipment is of limited use. The software must also be carefully designed so that the various media complement each other when reinforcing the material.

A most important feature of the multi-media classroom is the fact that the individual learner can work with different tools. It is therefore important to train the pupils to both select and make the best use of programs that they are interested in. Guidance is therefore vital in the multi-media classroom. It is also important to design the materials so that the same part of the course of study is presented in a variety of ways. Thus, individual learners are given the opportunity to find the system or medium that works best for them. This is, in fact, one of the major advantages of the multi-media classroom: it makes possible a more varied and individualized way of working. (See *Part Two*: Chapter Five, WHO, for a continuation of the discussion on individualized instruction.)

F. ASSESSING ACHIEVEMENT

The language facilitator must make many decisions about each learner's progress throughout the course. Some of these decisions are rather informal in nature and are made at many times during the daily teacher-learner interaction within the classroom. But these informal evaluations must be coupled with more formal measurements. Tests can be designed and administered by professional testing services or by teachers themselves. Here, we are only considering teacher-prepared tests.

Formal assessment means creating and using reliable and valid measuring devices. Such devices usually take the form of a test in which learners display their knowledge of language substance and language skills. It is the latter type of test, one which concentrates on skill areas, that gives the facilitator a more accurate evaluation of pupils' progress. It is the one which is discussed in this section. But there are other areas to testing and other types of tests. Diagnostic testing, attempts to ascertain learners' levels in particular areas of language substance, is discussed in *Part Two*: Chapter Five, WHO.

In order to create a good test, the facilitator must first know what the objectives of the test will be. They should always be listed as clearly as possible. Even if they are not stated in the test itself, they should be carefully thought through and written out by the test constructor, for his or her own use. Questions such as these must be considered: What skill area will be tested? What specific topics which were covered in the course of study will the test concentrate on?

Secondly, the facilitator must know what testing technique is most suitable. Some possibilities are the following:

a. The test as a whole, or in parts, can be of an objective, a subjective, or a semi-objective type. (A typical objective test is made up of blanks to be filled. A typical subjective test is an essay to be composed by the students.)
b. The medium used for administering the test can be a written form, a tape, or an overhead projector.

After the first draft of the test is completed, the facilitator must make sure that he or she has designed something that actually tests what was stated in the objectives. In other words, decide whether or not the measure effectively tests any of the following in an integrated way:

1. auditory comprehension
2. reading comprehension
3. speaking ability
4. writing ability

Preparing an achievement test therefore requires careful consideration of the language area, the language skill, and the testing technique which is to be used. The following examples will serve to clarify each of these aspects of a test item.

A   *Testing grammatical structures:*

(1) in writing

(i) objectively
Choose the word or expression that best fits into the empty space.
(a) Did you hear her _____ ? (to sing, singing, sings)
(b) When we were young we _____ walk to school every day. (had to, must, should)

(c) How long _____ in this country?
you have lived
are you living
have you been living
you are living
do you live
(d) "We want to sit at the table near the window." (customers)
"I am sorry, but _____ already." (waiter)
it took
it takes
it has been taken
it is taking
(ii) open-ended (semi-objective)
(a) Complete the sentence according to the pattern.
He can come, can't he?
You have finished, _____ ?
(b) Complete the following sentences using the words in brackets.
My brother succeeded _____ . (annoy, everybody)
I would have spoken to him if _____ . (I, see, him)
(c) Look at the picture and answer these questions.
What is the man doing?
What is the boy going to do?
(iii) not controlled (subjective)
Write five sentences using indirect speech.

(2) orally
(a) What would you say if . . .
(1) you wanted to leave the room?
(2) you wanted to borrow my book?
(b) Look at the picture and tell me . . .

B   Testing Lexical items: in writing, or orally

(1) multiple choice

The opposite of *strong* is _____ . (short, poor, weak, good)
Is your friend a *fat* boy?
No, he isn't. He is _____ . (little, round, short, thin)

Underline the word below that most nearly means *beverage.*
   drink, meal, animal, meat

(2) completion

A place where minerals are dug is called a _____ .

C   Testing pronunciation:

(1) orally

    I will read a list of words to you. Write (1) if the words rhyme (have the same vowel as . . .) with *seat* and write (2) if they rhyme with *Jim.*
        sit, eat, slim, lip, (etc.)

(2) in writing

    Which word in this list sounds different?
        blue, too, go, do, two

D   Testing comprehension:

(1) aurally

    The teacher or a recording presents a brief episode to the pupils. They can usually listen to it twice. Then pupils are asked to answer multiple choice questions about the content of the passage to which they listened. Although these questions are usually written, the test is really on aural comprehension of the passage.

(2) in reading

    The testees are given a passage to read. Following the passage there can be two types of questions:
    (a) multiple choice
    (b) essay type questions
The multiple choice questions are a better test for comprehension since they are not affected by the pupils' ability to express themselves in writing or speech.

    Additional ideas for testing items can be found in Part Two and of course in any text dealing with testing in ESL or EFL.
    If the facilitator considers all of the above carefully, he or she will be able to design a test that evaluates accurately. However, one must remember that any test is only a device. In the final analysis, the facilitator must be responsible for all value judgments made about the pupils' real progress, about the efficacy of the teaching materials, and about the teaching methods that are used in the course.

WORKSHOP ACTIVITIES

1. Plan a visit to an ESL or EFL classroom with the purpose of surveying (a) the teacher-made aids and (b) the materials for programmed instruction. What types of aids and materials did you observe which were not described in Sections A and B in this chapter?
2. Does either instructional television or the language laboratory play a part in the ESL/EFL programs you know? Interview two students and two teachers who have experience with instructional television and the language laboratory. Are the students' and teachers' opinions the same? Summarize your interviews in the form of a class report.
3. Collect five samples of teacher-prepared achievement tests from beginning level ESL or EFL classrooms. Point out what language skills the measures test. What testing techniques were employed? What medium did the tests utilize?

PART
TWO

INTERMEDIATES
AND ADVANCED

5

WHO

Refocusing on the Learner

OVERVIEW

In this part of *Facilitating Language Learning* the focus shifts to the intermediate and advanced levels. In some cases students move into more advanced classes after having spent some years studying English as a subject at school. In an ideal situation, they are people who have successfully passed through the stages of development which have been described in Part One. It is more often the case, however that intermediate and advanced students are making a new start at language learning in a new place. They might be recent immigrants who have had school courses in another country and are now studying in an ESL setting; they might be overseas students studying in technical schools and universities in the United States or Great Britain; or, they might be people taking courses in private institutes or lessons with tutors in non-English speaking countries.

Teachers who work with these levels must be prepared to expect a wide range of backgrounds among the students. In these kinds of classes people have usually had quite different kinds of preparation for intermediate and advanced materials. Some will have experienced only grammar-translation methods in their earlier study of English while others will have concentrated solely on literacy skills. There may be some who have had practice in oral and aural skills, but still need considerable exposure to the natural flow of speech in order to perfect listening comprehension and the ability to communicate with native speakers.

The WHO chapters in both this part concerning the intermediate and advanced levels and the previous one dealing with beginners and those beyond, bring the learner into the picture as the primary factor. When didactic teaching (telling the student how to do it) shifts to facilitating learning (helping students learn how to learn by themselves), then much more attention must be paid to the part played by the learners in the total picture. Too many methodological approaches to language teaching have concentrated on the methods of the art, but have overlooked the most obvious part—much like recipes which fail to tell the cook to include a basic ingredient such as seasoning. Even when considerable attention has been paid to questions of language *matter*, questions regarding the learner, his nature, and his needs, have only been taken into account indirectly.

Whether they are children, young people, or adults, whether they are beginners, intermediates, or advanced students, all people in our language classes are also members of a larger social community. So, in the following sections on the nature of WHO, learners are first viewed in relation to their place in the society in which they live. Next, intermediate and advanced learners are discussed in relation to their needs as individuals: how can we best facilitate their learning of language by placing them at the proper level? What are their optimum modes for learning language? How can we meet special needs in the areas of language skills through techniques of individualized instruction?

A. THE LEARNER IN A SOCIAL CONTEXT

Success in teaching and learning new languages is strongly affected by the community and the nation in which the teacher and the student live. This statement is as true of language courses for beginners as it is for those who are at the intermediate or advanced levels. To be effective facilitators, teachers must be able to work within the goals set by their particular society. They must, at the same time, be aware of the attitudes and aspirations towards language learning which are held by their students. Teachers who work with people who are making a new beginning at the intermediate level need to understand the social climate in which each person studied previously. Accomplishing these "musts" is not an easy task for one person to carry out. But, by first considering some of the social factors we can gain a better understanding of why some students succeed and others do not.

In certain cases, the goals, attitudes, and aspirations held by the larger society, by the school, and by the students are in conflict with each other. Sometimes such conflicts can be found within one teacher's classroom. When the curriculum of a school sets up goals which emphasize the teaching of language primarily by means of reading classics in English literature, the goals of students may have been overlooked. For the students, the themes in literary works may seem irrelevant to their own lives. Besides, the English language which students are more apt to hear is via television, films, or records. Skillful teachers are able to find strategies for facilitating learning within the context of their particular school setting. But first they must become aware of the possible underlying conflicts.

1. Societal Goals

The more deeply we investigate goals for language education in different countries, the more diverse appear to be the factors which must be considered. People who live in countries where everyone speaks one language are often amazed to learn that in other parts of the world there are strong political and emotional considerations tied to the use of one or another of the various languages spoken by the country's citizens. In locations as widely separated geographically as Canada and India, language teachers find themselves working with difficult questions of language choice which are tied to political issues within their societies. In Canada, a French-speaking minority of the population holds strong allegiance to their French language identity. They do not want their French-Canadian ethnicity drowned in an English-speaking sea.

In India, fourteen major language groups compete for political domination in different geographical areas. At the same time, English and Hindi are taught in most schools as languages which give people who belong to different sections of the country a means of communicating with each other. Teachers in India, as well as in other third-world locales, must deal with complex attitudinal and political questions in relation to the teaching of English.

Goals for English language learning differ among nations according to the size of the population that speaks the particular country's own language. For people who first acquire languages such as French, English, German, Spanish, Russian, or Arabic as their native tongue, the necessity of adding another world language is of less importance than it is for speakers of Finnish, Greek, Hebrew, Thai, or Korean. The number of speakers in the latter groups is comparatively quite small in the babble of languages spread over the world. In order to reduce their isolation from the rest of the nations, they must place a high priority on second language learning.

Over the past twenty-five years, the use of English as a fundamental communication tool has grown markedly in most areas of the world. The teaching of English for utilitarian purposes is often carried out relatively detached from teaching the culture, history, or literary traditions of English-speaking countries. It has proven to be the experience in many countries that English, along with other world languages, represents a key which provides entry into the modern world of ideas.

But there are multilingual countries which face internal planning problems of greater complexity than that of simply deciding on a shared world language. In such multilingual instances, a society must accommodate within its communications system—its radio, TV, newspapers, etc.—a variety of related and unrelated languages. Belgium, Indonesia, Malaysia, Yugoslavia, and the Philippines are all modern societies which must formulate language policy. In each of these countries, along with many other possible examples, decisions regarding language use must be made by the national government in order to help unify the nation. In each case it is necessary to make choices regarding which of the nation's languages will be used in various spheres of life—in government, in business, in schools, etc. It is necessary, too, in multilingual societies to set language policy in relation to both a shared national language and a language for broader communication with the rest of the world. So, for example, in Indonesia many students learn a second language, Bahasia Indonesian, as a national language together with learning English as a world language.

In many places, important national languages embody a cultural heritage which the nation wishes to preserve and strengthen through the education of its young people. In Iran, Afghanistan, Turkey, and Iceland, for example, teaching the important literary traditions embodied in the first language is a high priority item in the educational system. But, at the same time, young people need to have access to the scientific literature of the technological era, so they need to also acquire a world language, or a language of wider influence than their first.

In countries where two or more languages are commonly spoken, one finds that people are quite adept at language switching according to particular circumstances of time, place, and social setting. They may use one language for intimate family conversation, another for studying at school, another for shopping at the market or bazaar. In such communities, the learning of new languages, or of new dialects, has been a continuing process throughout a person's developmental years. Adding additional languages represents a relatively less difficult task for students in such circumstances than it does for people in monolingual countries such as the United States, England, or Japan where far fewer people have experiences in their early years with using alternate languages.

There seem to exist various common attitudes among people of a particular country concerning their ability to learn new languages. These accepted beliefs are frequently expressed in terms of comments such as this one made by a Japanese teacher: "It's such a problem for us . . . . English is the most difficult subject for our young people at school."

This attitude toward language learning contrasts strongly with a remark made by a Norwegian student: "Well, we all know how important it is to be able to speak to people outside of our own country. We all learn English in school quite naturally."

Certainly the first element teachers must consider is the role which English will serve in the lives of their students. That role will be crucially determined by the functions of language in the society in which the learner lives. The teacher must take into consideration questions pertaining to the ways in which language functions in the particular societal setting, for example, is the country monolingual or multilingual? Are people inclined to view the learning of new languages as a hurdle or as a natural process? Are there conflicting feelings within the country tied to the use of various languages? Is there a unified national language? Is it a language of limited use outside of the particular country? Does the learning of English represent the third or even fourth language which young people study in school?

2. School Goals

A student's need to use English as a communicative tool is more urgent when the language is used as the medium of instruction for teaching other subjects in the school curriculum. An example of this situation is the newcomer who is a student in an English-speaking country. If the person has little facility with the language he or she usually requires special instruction in order to move into regular classes. How, after all, can young people learn history or geography if they have trouble understanding the teacher's and the textbook's language?

But there are places in the world outside of English-speaking countries where school goals also call for children to learn various subjects through the medium of English. Usually in such instances the time spent on English language instruction is gradually increased in each successive year in school. By the time children are ready for grade three or four, many of the school subjects are taught in English. Such a program obviously greatly facilitates learning the language. However, societal pressures to preserve a local or national language often strongly oppose the use of a world language in the primary grades for instructional purposes. For example, by mid-1970 the use of English for instruction in elementary schools in the Philippines was restricted to the subjects of math and science.

The terms ESL and EFL have been associated with the use of English as a medium of instruction. An earlier part, *Clearing the Air,* has already set out some of the reasons for the confusion over the distinction between ESL and EFL. In considering the important matter of school goals, these terms again emerge. When using them it is important to remember the difference between the function played by foreign languages in the educational programs in different parts of the world. When American youngsters take French or Spanish in school, for example, it is true that they are studying foreign languages. In much the same manner, when Japanese or Egyptian students study English, they are learning a foreign language. However, it is in the area of the potential functional use which the foreign language will play in the lives of those students which makes the situations turn out to be quite separate from each other.

Americans study foreign languages more often than not for enrichment purposes. They foresee that they will be able to use the new language for travel, for living abroad, for other personal reasons. Adding a new foreign language certainly unlocks doors, but these are doors to quite different areas of life than those which the student of English in a non-English speaking country hopes to open for himself. It is hardly a matter of chauvinistic or nationalistic allegiance that makes the learning of English such a vital matter to so many young people.

School goals would do well to concentrate on the functional rewards which learning English can offer. It is probably through English that a Yugoslavian engineer speaks with an Ethiopian client in Addis Ababa. The same is more than likely the case with a Swedish demographer who wants to discuss professional matters with his Burmese counterpart in Rangoon, as it is the case with an Egyptian public health specialist holding a meeting with a Greek hospital administrator at an international conference in Geneva, and an Argentinean doctor speaking with a French-Canadian patient in a hospital in Montreal. This list could easily be expanded with similar examples. All of these, in fact, have been taken from actual incidents.

School goals sometimes fail to enunciate clearly enough the difference between learning English as a communicative tool for the purpose of interacting with other speakers of English and learning to be literate in the language, or being able to read and write. Often, too, another quite separate goal, that of gaining an understanding of the culture of English-speaking people through reading their literature is seen as the foremost goal in the English course. Too often it is the case that students who have studied English in schools which concentrated on one set of goals exclusively find that they are quite deficient in other areas. We frequently hear about people who even after years of studying English at school find it almost impossible to carry on a conversation with native speakers of the language. Yet they may be able to thoroughly understand quite advanced writing and be able themselves to produce well composed, accurate compositions.

Language learning is an extremely complex phenomenon. Much of what takes place in an individual's brain and nervous system connected with controlling language is far from being completely understood. However, one important feature of language learning has been shown to be generally true in a number of research projects which have examined the problem: learners master just those language skills upon which the curriculum concentrates. In a course which focuses on reading or writing skills, students tend to read or write far better than they can understand aural cues or produce speech. In a course which emphasizes hearing and speaking skills, students score lower on tests which examine their abilities to read and write the language.

Each one of the skill areas mentioned is of intrinsic value. But aural comprehension, speaking ability, reading, writing, and understanding a people by knowing its literature are all quite separate spheres of language competence. The important task for the school is to evaluate the focus of its English language program in terms of the realities of the larger community and in the light of the goals of students.

3. Student Goals

A generalization can never be made which would be valid for the goals of *all* language students in all countries. Certainly, even among different age groups there are striking contrasts. Child language learners have not as yet articulated goals for themselves. They normally go along with whatever classroom activity the teacher presents. Their reactions are spontaneous; they are involved in the language learning activity as long as it remains within their interest span and their attention span. On the other hand, many motivated adult learners have well-defined goals. They require an instructor who can bring together the materials for learning which best serve these goals. It is the students in the upper grades of school—often those who have reached the intermediate stage in English language learning—who need help in establishing goals for themselves. Coming to an understanding of one's own personal reasons for wanting to work at learning English frequently makes the difference between an individual who is unmotivated and a self-motivated student.

In many places in the world, the instrumental objective of adding English as a tool which helps a person move into modern life holds out the most important motivating pull to young people. Of far less appeal is the integrative objective of learning about the people and traditions of English-speaking countries as a stepping stone for entering into a new culture. Even though it has been suggested by researchers who are interested in people's motivations for language learning that success is more often brought about when the goals are integrative, in a practical sense there seems to be a great deal of overlap between the two categories. As people gain more confidence in their ability to comprehend and speak, they are more motivated to seek higher level educational and professional opportunities. Often these opportunities put them in contact with greater numbers of English-speaking people.

It is a great challenge for the teacher to try to present realistic objectives to the unmotivated young person. The task requires tact and understanding. Teachers who have investigated motivational goals among successful students find that these goals are often interpretable as both integrative and instrumental. But in the entire list, the goals which are conspicuous by their absence are the negative ones such as: to please parents or teachers, to pass the course, or to get proper credit for graduation or matriculation. These short-term instrumental goals seem to bear little significant influence on the successful accomplishment of the complex activity of language learning.

From various corners of the world, teachers report that good language learners usually want to add to their personal opportunities for a more productive and satisfying life. The following is a list of some goals which have been articulated by students as their reasons for wanting to learn English.

1. To acquire new ideas and to broaden my outlook.
2. To know more about modern life.
3. To understand films, records, and TV programs in which English is used.
4. To have access to English books, journals, and magazines.
5. To have access to technical literature.
6. To have more chances for getting a good job.
7. To speak with tourists and visitors from other countries.
8. To help me when I travel abroad.
9. To cope better with university classes.
10. To help me when I study abroad.

WORKSHOP ACTIVITIES

1. Find out what other languages are used by people in your community. What other languages do your students know? What other languages do students consider valuable? In what circumstances do students use other languages?
2. Prepare a questionnaire which will inquire into students' goals for learning new languages. Use the list of objectives which are given in the final paragraph of the section on *Student Goals* (above) as a starting place. Prepare similar questionnaires for use with parents and with school administrators. Do the results among the various questionnaires show similarities or differences among the three groups (students/ parents/administrators)?

B. ACCOUNTING FOR INDIVIDUALS

We recognize that humanizing and personalizing instruction must take the form of specifics, not just slogans. Since we place the needs of the individual learner at the top of the priority list, what are some ways in which this point of view can be carried out? One purpose of this section is to show how ideas for individualized instruction which have developed in other subject matter areas can be extended to the field of language teaching. We draw, too, on advances in language testing to construct diagnostic measures which aid the teacher in designating the skill areas each student needs to concentrate on. Diagnostic testing is an important preliminary step for organizing a classroom around an individualized plan.

These two topics, diagnosing levels and individualized instruction, are augmented by a discussion which touches on areas that the field of language teaching has begun paying attention to: individual learning styles and individual modes of learning. A personalized approach necessitates an overall scheme that is capable of encompassing materials which involve as many of the senses as possible.

1. Diagnosing Levels

When the teacher has not had an opportunity to follow an individual student's progress in learning English, when the student's previous preparation is unknown to the teacher, or, as is often the case in English-speaking countries, when students come from diverse language backgrounds, then the teacher (or the administrator) is faced with the problem: "Where does the student belong in our scheme of courses?" "Where should we place this person in our program?" These questions, of course, need not be considered where students follow a set plan of study, moving on into higher levels on the basis of passing achievement tests which examine their mastery of the material presented in each segment of the program.

One important consideration in determining the student's proper level must be clearly understood by both teachers and learners: it is impossible to define absolute levels of mastery—language learning is simply too complex. Assigning a student to any particular level, whether intermediate, advanced, or any other designation such as second, third, or fourth year is no more than a convenient fiction. The fiction is necessary for the orderly management of classes. The fiction is helpful for the bookkeeping job of grades and evaluations. But in terms of actual language competence, the assignment is only indicative of the student's relative degree of proficiency in particular language skills.

An important distinction is made today between discrete point testing and overall competence testing. A discrete point test is constructed on the basis of a check list of important grammatical topics. (For example, see the list in Chapter Six, *Developing Grammatical Sensitivity,* page 158ff.) Items such as selecting the correct grammatical form from among a group of possible answers and indicating a grammatically correct sentence among a set of sentences are often used in constructing discrete point tests. The TOEFL measure (Test of English as a Foreign Language, published by Educational Testing Services, Princeton, New Jersey) is a well-known example of a discrete point language test for English.

This type of test has certain important advantages. It can be administered to a large number of people who speak different languages; it can be rapidly scored; it is compatible with psychometric techniques for yielding reliable rankings of subjects in relation to each other; and it affords a degree of test security.

On the other hand, many specialists in language testing have pointed out the inadequacies of discrete point measures in terms of the depth and breadth of knowledge they actually test. Since it is impossible to catalog a complete list of items which go into what it is a person who speaks a language really knows (language competence), they say that what is lacking in discrete point testing measures is something which is greater than the sum of all the separate grammatical topics in language.

But even the advocates of overall competence testing are not at all satisfied that they can even approach being able to test what it is that native speakers know about their own language. However, they recommend integrative devices such as dictation, cloze procedures, oral interviews, and reading aloud as interim solutions to the problems. (Examples of these various methods are illustrated below.)

Recognizing that language learning does not consist of a closed set of grammatical facts about language, we must still devise placement tests to assess people's levels in a particular program. These measures do serve practical purposes. But teachers must be aware of the detrimental effects which can occur if either the teacher or the student believes too rigidly in the findings from them. All learning takes place on an individual basis, along a continuum. Experienced teachers know that within a class of intermediate or advanced students there are many differences among individuals in terms of their proficiency in the various language skills.

Carefully constructed placement tests are designed to cover a battery of language skills, including proficiency in both receptive (listening comprehension and reading) and productive (speaking and writing) language. For example, here is an outline of a group test, using pencil and paper, which has been used to place overseas students in English classes at an American university. The test makes use of both discrete point and overall competence devices.

(a) Listening Comprehension: The student hears four dialogs between two people, a male and a female. Each dialog is repeated once. After hearing the dialog, the student answers multiple choice questions referring to that dialog. The dialogs are meant to be colloquial, reflecting everyday situations.

(b) Dictation: The student listens to two dictation passages. In the first one punctuation is given. The reader indicates what punctuation to use by saying the word "period" at the end of sentences, "comma" at the end of introductory phrases, etc. In the second one the student has to supply punctuation. These dictations are intended to assess (a) skill in putting spoken language down on paper in grammatically correct units and (b) the ability to spell and punctuate accurately.

(c) Cloze: The student is given two written passages in which certain words are left blank. The student's ability to fill in these blanks in acceptable English (one word per blank) is a measure of reading and overall competence in English. One instance would be blanks for which the learner is

to supply a certain part of speech. In the example below, prepositions have been left out.

Example:

The cat ran _____ the rabbit and fell _____ a deep hole.
A second example consists of sentences in which every fifth word has been omitted.

Example:

Since the cat had _____ after the rabbit, it _____ the hole too late _____ stop.

(d) Grammar: There are two subtests of grammar. The first consists of sentences with four choices for completion. The correct one must be circled.

Example:

The ice cream cone _____ melting.
    a. are
    b. do
    c. is
    d. being

The second subtest consists of a series of sentences in which there may or may not be a grammatical error. The student underlines the incorrect word or phrase and writes the correct form at the right margin. If no mistakes are found, then the student puts a check.

Examples:

All the *boy* are here.   _____
Sally is her sister.   _____

(e) Reading Comprehension: Here, there could be a series of paragraphs, each paragraph followed by a multiple-choice question. The student chooses the statement that best expresses the main idea of the paragraph from four alternatives.

Many teachers, faced with assigning students to grades or levels, also rely on oral interviews for diagnostic purposes. Sometimes, too, the diagnostic interview is used to reinforce findings from a pencil-and-paper test. In the interview, the teacher, or some other experienced interrogator, asks the student a series of predetermined questions. The interviewer, however, does not feel constrained to keep only to the questions on the prepared list if it turns out that the student is capable of real conversation.

A basic list of interview questions should cover fundamental structures: yes/no questions; wh-questions; negative structures (do + not); verbs with *s*-present and *-ing*, etc. The semantic range should be within the immediate sphere of shared knowledge between student and interviewer: date of arrival in the city; place of residence; short-term goals for schooling or language learning; previous study of English, etc. In fact, the whole purpose behind the oral interview is to allow the student an opportunity to display two basic language skills: listening comprehension and oral production. A more lengthy test could include a sentence repetition section as well to further probe the subject's listening comprehension. The skills of reading and writing, if they are important components of the course or are necessary goals for the student, are ascertained through a pencil and paper test. It would include a reading section as shown in the sample placement test above and a short composition on a topic thoroughly familiar to the student.

The following is a sample list of questions for an oral interview which was used in a program for adults in a large city in the United States. The questions are structurally graded, proceeding from simple sentences to more complex ones. The students were asked to reply in complete sentences. The evaluator rated each student's performance on a zero to five scale as follows: *O*: No English. *One*. Able to satisfy routine travel needs and minimum courtesy requirements. *Two*. Able to satisfy routine social demands and limited work requirements. *Three*. Able to speak the language with sufficient structural accuracy and vocabulary to participate effectively in most formal and informal conversations on practical, social, and professional topics. *Four*. Able to use the language fluently and accurately on all levels normally pertinent to professional needs. *Five*. Speaking proficiency equal to an educated native speaker's.

1. What is your name?
2. Where are you from?
3. Did you stay in New York? Where?
4. Did your family come with you?
   Where does your family live?
5. Where are you living now?
6. Our English classes are at _____ o'clock and _____ o'clock.
   Which is the best time for you?
7. What is your biggest problem in English?
8. How did you get here this morning/afternoon? By car? By bus?
   –What time did you have to leave your house?
   –What time did you have to get the bus?
   –What would you do if you missed the bus?
9. Isn't it quicker for you to come by car/bus?
   How long does it take you by car/bus?
10. How long have you been in _____ (name of city)?

11. Have you gone to _____ yet? (Name of the most well-known local tourist attraction)
    Would you like to go (again)?
12. Before you came here, had you ever heard about _____ ? (the tourist attraction again)
13. Do you have any relatives or friends who live in other parts of the United States?
14. Are you planning to visit them?
15. What is your profession?
    Describe the kind of work you do.

A helpful result of an oral interview when it is used together with a paper-and-pencil test is that the teacher is able to quickly form a profile of the student's strengths and weaknesses in language skill areas. For example, here is a profile for a student who was enrolling in an adult program in an English-speaking country: "Mr. Kimoto understands written English quite accurately as indicated by the reading comprehension component. His writing ability is accurate but not fluent. (He did not finish the written part within the allotted time.) His knowledge of basic structures is adequate to place him in a class beyond the beginning level. His productive language and his listening comprehension needs considerable work. The report from the oral interview indicated that when he was asked basic yes/no questions—'Are you living with relatives here?'—Mr. K. asked the interviewer to repeat the question several times. His reply was overly careful, as though he was translating the idea from his own language."

This kind of profile, derived from both an oral interview and a pencil-and-paper test, can be effectively utilized by the teacher as an aid to selecting materials for use in a course of study. In a classroom which is organized around the concept of helping individuals work on the language skills in which they have the greatest weaknesses, it is important to give a diagnostic test at the beginning of the program. Individual testing should take place in on-going adult classes where students are free to enroll at any time. In some places a complete program is built on teaching the language skills in separate courses. Here, particularly, diagnostic tests are of extreme importance.

2. Modes of Learning

Along with a profile of each student's relative skills in the new language, the teacher must be aware of each one's capability for language learning and each one's particular style or way of learning. People who teach a language of which they themselves are not native speakers are in an advantageous position to examine some of the characteristics which describe a good language learner. All they must do is to look at their own personal case histories. Teachers who are native speakers of English (or of whatever language they teach) may or may not be good learners of other languages. They themselves are the best judges. A sensitive teacher is aware that some people have more talent for language learning than others, just as some people have better natural endowment for playing musical instruments, sports, for handcrafts, etc.

The teacher must also observe individual students to find out something about how each one learns best. Ways of learning do differ among individuals. All humans are endowed with the same senses, but their abilities to utilize their senses vary widely. We all possess the senses of seeing, hearing, touching, smelling, tasting. In most people, one or two of these senses are more acute than the others. Some people remember through strong visual cues: "I know exactly where that quote occurs in the book . . . ." Others have acute hearing. They can remember and sometimes mimic the tone and rhythm of another's speech.

Abilities related to language learning take on more precise characteristics. The ability to adapt to or meet the prevailing norms of the language we hear around us is probably related to phonetic discrimination. Success in reading skills is probably related to visual memory and visual phonetic coding, while an individual's willingness to make mistakes is undoubtedly related to deep-seated personality characteristics.

An application of the theory of individual learning styles has been utilized in programs which incorporate the extended listening period. In such courses, learners (particularly young children) are provided with a great deal of exposure to the new language before they are ever asked to speak—even to reply in short sentences. In some programs the extended listening period has even been as long as five or six weeks.

Through requiring overt physical actions such as picking out an object with the correct color or selecting the correct object from an assortment, the teacher can test if the learner's comprehension of the new language is developing. But the individual learner is in control of the more stress-producing activity of speaking, and will speak only when ready to. Extended listening is a strategy for providing individuals who require it ample time to take in the new language before they must begin to produce it.

All of the senses are used in learning, to some degree. But we are a unique species on this earth. We possess another vital endowment, one which is crucial for language learning. It is cognition, or the ability to perceive, to generalize, "to get the point." Some people cannot memorize if they do not see the overall design or pattern in the material first. The total language learning process is an exceedingly complex mosaic, with infinite individual variations. But for everyone, some thinking must take place. It cannot be done by rote repetition alone. Undoubtedly what makes our human species unique, and what makes our communicative system unique, is our cognitive ability.

In recent years, some teachers have accepted slogans of language pedagogy which concentrated on a small segment of skills and a small segment of the total human capability for learning. The audio-lingual approach is primarily concerned with hearing and speaking skills. The method for teaching these skills is through the use of listening and speaking. Too often listening has been limited to discriminating between sounds which contrast, and speaking has been limited to repeating memorized material. It is not difficult to realize that if we limit ourselves to hearing and repeating, presumably without attention to the cognitive process, we have taken an unproductive path to the goal of using language for communication.

Lately, criticisms have been made of language teaching methods which were based exclusively on techniques of pattern practice, memorization, listen-repeat, choral drill, etc. Critics have noted that these methods failed to utilize explicitly what is undoubtedly the most developed of the mature learner's senses—the cognitive ability. Even among children, the part of learning which involves "seeing how the thing works" is a vital one. For the young child, a good deal of acquiring the native language takes place through the process of formulating, unconsciously, a picture in the mind's eye of grammatical patterns and relationships.

An effective facilitator leaves learners free to make use of their own best ways to learn. A helpful facilitator allows each one every opportunity to experiment, to discover his or her own most productive way to learn. Skilled facilitators do not limit the presentation of material to one or two of the sense modalities, nor do they prohibit learners from using their full range of senses and skills. For some people, even the requirement of sitting in a classroom without occasional physical movement is not the best way for learning to take place.

"All very well," says the traditional teacher, frankly quite tired out from the task of *telling* but not yet quite ready to shift the responsibility over to the student for *learning*.

"How do I get learners to use what they have? I've had so many students who are bored, unmotivated. How do I get them to see learning— second language or anything else—as an activity in which they must move themselves, to find their own best way to learn, rather than to wait and be told (or pushed) by the teacher? How should I encourage an individual student to develop from being unmotivated to becoming self-motivated?"

This teacher's queries echo those of many others. Many point out that the self-motivated student will learn, despite what the teacher does. The self-motivated person learns despite the textbook and the content of the language course. We should concentrate our efforts on the unmotivated. Typically, they are young people in high school. How should we help these unmotivated students discover ways of learning which are best for themselves?

Any second language learner, if he or she is not really naturally endowed for the task, needs to feel a sense of success. Good language learners need to feel successful, too, but it is much easier for them to be "winners" in the game at school—certainly in language subjects.

One quite explicit technique which many teachers have found effective is to look at students' mistakes in the language classroom in a new light. Rather than concentrating on correcting, they concentrate on helping students gain a feeling of success when they use the new language for communication. The important goal is to communicate the idea; correctness comes later. Many people who are not natural language learners need this atmosphere of freedom—really a freedom from the fear of failure. In this atmosphere they can begin to speak a new language with attention to the meaning of the situation.

There is a place for corrections, if they are done constructively. One good method is called "doing expansions." When the student uses a form that is non-normal syntax, the teacher responds with a paraphrase expansion of the sentence in normal syntax.

Student: I asked my friend, *how* do you think about the way people behave here?
Teacher: Yes, you're right, it's important to ask, *what* do you think about the way people behave here?

Acute observers have pointed out that people who are talented language learners are not worried about making mistakes. They jump into the situation and use whatever language they know in whatever way they know. They are constantly on the alert for all of the communicative clues they can pick up, verbal and nonverbal. They watch gestures and facial expressions, They learn to make guesses about meaning. *They keep talking.* Most important, nobody in the situation stops to make corrections in such a way that interferes with communication. In a real conversation, if correction is ever done, it usually comes as an aside. But the central theme of the situation is not interrupted. If such an atmosphere could be simulated in a classroom, many students who have not had success in second-language learning at school might begin to regard the subject from a fresh perspective.

The unmotivated can become self-motivated and even the untalented can find within themselves talents which they never knew they possessed. It has happened when the teacher has created activities that gave everyone an experience in using the language presented in the textbook. It has happened when the teacher has planned activities in which all could participate. It has happened when the teacher made sure that each person left the classroom with a feeling of personal success. (Chapter Seven, HOW, presents detailed activities which stress the experiential and participational approach for the intermediate and advanced levels.)

3. Individualized Instruction

Rather than setting out a specific set of procedures, individualized instruction is a point of view towards the entire education process. In fact, many of the suggestions presented in this book under other headings promote the basic approach of individualization. The need to vary the pacing of instruction according to the learners, the need to introduce a variety of modes which appeal to various senses, the need to adopt realistic expectations towards second-language learning—all of these ideas along with many others are part of a philosophy of individualized instruction. Above all, by placing the learner, or WHO, as the basic component in the sequence of WHO, WHAT, HOW, and WHERE, we have underscored an attitude which places an individual's learning above someone's teaching.

In the field of second-language pedagogy, many practitioners are coming to recognize that organizing a classroom or setting up a course program around the concept of individualization is the only approach which will begin to cope with the fact that, particularly at the intermediate and advanced levels, students come to us with different backgrounds and different preparation. It is also apparent that the nature of language lends itself to compartmentalization. By looking at the separate components of language substance and language skills and realizing that students have unequal development in these separate components, we are led inescapably to the solution—individualized instruction.

The purpose of this section is to describe how the philosophy of individualization has been carried out for ESL and EFL in widely separated places. It sketches four different course designs. The first is an alternate-days plan, the second is based on the idea of skill stations within a single classroom, the third one is a year-program calling for self-placement in separate skill classes, and the fourth is based on creating levels within separate skill areas.

a. Alternate-Days Plan Some teachers have reported that they have had good success in alternating whole class and individualized activities in the following manner: about fifty percent of the total class hours each week are devoted to activities in which everyone participates together. Then certain class meetings are designated as individual learning periods when each student concentrates on the skill areas in which he or she feels weakest, usually two or three meetings during the week. The teacher sets out the materials; each learner spends time concentrating on one skill area. The room can have as many as four, five, or more separate activities taking place simultaneously. This type of alternate-day plan works well in classes which meet daily since it introduces an element of variety into the schedule.

The classroom plan for the days of individualized instruction might contain the following activities: in one corner there is a listening center with materials such as recorder, tapes, records, and earphones available for a few to use; some students are reading English-language books of their own selection; others are working on programmed-reading workbooks. A small group is holding a discussion, possibly with a more advanced student or a native speaker as the leader. (See Chapter 8, Section B, WHERE.) The participants in the small group discussion may decide to move out-of-doors under a tree so that they do not disturb the others who are working quietly in the classroom. Some students are meeting with the teacher for individual help in correcting a recent composition assignment. A few are busy at the games table playing word games such as Scrabble, with considerable oral help from onlookers.

In comparison with a five-days per week whole-class-moving-together plan, this one has the advantage of allowing for activities to take place simultaneously although at various levels of advancement. Not all are ready yet to participate fully in the small group discussion. There are some who still feel reticent in joining discussion groups. This plan gives them a chance to do other work and to use materials, such as the tapes, recorder, and earphones, which are important aids in developing more confidence in speaking-talking skills.

There are other benefits from balancing the total instructional time between activities devoted to individual learning schemes and activities which involve the whole group. When the teacher presents lessons for the entire class, they can include those which lend themselves to participation by a large class. For example, lessons built around songs are sometimes best carried out by the whole class. (See Chapter 7, HOW.) Lessons for improving reading and writing skills can be presented initially as whole group activities, then followed with individualized practice sessions. Similarly, listening-comprehension materials based on use of current media (see Chapter 7, HOW) can be introduced as whole-group activities. On subsequent days the tapes are available at the listening skills center for more individual practice.

b. Classroom Stations Plan   Course planners for an ESL program in a secondary school located in a large city were able to contend with the vexing problem of a continual influx of new students throughout the school term by instigating an individualized instruction program. The program was based on setting up skill stations within a single classroom. Students were placed in four levels on the basis of careful diagnostic testing. Within the classroom space, four locations were designated as the stations at which specific student learning activities would take place. A fifth location served to introduce all new students to the classroom procedures.

At Station No. 1, the teacher conducted grammar lessons using a core textbook. At Station No. 2, students used language-game materials and took part in freer conversation with peer tutors (see Chapter 8, Section B). Station No. 3 was devoted to a listening center. The audio equipment here was supervised by a classroom aide. At Station No. 4, students worked individually with workbooks and other materials for writing skills. The last station, No. 5, was also staffed by an aide and served as the entry point for new students. There, pencil-and-paper diagnostic tests were administered and, in general, newcomers were oriented to the plan of the classroom. Below is a sketch of how the classroom was set up.

	2. *Conversation-Games Center*	3. *Listening Center*
1. *Teacher*		*Tapes-Texts Library*
	4. *Written Work*	5. *New Enrollees*

In this scheme the students moved from one station to the next (among Stations 1-4) in 20-25 minute periods, thus affording each one an opportunity to work on all of the language skills during two class hours. The teachers found that planning for four different levels was not cumbersome since a plan, once it had been made for a more advanced group, was easily adjustable for the less advanced. The teacher held daily meetings with the classroom aides to check on the progress of individuals and to select appropriate materials for each of the five separate stations.

c. Self-Placement Plan   Teachers who are concerned with encouraging as much self-direction as possible among their students have recently been trying out methods in which learners place themselves in the class which they believe they will benefit from the most. The idea of self-placement in classes is a further extension of individualized learning procedures as carried out within a single classroom.

A successful plan for self-placement in a program for intermediate and advanced students took place in a college in a non-English-speaking country whose English department was staffed by both native and non-native speakers. The plan called for classes organized around skill areas in English rather than according to levels or grades. Following a diagnostic test and an oral interview, students selected a sequence of English classes during the year among the department offerings: listening-comprehension, reading, writing, and study skills. They remained in one class for about six weeks, then moved on to another skill area. Or, if they chose to do so, they could continue with the same class. Since the teachers anticipated an uneven turnover at six-week intervals, they concentrated on developing individualized activities.

An advantage for the teachers lies in the fact that each was able to spend more time preparing materials in the skill area of his or her special interest. One teacher—the listening-comprehension specialist—was able to develop an extensive tape library, which included textbook exercises, scenes from plays, and sample lectures, as a result of being freed from the time-consuming job of teaching and correcting compositions, really not an interest at all, but a necessary part of the overall curriculum. Another faculty member who was most interested in teaching reading, both remedially to improve basic skills and as a medium for the appreciation and study of English literature, was allowed more time to work individually with students in tutorial sessions. The students felt free to come to the reading skills center whenever they needed special help or wanted to borrow books for term reports in their other courses. The plan offered students more individualized instruction. At the same time it afforded them an opportunity to develop their independent judgment and their abilities to make decisions for themselves.

d. Separate Levels within Skill Courses   The English communication program for overseas students at a large university in the United States has organized its program around four levels: an intensive course consisting of thirty class hours per week, an intermediate "A" course consisting of fifteen class hours per week, an intermediate "B" course of ten hours per week, and an advanced course of four hours per week. Entering students are required to take a diagnostic test made up of objective sections, a writing sample, and an oral interview.

On the basis of the tests, program counselors are able to individualize each student's program. The course offerings at each of the levels include the four basic language skills: speaking, listening, reading, and writing. But the content varies according to the level. So, for example, a student may take listening-comprehension at the intermediate "A" level and writing at the intermediate "B" level, if the results of the test indicate that these are his or her needs. Or, a student may be exempt from taking courses in any skill area which the counselor determines unnecessary for the individual. The program thus affords a wide range of people, from entering freshmen to graduate students, considerable flexibility.

All four of the programs described above have acknowledged the fact that people come into language classes with different abilities and different backgrounds. A program which locksteps everyone into one mold has serious limitations. The fact that the four programs described do not look very much like each other captures the essence of the philosophy of individualized instruction better than any lengthy generalization could manage to do.

WORKSHOP ACTIVITIES

1. Gather copies of English language diagnostic or placement tests from as many sources as you can. What language skills do these measures evaluate?

2. Design a diagnostic or placement interview suitable for your particular school situation.
3. Interview someone who claims to be a good language learner (perhaps a co-worker). Find out what strategies that person feels she/he uses to achieve success.
4. Work out an individualized instruction plan for a school situation with which you are familiar. Can you either adopt or adapt any of the programs which were outlined in Section 3 of this chapter?

6

WHAT

Language Matter Grows in Complexity

OVERVIEW

What does the language class have to offer students who have already mastered basic, beginning structures in English? What can they gain from a class that they could not receive from just seeking out native speakers of the language to talk with? True enough, there are places where it would be difficult to find English speakers with whom to practice. But why shouldn't they try to improve their mastery of English by attending films, watching television programs, or listening to radio broadcasts? Essentially, what can we provide for students at the intermediate and advanced levels which justifies their coming to class at all?

There is certainly value in attending films, watching television, and listening to radio. But language learners need to do considerably more than passively attend, listen, and watch. At a film, or watching a television program, or listening to a radio broadcast, language comes to us in a fully synthesized manner. Everything is happening at the same time. There is no opportunity to examine structures or language form, there is no opportunity to learn meanings of new words and expressions. Further, there is no opportunity for the individual student to strengthen his or her abilities to use each of the separate language skills: listening-comprehension, reading, speaking-talking, and writing.

The essential thrust of intermediate and advanced courses is to give experience in both analyzing the parts and practicing the synthesis. We try to simulate real life in the language classroom. We know all the time, however, that it is not a substitute for real life. The difference between the class and real life lies in the fact that the classroom contains a facilitator, the teacher, who is available to stop the action and offer explanation. Moreover, the facilitator helps students select those language skills or topics in language substance to which they need to pay special attention.

The following sections present a breakdown of the course content which comprises intermediate and advanced programs. First, students need to expand their grammatical competence; they need to work at developing grammatical sensitivity. Second, they need to widen their range of semantic understandings in English, both through attention to words and expressions used in relevant stituations and through exposure to the social behaviors which carry meaning.

Third, at the intermediate and advanced levels there is a strong rationale which suggests that the four language skills can be linked effectively in a variety of relationships. Rather than proceeding step by step with listening comprehension coming first, followed by speaking, then relegating the literacy skills, reading and writing, to whatever time remains, we link together receptive-competence as manifested in the skills of listening-comprehension and reading to learn. Similarly, productive-competence as manifested in the skills of talking-speaking and writing to communicate are linked. (These relationships are illustrated in diagram 16 on page 176.)

Attention to producing the correct sounds of English is of less prominence at the intermediate and advanced levels. Mastery of native-like pronunciation becomes more of an individual pursuit since learners past the age of about twelve years seem to vary greatly in their ability to become proficient in a new sound system. At this level, pronunciation and intonation practice are worthwhile group activities only when a class is made up of speakers of the same first language background. Usually, concentrating on more significant cognitive areas makes better use of busy people's time.

A. DEVELOPING GRAMMATICAL SENSITIVITY

The presentation of grammar to people who are making a new start at studying English after a gap of time cannot be carried out in the same way as it was in their earlier years. Even if the teacher works with learners who have gone through an integrated course of study and are all speakers of a homogeneous native language, there are still compelling reasons to present English structure from a different approach than was appropriate at the beginning and just-beyond stage. Then, the most effective plan was to proceed slowly, breaking down large topics into manageable, bite sizes. Now we want to help students gain insights into the systematic nature of larger segments. In order to do so, we must have a plan of attack—a reason for picking and choosing the grammatical contents.

Learning a new language is a process which does not happen overnight. A person needs time to develop grammatical feeling for a new language—to arrive at the stage of having sensitivity to what does and does not sound right in the language. Reaching this goal takes many years of practice, work, and exposure. Too often we underestimate the amount of time required for language learning, particularly when the goal is the lofty one of native speaker "knowing."

Since the totality of native speaker competence—that sense of knowing what sounds right and what sounds funny—is so complex, it is easy to realize that no teacher, regardless of how much class time is available, can ever expect to present all of the grammar of English, or of any other language. Many teachers, when they come to this understanding of the nature of language, are able to relax. They feel less anxious about what previously they had viewed as a responsibility to teach everything; they begin to concentrate more upon what they can realistically present in a language course.

l. Selecting the Grammatical Contents

We cannot sequence grammatical topics at the intermediate and advanced levels since it is impossible to control the presentation of structures in the same way as at the beginning and just-beyond stage. How, then, do we decide what the grammatical content of language instruction should be? There are a number of strategies which skilled facilitators carry out: (1) They pay close attention to students' language, both in written work and during classroom interaction. (2) They make good guesses, based on consulting good textbooks. (3) They use the results of diagnostic testing to help individual students clear up areas of confusion.

When classroom activities are centered on spontaneous communication activities, the facilitator's important task at this level is to keep some kind of record of students' non-standard expressions as they occur. This is not an easy task, particularly when the group's focus is on the content of language rather than the form. Keeping a log or notebook of student errors must be carried out in an unobtrusive fashion. The attention of the group should never be diverted from the central activity. The notebook of language "curiosities" can be kept at the teacher's desk for students to consult at some later time. Or, each individual's attention can be drawn to specific grammatical problem areas by handing each person a page from the notebook at the end of class. Mature students usually want to know where their own areas of grammatical weakness lie and will welcome having the teacher point them out in a constructive, individualized manner.

Along with collecting students' non-normal utterances, alert teachers also look for avoidance errors. What important parts of the grammar of English does a student tend *not* to use, more than likely because of unsureness? For example, the present perfect tense (because the auxiliary verb—*have, has*—is unstressed in normal speech and therefore difficult for the learner to hear) is frequently an area that requires analytical attention at this level in order for learners to gain confidence in using it. An effective strategy for seeking out avoidance errors is to concentrate on an individual's use of a form such as present perfect tense while he or she is engaged in a communicative activity in front of the class.

Many of the grammatical problems students of English continue to manifest at the intermediate and advanced stages are difficulties in both form and meaning. These problems tend to lie in recurring areas of the grammatical system of English. (See Section 5, page 158 following.) The teacher needs to help students dig deeper into such perennial problem areas as the article system, tenses, phrasal verbs, relativization, etc. Even though these topics were introduced at the beginning stages, they contain many stumbling blocks. Reintroducing them at this stage does not indicate starting at the beginning. Instead, it represents an application of the cyclic approach: we deal with the same language substance, but now try to take in whole subsystems of the grammar. A grammar textbook for this level should offer explanations which cover considerably more ground than those given in a beginning book, even though there is a good deal of overlap in the table of contents of the two.

Selecting the grammatical content will also emerge from materials which are brought into the lessons for their content value. If the group is using selections taken from newspaper articles, the teacher sees the inherent language substance which the piece contains as the starting place for grammar practice and explanation. Songs can be an excellent source for introducing students to more subtle grammatical points. For example: the modal expressions in lyrics such as Alan Jay Lerner's "I Could Have Danced All Night," Paul Simon's "I'd Rather Be a Hammer Than a Nail," and John Denver's "I Guess I'd Rather Be in Colorado." An alert facilitator chooses material which contains inherent grammatical possibilities appropriate to the needs of intermediate and advanced students.

2. Interference and Interlanguage

The science of language analysis and those who practice that science—linguists—have been working to help us understand some of the processes which take place when people learn new languages. So, for example, most teachers of language are familiar with the concept of interference from the first language. They understand that learners are apt to exhibit both the pronunciation and syntax from their native language when they use the new language.

But along with interference, researchers in recent years have turned our attention to another concept which also helps to explain the process of learning languages—interlanguage. Think of young children acquiring their native tongue, their first language. Even though we have all heard stories about someone else's child, "Johnny," who, at the age of three or four-and-a-half finally began to talk and when he did spoke in quite lengthy, adult-like sentences, most children begin to babble around the age of six months. (Johnny was probably going through an extended period of inner language, cautiously trying out new structures before he was ready to produce them.)

A much more familiar pattern with young children is a series of developmental stages which all children pass through as they are learning to talk. At each of these stages they possess a grammar, a system which governs the classes of words and phrases which can occur with each other. Even children who are as young as six months or one year have been observed to possess "sentence grammars." Their small vocabulary—their inventories of meanings which are linked to series of sounds—are not used randomly.

Learning a new language, particularly by anyone over the age of eleven or twelve, is a very different process from first language acquisition. However, this concept of developmental stages in language learning is valuable for the purpose of grasping the difference between making so-called errors in the new language as opposed to having arrived at some intermediate, transitional stage where the learner uses his or her own system, an interlanguage. This interlanguage may not coincide completely with the grammar which the native speaker possesses, but it is a system which allows for communication, nevertheless.

When we are able to know more about the mental processes which actually control language, we will be in a better position to understand how an individual goes about learning language. Then we will know more about why it is relatively difficult for some people, easier for others. We will know, too, something about the tactics which the successful learner employs—probably unconsciously—to gain success in the pursuit. Until the time some day in the dim future when that part of the human brain which controls language has been scrutinized under a microscope, so to speak, we must use the working hypotheses, the pretty good hunches of language scientists.

They tell us that in the process of learning, people have developmental grammatical systems. Think of a continuum, a long line between "does not know the language" at one end to "native speaker control" at the other. At any point on the continuum, the learner possesses an intermediary system which, in certain ways, deviates from the norms of the standard language. This is interlanguage, or what is popularly described as "knows English but still makes mistakes."

What are some of the strategies which result in interlanguage? For one, the learner makes use of processes such as simplification. For example, the final -s ending on the third person singular of verbs in English is a tricky problem for speakers of many languages. It is a very asymmetrical grammatical form. It occurs in the singular but not in the plural; it is confusing for speakers of languages which have stricter systems of co-occurrence or agreement between subject and verb. Simplification takes place when the learner omits -s as in a sentence such as: *he see the bus.* Omission of the -s on *sees* constitutes his or her intermediary system, or interlanguage.

Other strategies which occur during the lengthy learning process have been observed. Spelling pronunciation: making the sounds correspond to one's idea of what the word sounds like based on the spelling. Historians of English tell us that the word *often* pronounced with a *t* sound in the middle came into custom through just such a tendency for people to pronounce words according to the spelling. Overgeneralization: since many English nouns are spelled with the letter -*s* in the plural, put it on all nouns. This type of overgeneralized rule overlooks the fact that English has two large classes of nouns. The countable nouns do add the letter -*s* for the plural form. However. uncountable or mass nouns do not. The speaker who overgeneralizes the rule is apt to add an -*s* to mass nouns such as *information*, *advice*, *music*, or *fun*.

It is obvious in some of the examples cited in the above paragraphs that there is a fine line between so-called mistakes which can be analyzed as interference from native language and those which constitute interlanguage, a developmental stage in the new language being learned. For the teacher, trying to decide the *source* of a transitional stage in the student's grammatical system of English is not a very productive approach. What can be helpful and valuable is for the teacher to develop a new point of view towards transitional language. After all, learners have not completely failed when they commit what we formerly called an error or a mistake. If they have managed to convey a concept, to communicate, they should be permitted, even encouraged, to keep on talking. The facilitator, at a later time, can suggest that the learner focus attention on that portion of the grammatical system which seems to be causing chronic difficulties.

Along with simplification, overgeneralization, spelling pronunciation, and avoidance of doubtful constructions, learners' interlanguage is characterized by certain fossilized features, remnants of an intermediate stage which persist and persist and take considerable effort to clear up. Sometimes, too, understanding the problem, trying to solve it by practicing it for a time, and then moving on to something else will still not have produced a long-lasting remedy. The fossilized form may continue to reappear in moments of stress, anxiety, or even complete relaxation. For example, a successful and highly fluent person whose native language was German had acquired a native-sounding pronunciation of American English. Only at those times when speaking about topics which brought to his mind associations with childhood, or with the experiences of moving from German to English during early adolescence was the presence of the characteristic uvular -*r* sound from German apparent in his pronunciation of English.

Viewing so-called mistakes from a fresh perspective has enabled many teachers to move into teaching at intermediate and advanced levels with a greater degree of confidence. They begin to see that developing the student's grammatical sensitivity can be aided by presenting topics in greater chunks. Reviewing the whole modal auxiliary system, not in one lesson, of course, but showing important contrasts in form and meaning in a series of lessons on all the modals, can often clear up fossilized confusions in a student's mind. (Other persisting problems in English grammar which lend themselves to presentation as topics for review are discussed in Section Five, page 158–163 following.)

3. Giving Explanations

Intermediate and advanced students are usually beyond childhood. As mature people, they need to see how overall systems work. It is at this stage of development that the teacher must bring activities into the language lesson which emphasize cognitive practice—perceiving, understanding, grasping the whole idea. The obvious place to bring in cognitive functions is in the presentation of grammatical explanations.

At this level, the teacher gives concise generalizations of how things work in the grammar of English, while avoiding at all times wordy, meaningless explanations, or explorations into the *why* of language systems.

Native speaker teachers usually need to build confidence in their abilities to look analytically at their own language. This confidence comes from a thorough grounding in modern language study. All teachers who have this background know that the only reasonable answer to a "why do you say it that way?" question that the native speaker teacher can offer is: "That's the way speakers of English say it. If you want to speak English, you'll have to say it that way, too." It is true, there are variations in the way English is spoken based on factors such as geographical dialects, age of speakers, social and ethnic backgrounds, etc. But these differences affect small, comparatively minor points. For the large, more productive areas of grammar, there is enough common, shared language to master to keep even advanced students busy for a considerable period of time.

Both the native and the non-native teacher must be able to say with perfect aplomb to students, "I really don't know how to explain such and such," or "I'm not sure, but I know where to look for a possible explanation. I'll do just that" or, "Why don't you see what it says about that particular topic in textbook X, Y, or Z?" Or, "Why don't you find out what Professor A, B, or C has to say about that question?"

We are not all scientific analysts of language. If we were, we would all want to write textbooks and grammars. But as classroom teachers, we must continually improve our ability to observe the formal features of language. At the same time we should be able to stand our ground firmly and with all confidence say, "I'm just not sure" or "I don't know. Let's try to find the answer together." No one loses face by saying "I don't know," in a classroom where a spirit of authenticity prevails.

4. The Textbook Is for Reference

At the intermediate and advanced levels, the teacher is freer to escape the tyranny of feeling tied to a single textbook. By this stage, one single textbook cannot realistically be all things to all students; a single textbook cannot cover all of the ground which the course of study at these levels encompasses. Frequently we find helpful grammatical explanations in one book, effective classroom language activities in another, and lively situational ideas for practicing language in a third. This tactic is quite different from the one adopted at the beginning level where careful control of vocabulary items and analytical sequencing of structures calls for the use of an integrated set of materials, or a core textbook. (See *Part One*, Chapters Two and Three.)

Many teachers who work with intermediate and advanced people have found that a good policy to adopt is not to think in terms of one textbook which will cover all of the content of the English language course. Besides, too much of what can be utilized for language practice at these levels resides outside of the classroom, out where the language is being used. At these levels we do not want to rely on textbooks alone to make the English language a live medium of communication for students.

But in the area of grammar or syntax, all teachers need to rely on good references and insightful textbooks. What is important is for the classroom library to contain as many sources as possible. The teacher can devise a lesson which makes use of students' interests, one which focuses on grammatical topics in which they need to develop greater security. If the classroom contains a good library, the teacher, after giving an initial presentation, can then say: "Okay, do you want to understand more about English tenses? Go read about it as explained by Author X, Y, or Z."

Many people, by consulting more than one authority, are able to free themselves from the constricting idea that there is one "right" explanation for every question under the sun, even in English grammar. Advanced language learners are ready to realize that a grammatical analysis, whether given by a textbook author or a scientific linguist, is a working theory. A sound theory attempts to tie together as much data as possible by showing how many separate facts can be explained concisely and accurately. The work of making statements about grammatical systems involves finding order out of the chaos of disparate data. As in all theory constructing, one person's explanation will stand up until someone else comes along to give us a better, clearer one. A good theory takes in more of the data and makes more order out of chaos than a prior one. That is one important reason why many teachers prefer to consult a small library of reference grammars and good texts rather than merely one source.

5. Important Grammatical Topics for This Level

A comparison among the table of contents of review grammar textbooks—by both British and American writers—indicates that there exists a shared pool of grammatical areas in English which seem to persist as stumbling blocks for intermediate and advanced learners. From these kinds of lists and from observation of their own students' problems, facilitators make decisions regarding the grammatical content of their courses. A list of grammatical topics which frequently turn up in the table of contents of remedial textbooks follows. A few of the chief features of each topic are briefly suggested below.

a. The modals (also called helping or auxiliary verbs): *can, could, may, might, must, ought, shall, will, would.*

Problems in form: No agreement with subject. Imperfect distribution in past and future.

Problems in meaning: One modal form can have various meanings depending on context.

Example:

would as a request: *Would* you come in?

would as volition: He *would* do it if he had the time.

Example error:

Here is a common meaning-form error in which a hotel clerk probably equated *can be,* the dictionary meaning for *possible,* as synonymous for the modal *can,* meaning ability at the present moment or in the near future.

Hotel guest: Where is the restaurant?
Hotel clerk: It's on the fourth floor.
Hotel guest: *Can* I take the elevator there?
Hotel clerk: Yes, that's *possible.*

b. Simple present time contrasted with continuous time (*-s* present contrasted with *-ing* present progressive):

Example:

John sings everyday/John is singing right now.

Problem in meaning: Verbs which do not take *-ing* for the meaning "right now"—*cost, forget, hear, know, like, love, need, own, prefer, remember, see, understand, want.* (Sometimes called "verbs of the senses.")

c. Countable and Uncountable (and the articles which accompany them)

Problems in form: a/no article goes with count/uncountable nouns respectively. Both count and uncountable nouns take *the* and *some.*

Example:

I eat an apple for lunch.   I eat rice for lunch.

I eat apples for lunch.	I eat two bowls of rice for lunch.
I eat the apple in my lunch sack.	I eat the rice I prepare.
I eat some apples everyday.	I eat some rice everyday.

Problems in meaning: Some nouns have different meanings when used as count or uncountable nouns:

Example:

I ordered a glass of tea.	The ambassador's wife gives many teas each year.
Iron is found in the ground.	Use a cool iron to press rayon.
The Secretary of State had talks with the President.	Prepare a talk to give to the class.

d. Tag questions: (Tags are a big problem, aren't they?)

Problems in form: The English tag is used similarly to tags in other languages. However, many other languages have tag expressions which do not change in form.

Example:

Spanish - *verdad*	Persian - *mageh-noo*
German - *nicht var*	Japanese - *soo desu*
French - *n'est-ce pas*	Hebrew - *nahon*

In English, however, a negative statement takes a positive tag and vice-versa. A common interlanguage expression is:

Example error:

You didn't spend much on it, isn't it?

Problems in meaning. Tags in English are a device to promote conversation. They do not ask for information but rather supply the hearer with information to talk about.

e. Phrasal verbs and prepositional phrases (phrasal verbs are also called two-word verbs):

Problems in form: The two forms are frequently confused with each other.

Example:

Two-word verb	*Prep. phrase*
I'll *go into* that matter later.	I'll *go into* the house now.

Prepositional phrases of time and place are frequently confused with each other.

Example Error:

I will meet you in 3 o'clock in Sunday.

All phrasal verbs are not the same. There are separable and inseparable ones.

Example:

inseparable	*separable*
I'll call on you.	I'll call (you) up.

arrive at	back (it) out.
depend on	take (it) off.
look at	fill (it) out.
complain about	hand (it) in.

Problems in meaning: The native speaker of English tends to use hundreds of phrasal verbs in everyday talking. The learner does not realize that the meaning of a phrasal verb is usually not the same as that of the verb alone without a preposition following.

f. Passive voice:

Problem of form: A passive sentence often deletes the agent. In natural passive sentences such as the examples shown below, learners frequently do not recognize the fact that the agent has been deleted.

Example:

English is spoken in many places.
Rice is served differently in Japan.

Problems of meaning: The passive voice reinforces the simple present and is used to describe generic facts. Often students are asked to practice indiscriminate transformations of active sentences to passive sentences. The results are unnatural passives, or sentences which are grammatically correct, but we cannot conceive of a context in which the sentence would be actually spoken.

Example Errors:

John read the book / The book was read by John.
I eat an apple everyday / An apple is eaten by me everyday.

g. If clauses (also called conditional or dependent clauses):

Problems of form: The two phrases of the sentence do not have tense agreement.

Example:

> If I finish, I'll see you.
> If I had finished, I would have seen you.

Example Error:

> If I'll finish, I'll come.

Problem of meaning: Confusion about real time vs. grammatical tense.

Example:

> If you're ready, I'll come now.

h. Perfect tenses:

Example:

> John has read the newspaper every morning since he was twelve years old.
> John had already read the newspaper when his wife came into the room and asked for it.
> John will have read the whole newspaper by the time the plane lands.

Problems in form: Present perfect tense in American English is only mandatory in expressions with *since* and *for*. British English uses present perfect more commonly.

Problems in meaning: Learners tend to use present perfect when specific time is indicated, or they misinterpret the rule they have been taught which calls for present perfect tense for "recent past" time.

Example Errors:

> I have been there yesterday.
> I have finished my studies in 1975.

i. Relative clauses:

Problems of form: The relativization process is a complex one of rearrangement, addition, and deletion of elements:

Example:

> 1. This is the book.
> 2. I mentioned it to you.
> 3. This is the book that I mentioned to you.
> 4. This is the book I mentioned to you.

Example Error:

This is the book that I mentioned it to you.

j. Contrasting verbal expressions: This list contains only a few examples of a large number of perplexing pairs of verbs. In each case there are difficulties in both form (syntactic) and meaning (semantic). Pairs like these are frequently called idioms and are overlooked or quickly passed over in teaching the English language.

Examples:

speak/talk   do/make   tell/say   bring/take   wish/hope
study/learn   lend/borrow   suggest/offer   invite/order
have to/used to/ought to   had better/would like

WORKSHOP ACTIVITIES

1. Collect samples of the writing produced by two or three intermediate level students. (A composition assignment would serve the purpose.) Analyze the non-normal sentences. Can you find any consistent errors which might be used to illustrate a particular student's interlanguage system?
2. Compare the list of grammatical topics beginning on page 159 with those presented in two review textbooks which are used in your country or your school. How does the list differ from those you find in the table of contents in the two textbooks? What grammatical topics do you believe should be added to the list?
3. How would you sequence the list of topics beginning on page 159, to best suit the needs of a group of students with whom you are familiar? (To work out the sequence, you should look back at *Part One:* WHAT Section A, *Language Substance.*)

B. UNFOLDING BROADER FACETS OF MEANING

One of the significant characteristics which divides this level from the beginner's is that intermediate and advanced students must grapple with intricacies of meaning. In all languages, form and meaning are intertwined with each other. We think of language so much in its totality that it takes a good deal of practice for a native speaker to be able to concentrate on the realm of form apart from the realm of meaning. But the process of separating form and meaning is what we must be capable of doing in order to effectively deal with language substance.

In its recent history, language teaching has been primarily directed towards presenting the *form* of language in a sequenced, organized way. There is at least one very good reason for this practice: we possess grammatical descriptions of languages, while our body of knowledge regarding grammars of meaning is far less developed. But form without meaning is dry bones without flesh. Meaning is very much a part of language and so must be included in language instruction.

The finesse in preparing language teaching texts, in fact the key to evaluating any materials, is the effectiveness with which form and meaning are meshed. How do we create a bridge between form and meaning in designing instructional techniques and materials? What do we do at the intermediate and advanced levels to take into account the fact that learners by this stage are no longer children? They have exceedingly well developed semantic systems which govern thought processes in their native languages. We must somehow tap this conceptual source and fuse it with the code of form and meaning which is manifested in the new language.

Just as form and meaning are completely integrated in real language, so, too, are the various dimensions of meaning. None of the aspects of meaning discussed here ever occur alone. It is all happening concurrently, like the playing of a symphony orchestra. Tackling meaning is like trying to take on the entire universe. Our aim here is far more modest. It is simply to point out some of the dimensions of meaning that are part of classroom materials and techniques.

Five aspects of meaning are briefly discussed in this section. First, *contextual meaning* is used as a term for describing the meaning inherent in grammatical structures. Another facet of contextual meaning is the shared web of associations, the implicit understandings which are held by the speaker and the hearer in any language exchange. A second type of meaning is *situational meaning*. We have used it to describe the setting incorporated in a particular language example, drill, or presentation. *Lexical meaning*, or knowing the words of a language, is a vital and ever-expanding part of a native speaker's ability. Another facet of knowing a language is being able to *paraphrase*, or to know when two similar ways of saying something mean the same thing. Finally, this section deals with *social meaning*, or the appropriate use of language in social situations.

1. Contextual Meaning

All grammatical structures contain inherent meaning. For example, verbs in English connote the aspect of temporal distribution. It makes a good deal of difference in meaning whether a person uses the *-s* present or the *-ing* present. So in the sentences below, we have an entirely different picture of what the person is doing in each of the two examples:

1. I eat cereal   (as an answer to: What's your favorite breakfast?)
   for breakfast.

2. I'm eating   (as an answer to: What's that funny-looking stuff you're
   cereal.   eating?)

At the intermediate and advanced levels, one of the most persistent problems for new learners is to take in the web of subtle meanings which are conveyed through language structure. The entire modal system, for example, delineates fine shadings of meaning.

1. You don't look well. You haven't looked well for days. You *should* see a doctor. (necessity)
2. You *should* call the garage to help fix the car. (advice)
3. They *should* be here any minute. (future possibility)
4. Take the umbrella in case it *should* rain. (possibility)
5. It's rather warm. *Should* I open the window? (suggestion-permission)

Unfortunately, too many textbooks at the beginning level present practice materials which cloud the meaning of structure. Drills which require students to change the indefinite article *a* to definite *the* abound in textbooks. Yet few devote sufficient attention to the shift in meaning which accompanies this shift in form. It is not too difficult to find drills which even ask the students to change a definite article back to the indefinite article. Even though this order (*the* to *a*) completely obscures the shared associations which the speaker and hearer hold when the definite article *the* is present. Erasing these associations is something akin to expecting the sun to rise in the morning from the west.

On the surface, looking at form alone, *a* and *the* appear quite simple. Yet the use of one or the other significantly changes meaning. If a person asks:

What do you keep in *the* bathroom medicine cabinet?

that person is implying a degree of intimacy between speaker and hearer by virtue of implicit shared information. But such information does not exist if one asks:

What do you keep in *a* bathroom medicine cabinet?

Even basic sentences in the earliest lessons in beginning textbooks convey a particular point of view held by the speaker. When we ask a student to repeat a sentence such as this seemingly simple one,

The table is big.

we actually know that the only context in which such a statement is likely to be made would be as a response to a question, or a request for information as an answer, for example, to:

Tell me something about the table.
or,
Describe the table to me.

Or, take the familiar type of drill found in many textbooks which tells students to change a statement to a question:

Statement	Question
This is a cup.	Is this a cup?

It is possible to reply with a question to the above statement in various ways which sound like real communication, but it is quite impossible to conceive of time or place in which a yes/no question would fit either the statement above or those found in many drill book exercises. Probably the most natural reply to a statement such as *This is a cup* is not a yes/no question at all, but rather another statement followed by a wh-question, as in:

I know that. What's wrong with you, do you think I'm blind?

In many textbooks, after the dialogues, narratives, or reading passages, come some kind of controlled exercises or drills. The purpose of this drill material is to offer further exposure to the grammatical focus of the lesson. Exercises which maintain the same contextual theme that was established in the presentation material are sometimes offered. More frequently, however, the writer seems to run out of steam when getting to the practice section, or perhaps the contextual possibilities contained in the initial presentation have been exhausted.

But practice materials which introduce entirely new themes—or what is too frequently the case, no continuing theme whatsoever, simply unconnected lists of sentences—are sorely deficient in contextualization. For contextual meaning also takes into account whether there is a thread of commonality or connected meaning in the lesson. If we want to have real language in the classroom, we should avoid having students practice structure drills which are lacking in connected meaning.

For example, if the first sentence in a drill which requires transformation from one expression of time to another deals with recreational events, then all of the other sentences should fall into the same field of meaning:

1. *cue*: Did you watch the tennis matches on TV last night?
   reply: Yes, and I'll watch them again tonight.
2. *cue*: Did you go to the football game last night?
   reply: Yes, and I'm going again tonight.
But not:
3. *cue*: Did you finish the last piece of cake?

Contrast the sentence transformation drills in (1) and (2) with the following examples which require the student to combine two short sentences into an expanded sentence which utilizes deletion.

4. *cue*: He's ready. I'm ready.
   reply: He's ready and I am too.
5. *cue*: Yesterday was sunny. Today is sunny.
   reply: Yesterday was sunny and today is too.

Unlike (1) and (2) above, in (4) and (5) no connected meaning has been established from one drill to another. The absence of connected meaning in language teaching materials detracts from their inherent interest value and must be as responsible for turning off students' attention as any other factor we might isolate.

Sometimes when we first read the drills in textbooks, we feel that we have no grounds on which to complain, "but that's not English." But at the same time we feel that the material sounds untrue, that there is something very unnatural about it. Consider this sentence:

John put the book on the table.

As it appears, it is certainly an "acceptable" English sentence. However, it stands out like a sore thumb as a typical "textbook sentence." In real life, such a sentence simply could not occur without some shared context of meaning between the speaker of the sentence and the hearer. There could be no "John" without both the speaker and the hearer knowing who John is. Unless, of course, "John" is the speaker's pet alligator, then the fact that he put the book on the table is, indeed, a feat to be noted and the intonation of the sentence would indicate such. Similarly, there could be no book and no table which do not hold connections to other associational meanings in the minds of both speaker and hearer. For it is an inescapable fact of language grounded in real life that when understanding takes place, the speaker and hearer share knowledge which goes beyond the domain of the sentence itself.

If a man who lives in Los Angeles says to his wife:

Hey, honey, let's take the subway train downtown and see a movie tonight.

the sentence is certainly "correct." It contains truth value within itself. However, anybody who knows the city of Los Angeles or even knows a little about it realizes that the man either lives in a mental institution or that there is something very odd about the utterance since there is no subway system in the city of Los Angeles.

All of the separate factors mentioned in this section are part of contextual meaning. They are the semantic elements which link the artificial classroom setting in which new languages are learned to the outside real world where language is spoken and used.

2. Situational Meaning

The term "situational meaning" is used to describe the actual setting or thematic ideas incorporated in a particular language example, drill item, or presentation. Situation is the whole gamut of people, places, and actions familiar to the audience who will use a set of materials. It is vital, of course, that thematic ideas be relevant to the learners' interests and concerns. Hopefully, they reflect the learners' level of understanding and their degree of sophistication. This is why there are beginners' texts for children and other beginners' texts for adults. Children and adults do not share the same spheres of interests—though there can be, of course, a certain amount of overlapping.

A frequent method for fusing situation and language substance is through the dialogue or brief narrative. Finding the relevant situation through which to exhibit particular language substance requires a high degree of creativity and expertise. It is an assignment which classroom teachers usually turn over to textbook writers. In most cases teachers trust the materials preparer to successfully embed selected structures in situations which will hold the interest of the learners. But people being as different from each other in tastes and experiences as they are, it is not always easy to find materials which are appropriate for all of the students in a given class. Expert facilitators find that they must continually edit materials. On the spot, they are able to adapt drills, for example, to their particular students' spheres of relevance.

A teacher who mechanically uses textbook drills that have unknown names of places and people, or that refer to actions which hold no relevance to the particular group of learners, is not doing a facilitator's job. That mechanical teacher could easily be replaced by a robot in this automated, computerized age.

But observe the opposite case, a skillful classroom facilitator. Take Ms. Smith, for example. She is drilling the present perfect tense using materials from a textbook. Without missing a word, she glances at the Teacher cue in the textbook she uses as a reference and changes the Mr. Brown and Miss Jones to names of class members. The settings become familiar places; she even alters experiences to characterize personalities in the group. Seeing that a member of the class is absent, she guesses the reason:

Mr. Gonzales has been visiting his relatives in Mexico since last Tuesday.

There are other elements of situational meaning which the teacher must look for. Examples of drill sentences which misfit the topic to the audience often occur in the semantic ranges of weather, climate, time zones in the day, directions, means of transportation, etc. It is absurd, of course, to practice sentences in which conditions of snow prevail if the learner is sitting in a classroom in Hawaii or Florida. To speak of "morning," "afternoon," and "evening" — the time zones of the day for most English speakers—requires some readjustments, too, for learners who equate morning as a period of time which extends until two or three in the afternoon, and evening as lasting until about 9:00 p.m. In this case the semantic timetable in English clearly does not coincide with those in various learners' first language.

Beyond the dialogue and brief narrative, there are other types of presentations which serve the purpose of embedding selected structures in situations which potentially will hold the interest of the learners. We use songs, poems, letters, riddles, everything and anything as presentation materials. In soundly constructed language learning texts, these various presentations are prepared so as to contain selected linguistic elements of structure and meaning. At the same time, they also control vocabulary items. The new words in the presentation are semantically related to its overall theme. In this way, the separate components of form and meaning are synthesized for presentation purposes but available for analysis in the language classroom.

The examples of situational presentations we have examined so far are appropriate for the just-beyond . . . intermediate stage. At the advanced level, it is much less necessary to limit presentations to a few key structures. Presentations at the advanced stage can be original materials, not structurally simplified, with key vocabulary words glossed for meaning. At this level, the facilitator is much freer to select materials which contain ideas of deeper significance for students: short newspaper items, selected paragraphs from magazines, even whole acts from plays. Selecting a relevant theme takes priority over maintaining structural control at the advancing levels. But the facilitator must remember that if the learners are to benefit from being in a language class, then some attention must still be paid to the structural complexity of the material they are working with in the new language—no matter how compelling may be the subject matter.

3. Lexical Meaning

Some time back, language teachers turned over a new leaf, one which flatly stated: I pledge not to teach long lists of new vocabulary items in isolation. But if words are not to be presented as lists of new items, how else can learners—particularly at the advanced stage—rapidly and efficiently add to their stock of word knowledge. How can they expand their inventory of lexical meanings in English?

Take the word which heads this section, *lexical*, otherwise known as an entry in a dictionary—a word. From the expression "lexical" we can expand to derivitives such as *lexicon, lexicography,* and *lexicographer.* Two worthwhile techniques for learning additional words in a new language have just been exemplified: (1) help learners expand their vocabulary by presenting them with new vocabulary items which they can associate with those they already possess, (2) help learners find the derivational possibilities which the new vocabulary item can generate.

Neither suggestion (1) or (2) are such new ideas; can we turn up anything better, anything fresher? Probably not. There is no magic formula. But we can predict that new vocabulary, new lexical items, are more likely to be remembered if they carry an association to familiar meanings. That association can come about through myriad ways. Words which appear in planned presentations give learners many more clues to work with so as to be able to fit them into their own internal systems of mapping sounds to meaning. New words are more apt to be remembered if they are used, if we turn them around in our mouths, so to speak. So much the better if we also turn them around in our heads and associate a new word with the thematic material in which we first encountered it.

One step beyond teaching mere lists of new vocabulary words is to teach organized lists of vocabulary words. An even greater leap forward is to have students make up their own lists and then organize the contents by consulting with the facilitator or another native speaker.

What makes a vocabulary list an organized one? (1) An organized list divides the items into content words and function words, or words which refer to objective events, states, or properties as opposed to those which function primarily as grammatical entities. (See *Part One:* Chapter Two, Section A.) For example: in the sentence below, the function words are italicized:

The cat *who* ate *the* rat sat *on the* mat.

(2) An organized list designates whether the given word occurs as a noun, verb, or adjective in a sentence. Further, it lists the derivational possibilities as well, for example:

travel (v.)   traveler (n.)   well-traveled (adj.)

The difference between teaching words, words, words at the beginning level and lexical items now rests primarily in the scope which is brought in at the intermediate and advanced stages. Now we pay close attention to helping people construct more intricate webs of meaningful associations by connecting related lexical items. Now we want to activate the learner's cognitive abilities to understand the productive processes which the new language contains for creating new vocabulary.

The structure of English lends itself to many productive possibilities in vocabulary building: the two-word verb constructions (*take on, take off, take over*... there are thousands of others) constitute an extremely persistent semantic problem for all new learners of the language. They should always be learned as units, verb + particle; they should be linked whenever possible to the meaning of the longer, often Latin-derived verb: *take on = accept, take off = remove; take over = expand.*

Various textbooks have developed worthwhile vocabulary-strengthening exercises which utilize the morphemic structure of English for the teaching of new vocabulary items. For example, such exercises give students experience in using the suffixes which change verbs to nouns *(-ance, -ence; -ation, -(t)ion, -ment, -ity).* So, *accept, acceptance; combine, combination; extend, extension; assert, assertion; enjoy, enjoyment; sense, sensitivity.* Similarly, the common suffixes which change verbs and nouns to adjectives *(-able, -ible; -al; -ate; -ful; -ous; -y).* So, *remark, remarkable; sense, sensible; nature, natural; passion, passionate; doubt, doubtful; danger, dangerous; risk, risky.*

Another valuable vocabulary exercise is the type which helps students become conscious of the difficult verb + particle pattern in English. Effective exercises often point up the contrast in meaning between such pairs which appear similar, yet are semantically quite distinct: *talk to/talk about; agree with/agree about; begin with/begin by; related to/related by; preferred to/preferred by; present to/present by.*

Learners need to become sensitive to these morphemic expansions and contrasts in the structure of English. In fact, gaining word sensitivity is another facet of grammatical sensitivity, or the internal knowing of what sounds "right" as opposed to what sounds "wrong"—or not English at all.

At a certain level of competence, word building is determined, too, by the individual student's interests and goals. If the learner uses English as a professional tool through which to read or study in a field of knowledge, he or she unconsciously learns new vocabulary which relates directly to those interests. Learning vocabulary in this fashion is accomplished with relatively little blood, sweat, and tears. At all levels of instruction, however, people probably learn what they need to learn; they remember what they use. Words memorized but not used tend to be quickly forgotten.

4. Paraphrase and Meaning

One of the important characteristics of knowing a language is the ability to paraphrase. If we say something one way in a language in which we are competent, it is almost always the case that we can rephrase or paraphrase the idea: we can say approximately the same thing as far as the meaning of the message is concerned but use different words and different syntactic arrangements. An ultimate objective in learning a new language is to reach the stage where the ability to paraphrase operates as surely.

The following set of sentences illustrates the "knowing" which comprises paraphrasing:

Seymour sliced the salami with a knife.
Seymour used a knife to slice the salami.

It was a knife that Seymour used to slice the salami.
It was the salami that Seymour sliced with a knife.

In each case the person doing the action, the action itself, the object acted upon, and the means by which the action was performed are all the same. Even though the sentences look and sound quite different, yet all four mean the same thing. The emphasis may be different, but all four deal with the same occurrence.

When used in connection with single lexical items, the ability to paraphrase is called synonomy (fall/autumn; sofa/couch, etc.) A way to build a large vocabulary is to increase one's fund of synonymous words. And, of course, learning synonyms is a basic device of vocabulary instruction in language teaching. An important part of learning two-word verbs in English consists of learning synonymous words: *look over/examine; keep on/continue; look like/resemble; go over/review; talk over/discuss; try out/test; use up /consume; pick out/choose; make sure of/verify,* and hundreds of others.

There are a number of ways in which the technique of paraphrasing can be an important classroom activity: when we ask students to retell a brief narrative in their own words, to give the gist of the meaning of material listened to, to offer equivalent ways to say the same thing. In correcting pronunciation, paraphrase can be a useful tool. Instead of telling a student, "No, that's not the way to say *marijuana*; you shouldn't make the sound of the letter 'j'." Rather, the skilled facilitator rephrases the learner's sentence and presents a correct pronunciation model for the student: "Oh, of course, you're interested in reading more about marijuana."

We teach dialogues, not for learners to repeat them like parrots, word-for-word, but rather so that people will first grasp the overall idea in the dialogue and then rephrase that meaning in their own words. A technique for stimulating this ability can be carried out by actually presenting alternate ways of saying the same thing within one basic dialogue. Paraphrased extensions of a basic dialogue take into account the concept that language competence is not a strictly linear function. What really counts is the overall meaning of a segment. Paraphrased dialogues present whole chunks of language which carry meaning.

The material used in paraphrase exercises should be kept quite short. First the learner is introduced to a basic four-line dialogue. This takes place through listening, repetition, and memorization. When the basic meaning and information exchange contained in the dialogue are well understood, variations of the basic piece are introduced. The following example shows the variations possible in a brief, four-line exchange.

Original Version

Speaker 1:	Can you go with me to the concert on Saturday night?
Speaker 2:	Oh, I'm sorry, I'm busy Saturday night.
Speaker 1:	Well, what about next Saturday?
Speaker 2:	That would be fine. I'd really like to go.

Variations

Speaker 1: Would you like to go with me to the concert?/Can you make it Saturday night?/Are you free on Saturday night?/Would you like to hear the concert with me on Saturday night?

Speaker 2: Oh, I'm terribly sorry, I have a date on Saturday night./ Oh, I'm really sorry, I'm busy Saturday night./ Oh, I'm awfully sorry, I'm not free this Saturday night.

Speaker 1: Could you go next Saturday, a week from now?/Could you make it next week when the orchestra plays?/Are you free next Saturday?/How about next Saturday?

Speaker 2: Yes, I'd like that very much./Yes, I'd love to go with you next week. /Yes, Saturday of next week would be great./Next Saturday sounds fine.

5. Social Meaning

Just as the understanding that neither words alone nor sentences in isolation constitute the only type of meaning, similarly have language teachers recently begun to recognize another whole facet of competence in using language—the knowing which enables speakers to use language appropriately. This knowledge, which is as complex as the phonological, morphological, and structural systems with which language teachers have been traditionally concerned, is referred to as communicative competence. When we expand the skill of speaking to include talking as well (see Sec. C.), we are taking into account the whole gamut of abilities necessary for communication which social meaning implies. Native speakers in all languages possess a formidable system of implicit understandings which they utilize in communicating with each other. In fact, much that goes on during the ordinary, everyday acts of both talking to and of understanding the other person in a conversation rests heavily on the cultural code of communication, the system of shared social meanings.

If it is *not* the same as knowing the grammatical structure of a language or knowing how to make the sounds of a language, what aspects does communicative competence actually include? Why should we try to incorporate features of social meaning into our instructional programs for facilitating English language learning?

The answer to the first question is that communicative competence is made up of all the characteristics of language behavior which enable speakers to judge what to talk about, with whom, and in what way; it includes the ability to judge when and where to speak and when and where not to speak. Why should we be interested in social meaning in the classroom? Consider this fact: Misunderstandings certainly occur when learners use the new language for real-life communication with native speakers. Misunderstandings can arise because of a person's incorrect pronunciation, or incorrect syntax. But misunderstandings based on the linguistic code alone are trivial compared to those which can occur when, for example, the new speaker of English is not able to make judgments about the use of particular slang expressions with particular groups of people. What good does it do for a language learner to memorize countless dialogues in English if he or she does not know when it is appropriate to use bits of dialogue material which have been learned? We place an inordinate amount of trust in the textbook writer when we offer to learners as accurate models of the way people talk the examples which fall into many of our texts.

How should we go about the task of augmenting intermediate and advanced courses of study in English language to include material on social meaning? What must we add to English language course content which is not there now? The understandings of language-based social meanings which need to be included in intermediate and advanced programs would encompass communicative skills such as those outlined below. In most cases the goal of receptive understanding, an awareness of stylistic shifting, for example, as opposed to the goal of productive skill or actually being able to talk in more than one register, is a worthwhile objective. It is usually the case, however, that as people's sensitivity to social meaning grows, their productive capacity will increase, too.

a. Awareness of differences in English language registers.　Can our students hear the contrast between formal and informal styles of speaking? Can they push out their parameters and hear the difference between frozen and informal talk? (As coined by Martin Joos in *The Five Clocks:* Professor Joos points out that most speakers of English have five styles or registers of speaking which vary according to occasion, topic, situation, etc. These five styles range from an infrequently used "frozen" language through the intermediate band of "formal," "consultative," and "casual" styles to the other end of the scale, "intimate" style.)

b. Awareness of geographical dialects.　Can our students hear the difference between people from varying English-speaking locales in the world? It may prove valuable to select two or three regional varieties of English which your students might come into contact with as models: American/British; American/British/South African; Indian/British; Trinidadian/British; Philippino/American.

c. Awareness of appropriate topics of talk at particular occasions and with particular people.　Material in TV programs and films can serve as illustrations. How do strangers in English-speaking countries address each other? How do husbands and wives talk with each other? Parents and children? Teachers and students? Shopkeepers and customers? Employers and employees?

d. Awareness of the physical signals which accompany language messages.　Using examples from TV and films, can our students pick out characteristic non-verbal communicative features of English-speaking people such as the following: hand gestures, facial expressions, laughing, smiling, hand shaking, bowing, body movements, etc. (See as reference, E. Hall, *The Silent Language.*)

Although the field of language pedagogy is just beginning to consider how to teach sensitivity to the social cues conveyed in language, intermediate and advanced learners need to learn communication skills as much as they need to develop competence in language substance. For this reason, creative facilitators will find themselves developing their own materials for teaching social meaning.

WORKSHOP ACTIVITIES

1. Examine the drills contained in at least two English language textbooks which are used in your school, community, or country. Try to find examples of materials which make effective use of the concept of situational meaning. Why is the theme relevant for some particular group of students? Next, look for examples of drill materials which have no situational theme, even though they share the same structural pattern.
2. Select an English language novel which contains ample dialogue between the various characters. Can you point out contrasting stylistic registers? Try to find examples of certain characters talking in formal style, in informal style. Does the novelist ever allow the characters to talk with each other in an intimate style? It is advisable to carry out this activity using a novel with which you are already familiar.

C. ENLARGING THE SCOPE OF THE LANGUAGE SKILLS

The four basic language skills each take in a wider scope at the intermediate and advanced levels. For beginners, it was necessary to carefully control the sequence in which language skills were introduced. It was important then to concentrate on having learners acquire basic, mechanical abilities necessary for all of the skill areas—listening and speaking, reading and writing. Diagram No. 2 in *Part One:* Chapter Two, WHAT on page 53 indicated the central areas of attention in the early levels of new language learning. During the period of time required for developing basic skills, competence in the new language has been deepening all along.

The expanded Diagram No. 16 on page 176 shows how the various skills have become enlarged at the intermediate and advanced stages. A deepening of the learner's competence in language substance is implicit in the model itself. Beyond that, each skill area takes in a greater scope, enabling us now to be more flexible, to look for new ways to combine and link together various pairs among the four skills.

In the area of listening, learners can now distinguish sound contrasts in the new language; they have developed the necessary inner ear to be able to hear meaningful units. They remember short segments when they hear the language spoken. Intermediate students produce the sounds and words of the language in connected sentences as well. As for literacy, reading and writing, students have mastered the basic fundamentals. They know the system of English writing; they are able to produce moderately accurate representations of the language. In the basic skill areas then, Diagram No. 16 assumes that by the intermediate and advanced levels, learners have grown both in their depth of language competence—listening and speaking, and in literacy—reading and writing.

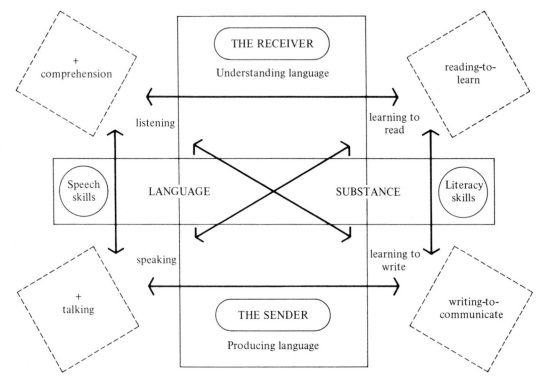

Diagram 16

(Note: Those parts of the diagram which were included in *Part One*, Chapter Two, are listening, speaking, learning to read, and learning to write. The developments which occur at the intermediate and advanced levels are listening + comprehension, speaking + talking, writing-to-communicate, reading-to-learn.)

Even though we are no longer concerned with practicing basic skills, if an individual is weak in the ability to perform any of them, the facilitator should provide assistance for that person. Such individualized attention can smoothly take place in classes where a portion of the time is devoted to individualized activities. (See Chapter Five, WHO.) For example, while some are taking part in small group discussions, people who need to improve basic skills areas could be working with tapes for listening-comprehension or with workbook materials for reading and study skills.

1. Expanding Each of the Skills

One important contrast between the skills Diagram No. 16 on page 176 for the intermediate-advanced levels and the one in *Part One,* page 53, shows how each of the four skills have expanded at this stage. It is no longer necessary to simply distinguish the sounds of the new language. Now, listening encompasses hearing and understanding of longer segments. We want learners to be able to follow the gist of a conversation, even though they probably miss words or lose the thread here and there. We want them to be able to understand the main topics, the themes in a news broadcast, for example. We want them to be able to hear and comprehend a good deal of the new language when they encounter it in natural settings outside of the classroom situation.

A significant development in language use occurs in speaking skills. In this area we expand the parameters of language to include real communication. For that reason, the box in the diagram is labeled [speaking]+ talking. The term *talking* sums up the abilities which go along with using the new language for communicative purposes. Talking is different from speaking in that now the learner freely initiates the response rather than repeats or completes a set piece of language. The goal in talking is to be able to interact, to communicate meaningfully in a realistic setting. An important aspect of talking involves sensitivity to the social rules for interaction which characterize how people behave when they speak with each other.

At the intermediate and advanced levels we plan instructional activities which give learners opportunities for participating in controlled, interactional situations. These activities are first simulated in the classroom. Then we provide tasks which take the learner into realistic situations with English speakers. (See Chapter Seven, HOW.)

The literacy skills at the intermediate and advanced levels are focused on comprehension and communication. Reading-to-learn implies the reading of any and all materials which are suited to the particular interests and concerns of the learner. Now English is a medium through which to gain knowledge and to broaden horizons. However, it is quite possible that the learner still needs special materials for learning to read. The intermediate students benefit from using structurally simplified reading passages, or original articles which contain a glossary of unfamiliar vocabulary items. The goal is to push toward reading as much and as frequently as possible. It is only through reading widely that the learner's reliance on edited materials or on a bilingual dictionary will gradually diminish.

Now that the mechanical skills connected with writing are under control, the focus is on writing-to-communicate. But students' goals and concerns vary widely. All do not need to acquire the same degree of proficiency in written communication in English. Obviously, students who plan to work for higher educational degrees, particularly those whose personal objective is to study in places where English is the medium of education, need to handle writing skills with ease. Others may have less ambitious goals and needs.

Native speakers of any language spend years in school learning the conventions which are part of the written form of the language. In English, spelling, punctuation, and paragraph construction are the basic mechanical skills beyond learning to form the letter shapes. But besides the mechanics, writing well is a fairly abstract form of communication. It requires organizing ideas, outlining thoughts, giving attention to stylistic usage of words. Facilitators, in working with new language learners, must be aware of the vast area they step into when writing is included in the second language curriculum. Standards should be set which are realistic. Short, informal notes or letters, brief descriptions of personal background, summary paragraphs based on experiences outside of the classroom are all good places to begin writing-for-communication.

Many facilitators find that having students write frequently is the best way to help them feel a growing sense of success in the skill. Like so many other pursuits which require intricate meshing of intellectual and, motor processes, writing flows easier when it is practiced consistently. Facilitators who have learned the benefits of frequent, short writing assignments have also learned not to let themselves become overburdened with the job of correcting papers. Even if students write daily, some realistic procedures should be carried out which do not call for the teacher to mark every error on every piece of written work. Some teachers try to strike a balance between frequent assignments and careful correcting procedures by recording all papers turned in by students but only periodically, perhaps on a revolving monthly basis, scrutinizing written work for all of the errors contained. In those classrooms where frequent writing and periodic correcting take place, both the facilitator and the learner realize the value of writing often, as well as the considerable labor involved in careful correction of all errors.

2. Linking the Skills in New Relationships

Both the parallel and crossed arrows represent a third dimension of Diagram No. 16. They draw our attention to more flexible ways in which to link the various skill areas. At the intermediate and advanced levels there are at least two important reasons why we want to take advantage of all of the possible linkages between the skills. First, we know that learners can help themselves is they employ one skill area with which to practice another. There is nothing unnatural about utilizing the skill to read, for example, as an aid to listening comprehension. The learner who follows spoken language while reading the same material is clearly attacking on a broader front, since understanding is the basic requirement for both listening and reading comprehension.

Second, in real life there is no strict compartmentalization of listening or speaking, reading or writing. These skills tend to overlap and spread into each other in numerous instances. So, we want to be able to connect them in activities which recreate real life language situations in the classroom. The model helps us to see possibilities for moving in directions which we may not have taken advantage of before.

When we regard understanding language as having a separate function from producing language, we begin to think of many classroom activities which interrelate the possible connections between the two skills. The diagram enables us to make use of the important difference between those skills which are used by the language *receiver*—listening-comprehension and reading-to-learn—as opposed to the skills which are used by the language *sender*—speaking-talking and writing-to-communicate. The diagram labels the connection between listening-comprehension and reading-to-learn as "understanding language." The connection between speaking-talking and writing-to-communicate is labeled "producing language."

There is nothing inherently passive about either listening-comprehension or reading-to-learn. In both, active skills are involved, even though the original stimulus, the idea, comes from another source. Listening-comprehension is not accomplished without active concentration on the underlying meaning which is conveyed, just as reading-to-learn does not take place without actively thinking about the content of the material. True, there are degrees of active concentration which are necessary. But the new language learner, in order to listen and comprehend and in order to read and comprehend must pay close attention in order not to lose the thread of meaning.

Producing language implies initiating the idea. In the language learning situation, the facilitator's chief role is to supply the context and the situation for producing language. Learners should practice both speaking-talking and writing-to-communicate using, as their basic fund of ideas, those facts, opinions, and experiences which are already a part of their knowledge. We can send native speakers to the library to do research on some topic, then ask them to report back in a medium which requires them to produce language: an oral talk, a composition, etc. In contrast, it makes much more sense if we let new learners of English discuss or write about subjects with which they are already familiar. For younger learners, the topics should be immediate concerns: interests, hobbies, everyday experiences. For more mature students, questions of the day, politics, popular advice—anything which suits the interest level of a particular group of people can become the fund of information for the production of language.

The linkage from talking to writing forms a natural sequence of activities in intermediate and advanced levels. Talking out ideas, airing opinions, getting ideas into the open, all are part of a process which makes writing flow more easily. For many, the activity of group discussion before a writing assignment brings into focus ideas which were beneath the surface but needed to be activated by an external force.

Many experienced teachers know the benefits of the oral composition as a vehicle for helping students express ideas in English. In the oral composition, the sequence of activities moves from writing-to-communicate to speaking before the class. Students prepare for an oral presentation by first writing out their ideas on paper. Often, the teacher will read through the written version before it is presented in the classroom. Many teachers insist that some degree of memorization take place. Students are encouraged not to rely on the written version when they give prepared talks, but to speak as freely as possible.

It is important for the facilitator to help learners find a stylistic level for the oral composition which is a comfortable adjustment between the informal register of real interactional talk and the tighter, more controlled style of informal writing. When we read actual transcriptions of free, spontaneous talk, even discussions on highly intellectual topics, we see that talking utilizes a style of language which is quite different from writing. For this reason, the facilitator should never give learners the erroneous impression that a prepared talk is the same as interactional talk.

As a further step in the direction towards spontaneous talking experiences in the language classroom, students join small discussion groups in which the main ideas contained in either one or a related group of oral compositions are open for comments and questions. In a language class made up of twenty or more students, dividing the entire class into smaller groups for the discussion part of oral compositions is a beneficial procedure. Many feel less inhibited about taking part in freer talk when they are grouped together with four or five fellow students.

What other possibilities for moving in new directions do the diagonal relationships shown in Diagram No. 16 on page 176 suggest? Are there other useful connections, first between listening-comprehension and writing-to-communicate and, second, between speaking-talking and reading-to-learn? Inventive teachers will quickly see many useful ways in which to capitalize on these possibilities. In an adult's life, listening-comprehension and writing fall together in numerous circumstances. We often find ourselves reaching for a pencil or pen while listening. True enough, writing in these instances is not the polished kind which we want to achieve in a composition, but the two skill areas are linked as a communicative medium when we examine language grounded in life.

Many classroom activities which utilize role-playing make use of the link between listening and writing. Note taking, message writing, and dictation are some of them. As much as possible, when these activities are introduced, they should be tied to the situations and settings in which we naturally find them. If the activity is note taking, the material should have relevance to the students' interests and concerns. Let them hear a reading of a brief magazine article on a subject of current interest. Have them take notes during a first and second reading of the article. By then most will be ready to write a brief summary statement about what they have heard.

In all three of these listening-linked-to-writing activities—note taking, message writing, and taking dictation—listeners actually utilize the product of their efforts. The listener needs to use notes to remember what the speaker said on a particular topic; the receiver of a telephone call wants to remember the information the caller delivered; the secretary needs to read the notes when writing the letter which the employer dictated. In all three instances, it is the listener's responsibility to understand not only the oral message but also the written product which resulted from understanding that oral message.

Sometimes new language learners find themselves in situations where they can utilize the skill of writing in order to make communication possible. Take the case of someone trying to talk with a native speaker of English. The learner is asking for directions, but the native speaker has not made any accommodation to the questioner's foreign-sounding pronunciation. "Here is a piece of paper. I'll write the name of the street I'm looking for. Then perhaps you'll recognize it," the learner says.

WORKSHOP ACTIVITIES

1. Suggest three classroom activities for intermediate and advanced learners which concentrate on the skill of listening-comprehension utilizing sources of natural language spoken by native speakers. For example, using radio broadcasts, phonograph records, or television programs.
2. Observing people in actual communicative situations helps us become sensitive to cultural patterns of talking. Try to attend a film or watch a television drama as a group. Afterwards, discuss occurrences of significant interactional behavior. For example: Did you notice any culturally characteristic hand gestures, head nods, or other body movements? Did you notice switches in language style between occasions when parents spoke to children contrasted with parent to other parent?

7

HOW

If It
Works,
Use
It

OVERVIEW

How do we select classroom procedures for intermediate and advanced programs? One way is to set out a basic formula: if we take WHAT, or language substance plus language skills, then add the appropriate answers to WHO, the nature of the learner, we find that the resulting integration of content WHAT and learner's needs WHO gives us criteria for creating effective HOW. But the formula is not simple. Actualizing it requires both knowledge and experience on the part of the teacher.

This chapter presents some techniques which have worked in widely contrasting circumstances. They have been used in classes for newcomers to English-speaking countries; they have been used in classes for adults and high school age students in non-English-speaking countries. But there is no reason to feel that they must necessarily work in all settings. Facilitators must be ready to try them out, to adopt whatever works, to adapt for their students what works partially, to throw out that which is irrelevant to their situation. By feeling free to adopt, adapt, and discard, the teacher's ability to facilitate the learning process will grow. Qualified facilitators work with both knowledge of the language field and an appreciation for their own creativity in the classroom. Real facilitators need to have a solid background in the subject area, but they must be artists as well as trained technicians.

To the artist-practitioner, we say: if it works, use it. It's okay. Do not worry about the methodological label attached to what you do. Trust in your own method, particularly if it is built upon successful results. But be prepared to be critical of those results. Good facilitating is not ego-tripping. Good facilitating is not rigidly tied to quoting methodological sources. Be open to new ideas and fresh insights; do not feel that it is necessary to follow one rigid path. Be secure in the knowledge that no one has found an easy, foolproof road to success in language learning.

There are a few basic principles to keep in mind at the intermediate and advanced stages: the first one is well-known, but sometimes is overlooked now that the learner has real ability for communication in the new language. The principle is this: the classroom experience must give the learner an opportunity to take one step at a time. The principle is important enough to fill up the first section of this chapter.

For the most part we have been dealing with the intermediate and advanced stages as a conjoint level. However, there are times when we want to look at these levels separately. What can be assumed as comfortable steps for the advanced student are often too large for the intermediate student to take. We want to be able to provide the intermediate learner with more intervening steps. The facilitator keeps in mind goals which are appropriate for learners at various stages. For advanced people the ultimate goal is to discover how to help themselves be good language learners in a manner which suits their own particular style of learning. The facilitator wants to help advanced students find their own materials, their own method, and their own way to ultimately leave the classroom and move into real-life language utilization.The goal for the intermediate level, on the other hand, is plain: it is to reach the advanced stage.

A prevailing problem is to locate materials which are appropriate for students' interests. The second section in this chapter on HOW points out some vital sources—the popular, and possibly overlooked, mass media. The third section outlines communicative activities for the classroom. We can simulate lifelike language situations right in the classroom; we can involve students and make the time spent in class profitable if activities are varied. The types of activities discussed in Section C are not just end-of-the-week time-fillers. At the advanced level, they are presented as part of an overall plan for activating language use.

The next step towards the goal of finally leaving the classroom behind is to use the new language in facilitator-initiated learning tasks. Section D in this chapter presents some ideas for sending students out of the classroom and into the surrounding community to use the language which they have been practicing for years at school.The selection of these tasks necessarily varies, depending on whether the student is in an English-speaking or non-English-speaking setting.

A. ONE STEP AT A TIME

Now that the learner has moderate competence in English, there is a tendency for the facilitator to make demands upon this ability which push beyond realistic expectations. Learners should feel justifiable pride in how far they have come rather than to sigh and be overwhelmed with how far there yet remains to go. The facilitator's important job is to help students pass through these upper levels as constructively and productively as possible. Facilitators are not performing their role when they nudge learners into unstructured language situations without adequate preparation. Learners can find plenty of these for themselves without bothering to go to class at all. Facilitators at this level must justify what they can offer in the classroom. The urge to plunge the learner into free conversation of the "lets's talk about some interesting topics" approach should not be indulged in without attention to the fact that, as appealing as it might seem, free conversation and all other activities must be undertaken with a plan and a purpose. It is the object of this section to point out a useful, underlying scheme of organization which is applicable to a wide variety of activites at both the intermediate and advanced levels.

Following the motto, "if it works use it," we will not turn our backs on what has proven to be effective for language learning in the past. So some of the steps in the outline for intermediate lessons which is presented on page 188 ff. are known to teachers who have worked within the audiolingual framework. These steps—really a checklist of the separate components which go into a good plan—can be adapted either to topics in language substance (for example, lessons on a grammatical problem) or to topics in language skills (for example, controlled composition or reading comprehension lessons). The concept of the organic plan has evolved in a natural way from the framework for planning activites which was outlined in *Part One,* Chapter Three, HOW. But now there is less attention to controlling all elements and more concern with encompassing a larger scope.

1. The Organic Plan

We want to expand on the static quality of the familiar audiolingual format, as valuable as it might have been. So, we utilize it as an organic structure, one which we can, by applying the principle of "one step at a time," adapt to various levels of student capabilities. The steps which appear on page 188 ff. are built around ten basic components. These steps are the core of effective planning. But at more advanced levels, it is no longer necessary to take such small steps. The organic plan can change and be abstracted into larger steps which are more useful for advanced level classes. So, at the advanced level the ten-step plan is reduced to four, as shown on page 189. The four steps of the advanced plan do not simply repeat the same ones which were appropriate at the intermediate level. Rather, each one of them offers greater flexibility and a greater opportunity for integrating a wide variety of communicative activities, inside and outside of the classroom. Many teachers have found that it is time well spent to actually sit down and write out a plan following the organic scheme on pages 188 and 189. Others simply work with these steps in mind. But whether the plan is on paper, or in the teacher's head, the classroom activities are conducted according to a recognizable structure.

The ten steps of the intermediate plan are at times presented in a slightly different order depending upon each teacher's assessment of the needs of a particular group of students. Adults want to have explanations of the grammatical focus contained in a presentation much earlier than do younger learners. Checking for understanding enters into classroom activities more than once, particularly when material is being presented for the first time. Clearly, the steps in the plans for both levels represent convenient checklists for the facilitator who wants to make sure that only one step has been taken at a time.

The advantage of the organic plan for the advanced levels is that it offers flexibility to suit a wide gamut of instructional activities. Learners in an advanced class no longer need to begin with a structured presentation which contains exemplary language. So the facilitator working with an advanced group can branch out and try to utilize as many communicative activities as possible. Wise facilitators, of course, will realize that they can combine parts of the intermediate and the advanced plans depending upon the particular material which they are presenting. And, of course, many communicative activities can be introduced into the format of an intermediate program as well.

2. The Facilitator and the Learner Share Responsibilities

An extremely important feature of the organic plan is that it can delineate those steps in which the facilitator's responsibilities are primarily active as opposed to those in which the learner's responsibilities are active. No plan can be successfully actualized by the teacher alone. Learning only takes place when students decide for themselves that they want to learn. Each learner has responsibilities. Sometimes a statement of such responsibilities is carried concretely in the form of a student contract: students put into writing a list of specific goals which they hope to attain in the period of time they will spend attending the particular English language course. A student contract is an effective method for involving learners in the idea that success requires input from *two* sources in the classroom—facilitator and learner.

The facilitator's reponsibilities are active in the earlier stages of both the intermediate and advanced versions of the organic plan. Then the chief responsibility lies in the area of selection. Based on training and knowledge, he or she is usually the person in the language classroom who decides what element of language substance and what areas of language skills either the entire class or subgroups within the class need to work on. However, the facilitator encourages and appreciates input from the learner as well. Often learners need the facilitator's help to crystallize for themselves the language areas on which they should concentrate. Beyond remedial attention to language content and language skills, the facilitator utilizes the organic plan to bring a wide variety of participational activities into the program. The facilitator is the person responsible for keeping up his or her sleeve, or tucked into his or her bag of tricks, a healthy assortment of activities which make students genuinely look forward to the time spent in class.

The learners' initiative becomes active in the middle and latter parts of the organic plan. In the intermediate version, the learners' responsibility comes to the fore at the time they let the teacher know quite explicitly whether or not they understand the language presented in the lesson. If there are words or expressions in a dialogue or narrative which are unfamiliar to them, they must realize that there is no shame in revealing their lack of understanding to the teacher. Indeed, it is their responsibility to speak up. From that point on, the learners' obligations grow with each of the steps. By the final step, even through the teacher initiates a classroom activity to review the material of the lesson, it is ultimately the learners' duty to themselves to incorporate the content matter of the lesson into their own consciousness. There may be any number of acceptable explanations why, up until step No. 10, a person had somehow failed to focus on the new material in the lesson. But by the time it is repeated or reviewed for final reinforcement, each learner faces a moment of truth: get it now or your chance has passed by. It's your responsibility to yourself.

At the advanced level, the learners' responsibilities enter into the picture in an active sense during the participation phase. At first, in the anticipation and preparation phases, the facilitator was the chief initiator, the one who brought into the classroom the appropriate designation of task, activity, or resource. It was the facilitator's responsibility to sketch in necessary background information for the learner. During the anticipation and preparation steps, the facilitator set out the procedure and explained the parameters of the activity.

The advanced learner has unique obligations. For now, by participating in language activites, by actualizing those activities through sharing experiences, the learner uses the new language for purposes of interacting with other people. In this way advanced learners' responsibilities are both to themselves and to other members in the group. Thus, language learning at this level is more tied to real life. At the advanced level, language learning is manifested by both individual and social behaviors.

The communication goal in the language class is ultimately achieved when the learner joins with the facilitator in the creative aspect of activity planning. Any game can be modified or altered. The learner shares the responsibility with the facilitator for adapting, adopting, and discarding. Any task which is carried out outside of class can be done in a different way depending upon local circumstances. The learner shares the responsibility for offering suggestions for improving upon language practice tasks which the facilitator has suggested. Real communication is ideally experienced when the learner *and* the facilitator work together as responsible partners in both planning and actualizing undertakings which facilitate language use.

3. Steps in the Intermediate Level Plan

This checklist of steps for planning instructional activities is appropriate for either intermediate level ESL or EFL. We carry out all ten of the steps although the order in which the steps are used might differ depending upon the particular setting.

The Facilitator's Responsibilities Are Active

1. *Planning:* The diagnostic phase. What is the element to be taught? What indications for planning appear in the results of tests, attention to errors, and avoidance of errors?
2. *Stating Objectives:* The definition phase. What are the limits to the material covered in this particular plan? What does the facilitator expect the learners to be able to do at the end of the lesson that they could not do before?
3. *Presenting Language in a Situation:* The embedding phase. How shall we present the language problem in a situation which is meaningful for the students?
4. *Modeling the Language*: The initial performance. The learners meet the presentation for the first time.The form of presentations should alter during the course. Dialogues are fine, but let's introduce some variety.
5. *Stating the Rules:* The answer to everyone's question: Why are we spending our time with this lesson? What is the systematic aspect which we can grasp about the language problem that we are practicing?

The Learner's Responsibilities Are Active

6. *Checking for Understanding:* No one hides behind false pride now. We ask for useful meanings of unfamiliar words or expressions in the presentation. What is the point behind the story line in the presentation?
7. *Practicing, Drilling, Internalizing:* Use any technique that suits your own style of learning. We don't drill simply for the sake of drilling. We want the language substance to stick in our heads. How will we connect this bit of language substance with other patterns we already know and use in English?
8. *Moving into Independent Communication:* The facilitator sets out some additional ways to use the new language. We are freer now to utilize the new patterns in a variety of contexts. What can we read

or write which will also help us to make the new language a working part of us?

9. *Testing the Objectives:* A quick appraisal of the overall success of the procedures in Steps 1-8: Who needs individual help now? Who failed to grasp what the essential point of the entire sequence has been? Step No. 9 works in connection with Step No. 2.

10. *Reviewing, Restating, Reinforcing:* Neither facilitator nor learner is ready to put the problem aside. We look together for further utilization of the language substance or language skill embodied in the lesson. How else can we extend the activities so that the new language is part of our communicative system in English?

4. Steps in the Advanced Level Plan

At this level we can reduce the plan to four broad steps or phases. The plan is more appropriate for ESL settings, but nevertheless can be used with EFL students in the final years of secondary school or in college or technical courses.

The Facilitator's Responsibilities Are Active

1. *Anticipating:* An assessment of the learner's needs. What are the objectives of the plan regarding substance areas, regarding language skill areas? What are the resources and materials which will most effectively help us to achieve the goal of the lesson? What will we need to do to motivate learners so that participation in the activity will be largely a voluntary affair?

2. *Preparing:* The facilitator acquaints the learners with all phases of the activity. Everyone gets ready for the task by becoming familiar with the rules for carrying it out. Learners come to understand the reason behind the activity. Key grammatical structures, important vocabulary words are reviewed. The steps of the tasks are broken down and analyzed. Before doing the whole, we make sure that everyone can manage the separate parts of it.

The Learner's Responsibilities Are Active

3. *Participating:* All of the learners who feel they will benefit from doing so take part in the activity. The happening takes them outside of their own concerns and engages them to such a degree that they lose themselves in the doing of it. Their use of English is not limited to a set of specific patterns.

They must use everything they know in order to communicate and interact.

4. *Actualizing:* This is the period for assessing the results of the activity. Learners can share experiences, reporting on incidents, give a review of the investigation, summarize the consequences which took place. Next, they get ready to carry out the task, play the game, or participate in the action once more. Learners know that the second time around the activity and the language necessary for it will feel more like putting a hand inside of a glove which really fits.

WORKSHOP ACTIVITIES

1. Select a grammatical topic from those listed in Chapter Six, WHAT, Section 5, page 158. Work out a sample of the intermediate level plan utilizing the task you have selected and showing the ten steps discussed in Section 3 of this chapter.
2. Select a communication activity from Section C (page 201, following) of this chapter. Work out a sample of the advanced plan which follows the four steps illustrated in Section 4 of this chapter (page 189).

B. OUR GREATEST RESOURCE

The key to providing a successful intermediate or advanced program is to find means by which to help learners develop fluency in the new language.The goal is for learners to move from using fixed language to using freer language. Fixed language consists of the set patterns, phrases, and expressions found in beginning level text books. Freer language is the utilitarian tool which enables people to participate in actual communicative situations. If we want learners to deepen their overall competence in the new language, then the English which we present in the classroom must be drawn from the real world.

At the beginning levels, most of the language examples were carefully controlled, typically taken from textbooks and other auxiliary classroom materials. One of the perennial dilemmas of intermediate and advanced facilitators is how to present learners with examples of language which are both lively in terms of content and reliable in terms of language substance. Where should we look for an ample source of language samples to incorporate into our programs, particularly when we are facilitating language learning outside of English speaking communities? An overlooked, or at best neglected, resource for English language instruction is the popular communication—the mass media. In this section, this extremely valuable source is discussed under the following headings: 1. radio; 2. TV and motion pictures; 3. newspapers, popular magazines, and paperbacks; and 4. pop, rock, and folk music.

The suggestion to incorporate the mass media in language teaching is hardly news to most professionals. But, more often than not, these resources are thought of as extra activities rather than as basic elements of an English language course. In English-speaking countries where all of the media abound, it is of paramount importance to bring them into the classroom. However, even in those parts of the world where English is a foreign or an auxiliary language, most of the sources which are described in this section *are* available. Gathering them together represents a vital element in the anticipation stage of planning.

The availability of English language media is likely to seem to expand as the facilitator pays attention to the possibilities inherent in these materials. Once we start to remember the hours of the broadcasts, look for ways to beg or borrow a tape recorder, bring our small radios into the classroom, clip the current film announcements from the newspaper, remember to ask friends and relatives for their soon-to-be discarded magazines and paperbacks in English—the more we keep these gathering tasks in mind, the more we are carrying out our responsibility to the learners.

Beyond merely outlining which resources are valuable for utilization in English language courses, this section will also suggest some of the specific skill areas which can be practiced by means of using media resources in the presentation or participation steps. However, the wary facilitator is warned that there is no guarantee that all the ideas suggested in the following pages will work out in his or her particular setting. Remember, try them out; if they work, then use them. If not, then develop your own activities using whatever media resources are plentiful in your own locale.

1. The Radio and the Tape Recorder

Many teachers have found that it is valuable to keep a small battery-operated transistor radio in the classroom. The radio lends itself uniquely as a model of a particular level of English language usage, that which is appropriate for the delivery of news and announcements. The radio is an excellent source for contemporary vocabulary. The skill of listening comprehension linked with reading and also with writing-as-dictation can be practiced by means of language examples taken from the radio. The most common content of radio language is current news items, usually of genuine interest to intermediate and advanced learners. Facilitators should find out about all possible English language broadcasts in their locations, both from the British Information Services (BBC) and from the U.S. Voice of America (VOA). In addition, in many countries there are English language news broadcasts at specific hours produced by the local broadcasting authority. If the hours of these broadcasts do not coincide with the meeting time of the class, then the teacher should attempt to use radio broadcasts in connection with a tape recorder, either reel-to-reel or cassette.

An instructor in a college-level EFL program has reported on a successful procedure for combining the radio news broadcasts and the tape-recorded version of the same broadcasts:

"One technique which proved useful was listening to radio news broadcasts in class, while simultaneously recording them on tape. Concurrently, on the blackboard, I made notes of words and phrases that were spoken in the broadcast. As the news went by the first time, the students understood relatively little of it. Then the words and phrases that had been noted on the blackboard were explained and defined. This process was repeated as the tape recorder was played over several times. By the time they had listened to the several repetitions and explanations, with additional words explained each time, the students understood what had only minutes before been considerably beyond their comprehension."

A word of caution is necessary. The language used in many news broadcasts is surprisingly sophisticated; therefore, many repetitions and explanations are necessary. This is not an exercise for beginners, but when it is used carefully and patiently with intermediate and advanced learners they themselves feel a great sense of accomplishment when they realize that they can understand a short segment which, on first hearing, was beyond their grasp.

The facilitator should consult the newspaper announcements and try to discover the hours of the English language broadcasts which are presented as a special service to learners of English. These special programs are helpful, but the instructor must realize that usually their only concession to the non-native listener is the rate of delivery which the news broadcaster uses. Vocabulary items and grammatical structures are not modified in any appreciable manner. Therefore the job of the facilitator is to pull out new or unfamiliar vocabulary words and expressions. This procedure is a vital necessity, even when the source is a slower-paced "special news in English" broadcast.

Radio news broadcasts have been utilized successfully in a technique known as the frame paragraph: A short news item, approximately 75 words in length, is taped from a news broadcast. The item is first heard by the class, directly from the radio if possible, using the simultaneous taping technique described above. Then, perhaps at the next meeting (or concurrently if it can be written down that fast), the item is re-read to the class by the instructor and understood as much as possible by the listeners. The instructor answers questions about content words first, then the listeners are themselves questioned on their understanding of the news piece. Next, probably at the following class meeting, the process is repeated using substitute paragraphs in which the basic content or story-line of the original is retained, but the details are changed (i.e., names, dates, places, numbers, etc.). Finally, some slight modifications are made in the grammatical patterns, for example, shifts from past time to the recent past as expressed in the present perfect. The following is one example of the frame paragraph technique developed by a teacher using, as the base frame, an item taped in the classroom from a radio news broadcast:

Base Frame Paragraph:

The foreign ministers of *Britain* and *Spain* ended three days of talks in *London* without making any progress on the *Gibraltar* dispute. They agreed to meet again in October, probably in *Madrid*. *Spain* has demanded the return of *Britain's* fortress colony which sits on a *Spanish* peninsula. *Britain* has refused.

Substitute Paragraph No. 1:

The foreign ministers of Argentina and Britain ended several days of talks in Buenos Aires without making any progress on the Falkland Islands dispute. They agreed to meet again next month, probably in London. Argentina is demanding sovereignty over the group of islands, which are 300 miles off the coast of Argentina. Britain has so far refused.

Substitute Paragraph No. 2:

Indian and Pakistani foreign ministers finished a week of discussions in New Delhi, without coming to an agreement on the Kashmir problem. They agreed to another meeting in September, probably in Lahore. Pakistan wants possession of the region, which was seized by India after Independence in 1948, but India is reluctant to give it up.

In the above example, the base frame paragraph is taken from an original radio news item. The teacher can facilitate the intermediate learner's aural comprehension of the item by putting it on the blackboard or on a dittoed handout following the initial hearings. For advanced learners, probably all that is necessary is to present the basic structure of the four sentences on the blackboard. Then the instructor introduces the substitute words. What is important is for the students to understand first the basic concept of the entire paragraph, then the sequence of the separate sentences.

With an advanced group, this basic paragraph would lend itself to a further step as well, one which calls for independent communication. This step would be carried out by leaving the four basic sentences on the blackboard, but asking students to prepare their own list of substitute words to insert into the basic sentences. Ample time is allotted for the activity so that the original paragraphs can be shared with the whole group. Making up fictitious names for mythical countries and places adds to the interest.

A final step in this series which expands on the basic frame paragraph would be to ask students to take turns giving substitute words to each other with the instruction: "Now, tell us what happened." The list of substitute words could be written on slips of paper, each member then draws a slip at random. During this final step, each member of the group would retell the basic idea of the frame paragraph, inserting the new vocabulary items which appear on his or her slip of paper. Substitute words could make use of either local events or those of world-wide interest, as in the examples above. They could even deal with sports events, either local, national, or international.

The Tape Recorder The extreme flexibility of the tape recorder when used in connection with other media sources has been illustrated above. In fact, many language teachers claim that they can make greater use of one tape recorder than they can an entire language laboratory arrangement where each student works at a separate booth. (See Part One, Chapter Four.) The tape recorder, too, is uniquely adaptable to individualized instruction. Small groups of students can work with the recorder while other activities are going on elsewhere.

The tape recorder used in connection with the radio can bring a wide gamut of language vehicles into the classroom. Some teachers have had good success with taping radio plays or taping scenes or selected acts from recordings of contemporary plays in English. (Often such recordings are found in U. S. and British libraries located in larger cities throughout the world.) Tapes can be played either before or after students have read passages from the original plays. At some later time, students are then encouraged to produce the play themselves. The play production unit can be a worthwhile small group activity during individualized instruction periods.

2. TV and Motion Pictures

An important distinction exists between countries where motion pictures are shown in English almost exclusively, and elsewhere in the world. Local practices differ in their dissemination of English language films and TV programs from abroad. In some places, the original language is maintained with titles given below in one or more of the local languages. Obviously, for the purpose of language learning, this method is preferable to one which replaces the original sound track with the local language as spoken by native-speaker actors.

In English-speaking countries in which TV watching is a normal, everyday pursuit of much of the population, the facilitator who does not incorporate television into the language program is overlooking an extremely vital connection to the interests of the vast majority of people. Since motivation among new language learners to understand British or American television programs is high, the facilitator who makes use of either the content or the format of television programs is capitalizing upon the wide appeal which television holds for most people in today's world. For example, classroom activities can be modeled along the lines of television quiz programs; interviews can be held which follow, to some extent, the format of well-known television programs.

Both TV and motion pictures are readily available media through which learners can gain experience hearing and understanding the English language. Teachers, however, should not stop at the obvious benefits to be derived from just watching TV or attending movies. There are some definite responsibilities which facilitators must carry out if these media are to become functioning elements in the program. An important guideline to keep in mind is that effective facilitators do not try to impose their own tastes, standards, or critical opinions on their students. In the language-learning situation, it is the examples of English which count above all else, not the benefits or demerits of the vehicle itself. So, if students find interest or value in a particular program or film, that is sufficient reason to encourage them to view it or to attend.

Also, it is the facilitator's responsibility to keep himself or herself, and in turn the students, well informed about current offerings in the community. Clip newspaper announcements and schedules. Find out in advance what is coming to the local cinemas. Be sure, always, to give students accurate information regarding time, hour, channel, place, etc. Help the students understand the content of a particular offering by giving them a synopsis or a brief summary before they attend or view. In the case of a film, this might mean that the facilitator attends the film when it first opens. Based on previewing, the facilitator gives students not only a summary of the main ideas contained in the program, but can also prepare a vocabulary list of possible new words or expressions. In the case of a TV program, the facilitator might be able to obtain a summary of the story or an outline of the program from the station manager or local TV authority. Often these are available to educators when a specific request is made.

Counsel students, when they attend films, to listen for total comprehension. Urge them not to depend on the sub-titles supplied in the local language. Give assignments, brief ones, which will help them look for specific items in the offering. For example, in a serial TV program, students can prepare brief descriptions of characters who appear regularly. Or, for detective programs, have students write out short, "who did what to whom" assignments. Give them a sample character sketch of a key figure in the story before asking them to prepare their own. Similarly, work out a sample "who did what to whom" report based on a telecast which all have watched before sending them out to do the assignment.

Television news programs have special features which can be utilized in the language classroom. The following report of a classroom procedure is based on the experience of a teacher in an English-speaking setting.

"The evening television news was assigned as a listening-comprehension task. The students took notes and brought them to class the following day. Even if they were unable to understand the details of the broadcast, they were generally able to note the topics which were discussed. From their notes a list of the topics which were included in the evening news round-up was assembled on the blackboard. The topics were discussed by the class as a whole, with guidance and explanation by the teacher. Thereafter, when the class listened to the day's current news broadcast, the topics were familiar to them and they started to understand a little more than they had on the previous day. The cumulative and repetitive character of the news from day to day made it possible for the students to progress over the period of the activity."

3. Newspapers, Popular Magazines, and Paperbacks

The appropriate selection of materials in print depends to a large extent on whether the students are learning in an English-speaking country. But even in non-English-speaking areas, distribution of international newspapers and magazines in English is wide. Paperback editions of good reading matter published in both England and the United States are also generally available throughout the world. The facilitator's task is to serve as a collecting agency by continually looking for sources of reading supplies. Some teachers in non-English speaking countries are able to have local residents donate their popular reading materials in English for educational purposes. Frequently, local libraries constitute another resource.

For intermediate and advanced English learners, the availability of interesting, popular reading material in the classroom is extremely important. Some teachers set up special displays of books. A reading corner in the classroom with an assortment of newspapers, magazines, and paperback books becomes another possible choice when the class works on individualized learning activities. There are always some whose objective in the course is ability to read widely and copiously in English. The skill of reading comes about in one way only: through reading. Frequently, the skill of reading rapidly in the new language can begin in a classroom which affords the learner a wide selection from which to choose.

In those places where the English language teacher goes from class to class rather than having the students come to an established room, some space must be found for making newspapers, magazines, and books available for students' use. A shelf in the library or in the principal's office, a table in the recreation hall or in the teachers' lounge, even an unused storeroom could serve as such a center. Then it is up to the English language facilitator to ensure that learners use this resource as a central feature of the course itself. Learners, too, can help to contribute to the collection by bringing magazines or newspapers to share with fellow students.

As in the case with films and TV programs, the wise facilitator realizes that reading choices should not be prejudged for students nor preselected for particular contents or ideas. It is the new language alone which is important. If some students prefer *Rolling Stone* or *Playboy* magazine to Shakespeare's sonnets, it should be their own option which counts, not the instructor's. Individual learners know better than the teacher what they prefer to spend their time reading.

It is true that many schools do not have funds available to allow teachers to organize attractive reading centers. Here is an account of what one teacher on the Caribbean island of Jamaica did to find popular reading material for the students in his classes, as follows.

(from "Read Bambi? De Letter Dey Tiny, Sir, and So Many Pages, Too," by Andrew Briggs, *Los Angeles Times*, January 8, 1974.)

...At Frankfield High (Jamaica), no money whatever was budgeted for any library books. What funds we did have went toward purchasing books for classroom use. Only 40 copies, for example, of an abridged version of 'Treasure Island.' We would haul these sets from class to class, never allowing them to be taken home because the books were too expensive to replace if they should be lost or, more likely, 'borrowed.'

Despite these hindrances to reading, the future lives of my students would hinge importantly on their ability to speak and write standard English: Entrance to almost any respectable job or career—to Jamaica's emerging middle class—requires its mastery.

Such mastery, under the circumstances, seemed out of the question. Some three months into the academic year, I had a keen sense of failure and was tempted to quit. But then I had a brainstorm, incited by a parcel of books from home.

In opening the package, I noticed that the postage was only 36¢. Since the rates were so low, why shouldn't I solicit books for the Frankfield library from friends and relatives in the States? I immediately composed a form letter for that purpose, describing the school and its needs as well as providing exact figures on shipping costs, and sent mimeographed copies far and wide.

'From children's fairy-tales to song books to James Bond to science to sex education,' I wrote—'send them all.'

...when school reconvened there was a virtual stampede to check out books, which we had simply piled on two tables so that the gaudy covers were fully displayed—love, sex, violence, adventure, and fantasy.... The experience of reading and more reading encouraged the students, as I had hoped, to improve their tastes.

So the principal has again set aside $300 for buying paperbacks, and faculty members are planning another extensive mailing campaign—they call it, simply and directly, 'Shake Down Family and Friends.' It is the kind of shakedown that can pay off handsomely wherever students need help—books, lots of books—in broadening their horizons.

Items from newspapers and news magazines are valuable sources of material because of their appeal to a broad range of interests. They can be used for classroom practices and provide a combination of the four skill areas. Sequences can be worked out based on items taken from international news magazines. For example: the facilitator selects an appropriate piece, probably two or three paragraphs in length, paying careful attention to the known interests of the members in the class. The item is read aloud (listening-comprehension), the item is duplicated so that all students can read it for themselves. From that point, the subject area can become the central theme behind a writing assignment. Or, using the same sequence, the theme can become the topic for preparing an exchange of opinions in a small group discussion.

Sample paragraphs taken from magazines are effective models to present for writing lessons. They can be used to illustrate how to compose a sentence, how to organize ideas in a paragraph, how to use transitional expressions, and how to write different types of paragraphs. Popular magazines are useful, too, for finding materials which show students how to skim for the main ideas in a paragraph and how to read for topic sentences. Actually, the variety of skill activities which can incorporate popular magazine and newspaper sources are virtually without limit. Here are two examples: (1) Use magazine or newspaper articles for dictation practice. After the dictation, put the sample paragraph taken from a media source on a screen by means of an overhead projector. Students correct their own papers. (2) The instructor reads an item from a media source. Students take notes during the reading. Their notes become the basis for small group discussions, or a "quiz" on the main ideas using the notes, or a writing exercise in which notes are used as references for recomposing a paragraph which contains the central ideas of the original.

Both newspapers and magazines lend themselves to a variety of writing assignments: an editorial can become the reason for writing a letter to the editor; the advice columns "Dear Abby" and "Ann Landers" can be used as models of informal letter writing; classified advertisements can be followed up through writing letters or making telephone calls. Aside from the skill areas themselves, facilitators can frequently bring to the learners' attention features or regular contents of newspapers about which they were not previously aware. It takes experience to be a newspaper or magazine reader, to know where to find the daily index, to know where certain types of information always appear, to understand the styles of writing, news vs. editorial, feature writing vs. critical reviewing, etc.

The media in print are themselves vehicles through which to present a variety of subjects which contrast particular cultural backgrounds. "How to read a newspaper" is one such topic that could be worked out as a unit of study following the outline for the Advanced Level Plan. (See page 189 in Section 4.) Samples taken either from principal newspapers in the United States, Great Britain, or other English-speaking countries contain unique characteristics which are peculiar to that specific locale. United States papers, for example, discourage placing editorial opinions on the front page, while in some parts of the world that format is accepted style.

4. Pop, Rock, and Folk Music

Experienced language teachers for years have realized the effectiveness of utilizing songs in their classrooms. Because music is a pleasurable outlet which is shared by almost all people, singing is a good way for students to relax and feel more at ease in using the new language. As viewed by many teachers, however, singing is a fun-and-games activity, something to do for the last five minutes of the hour or at the end of the week when serious work in the language class is completed. In many classrooms, too, teachers only introduce songs which they themselves select as most appropriate. They tend to overlook the music which their students listen to—the songs which young people sing when they are outside of school.

For others in the language-teaching profession, singing is regarded as more suitable for children than for older students or adults. So, when textbook writers do occasionally include a few songs, the selections are geared to the interests of younger people. Often, these selections in textbooks are drawn from traditional songs in the English language which are infrequently heard outside of the classroom.

There was even a time during an earlier era in the language teaching profession when pedagogical advice warned against songs for language instruction. Taking its cue from a theory of language which was primarily concerned with performance or surface features of language, this admonition cautioned that, in most instances, song material gives learners an incorrect model of spoken language since the songwriter is free to distort normal intonation in order to comply with the requirements of the rhythmic pattern of the musical line or phrase.

At face value this statement is true enough. However, we now look upon the knowledge which the learner must acquire from quite a different perspective. Today's concern with both the semantic element in language—meaning—and the motivational requirements for successful learning go a long way toward overriding some of those earlier, more simplistic warnings.

Pop, rock, and folk music is an idiom which is embraced by a broad span of young people—and not just those living within English-speaking countries. It is familiar to students both in academic and non-academic settings. In many places in the world, the pop music of the United States, England, and other English-speaking countries is known because it is translated into the local language and recorded by local artists. In those parts of the world where governmental pressure frowns on pop and rock music, it has become, probably by virtue of its exclusion, the forbidden but highly-prized fruit.

For the English language learner who roughly falls into the span of years from 10 to 35 (though a person's age is more apt to be determined by spirit than by years alone), modern music represents a different element in life than do some of the other mass media which have been recommended for inclusion in intermediate and advanced language courses. Most newspapers, television programs, and the majority of commercial films do not hold out the same generational pull which pop-rock music represents. In many ways, too, culture heroes who play such important roles in the music scene do not have counterparts of the same magnitude among newspaper columnists or even comic strip characters.

The songs of modern troubadors such as Judy Collins, Paul Simon, James Taylor, and scores of others often turn out to be the examples of English language which are already familiar to young people who want to learn and improve their knowledge of English. These songs turn out to be the material in English which students want to understand; they want to be able to sing along. So, why not help them by bringing pop, rock, and folk music into the English language course curriculum?

Suggestions have been made before in the English language teaching profession regarding the effectiveness of using teacher-written songs for the language classroom. But somehow, as earnest as the teacher's own efforts might be, these songs usually cannot hold out the same pull of generational identification which a recording of a name entertainer evokes. Familiar voices of favorite singers plus the total musical experience which well-known arrangements of songs produce are qualities which are beyond a single teacher's ability to match.

Language teachers who have reported good success with using pop, rock, and folk songs in their classrooms advise that the best source for recorded material is often among the students themselves. They ask their students to bring in favorite records so that everyone in the class can learn the songs in English.

The teacher can transcribe the words. For it is the language—the words of the songs—which makes the activity worthwhile. When students are provided with duplicated copies of the words to songs, or even if the teacher puts the words on the blackboard, motivation to understand and to learn is more readily assured.

Song material is adaptable to any number of possibilities in the language classroom: songs can be utilized as presentation contexts, as reinforcement material, as vehicles through which to teach all of the language skills, as a medium through which to present some of the most important cultural themes which pervade language and modern life. Some songs are more applicable to lessons which stress pronunciation or speaking skills, as for example, those which contain frequent repetitions of particular words or phrases. Other songs provide contexts for teaching particular grammatical points. Structural elements such as the present perfect tense and modal verbs frequently turn up in song lyrics. Many songs contain a brief narrative. For example, folk songs and ballads often carry explicit story themes. The alert facilitator is constantly on the lookout for these kinds of materials to utilize in the English language program.

WORKSHOP ACTIVITIES

1. For EFL:
    a. What English language news or feature programs are regularly scheduled on either radio or TV in your city/country? Select one pro-

gram and work out a classroom activity which incorporates having students listen to or watch the program outside of class.

b. What English language newspapers are available in your city or country? Bring samples. Select one news or feature story. Work out a classroom activity which makes use of the material you have selected.

2. Find five popular songs which you believe would be effective for English language teaching in a particular setting you are familiar with. Why are the songs effective vehicles for language instruction?

C. LANGUAGE IS FOR COMMUNICATION: TALKING WITHIN THE CLASSROOM

Many teachers hesitate to devote too many hours to communication activities, feeling somehow that they are not performing their responsibility if they fail to spend the bulk of time pulling students through a predetermined outline of language structures. But successful facilitators in a wide range of circumstances have found that with advanced students, those who have had a grounding in basic structures, increasing attention should be devoted to activities which encourage free and spontaneous talk.

The distance between practicing structures—or language substance—in a classroom and using the new language in real life is a vast no-man's-land which some never manage to cross. Communication activities in the language class are a vehicle through which to help many along the road to fluency. Unfortunately, often unplanned conversation periods either end up by allowing the teacher to do most of the talking or by letting a few assertive people dominate. To be successful, communication activities, too, require the facilitator's active input—anticipating and preparing. (See Page 184, Section A, One Step at a Time.)

The purpose of this section and the following (D. Broader Opportunities for Communication), is to present a framework for creating effective communication lessons. A teacher can control, vary, and expand these activities by paying close attention to the dominant classroom participation structure which is inherent in the activity itself. Reacting, interacting, sharing-discussing, and improvising represent different types of participational configurations. Each one lays the groundwork for the next.

The framework, therefore, begins with activities for REACTING: the teacher and the whole class carry out the communicative task together. Since the response is a voluntary act, a hesitant individual has the most amount of "cover." Activities for INTERACTING are those in which the teacher presents a model to the whole class and then becomes an observer allowing others to assume the role of leader. Often the activity is based on pairs or teams interacting together. Activities for SHARING and DISCUSSING allow opportunities for students to work in small groups—a different type of participant structure, one in which each individual is responsible for some part of the joint effort. Finally, activities for IMPROVISING are those in which students assume the greatest amount of personal accountability. Typically, small groups work together and then perform before the whole class. Improvisations are not at all restricted to advanced learners. At all levels, students enjoy and benefit from language activities built on simulating a small part of the real world within the classroom.

In order for communication to take place, everyone needs to feel relaxed, to lose oneself in the activity without concern over grammatical or pronunciation errors. When too much pressure to perform, to talk, is applied too soon, communication breaks down. Here, as well as in other aspects of language teaching, the principle of "one step at a time" applies. Reacting is a step towards being able to interact. Interacting, in turn, prepares the way for more intensive small group "brainstorming," or sharing and discussing. Finally, improvising, originating as a small group activity, calls for the greatest degree of spontaneity and creativity in both language competence and behavior.

Communication activities usually improve with use, just as our performance of games improves through practice. Don't be dismayed if a bright idea falls flat the first time it is tried out. Try to analyze what went wrong. Why didn't the group respond to the activity with enthusiasm? Was there a lack of adequate preparation? On the other hand, don't hesitate to repeat activities which have been successful. Some teachers regularly play language games with their classes as warmups to other types of work. Try jotting down ideas for expanding or altering activities while they are actually in progress. Keep a notebook handy so that you won't forget the good ideas that pop into your head during class hours.

1. Activities for Reacting

A wide variety of techniques for evoking language responses call for the teacher to participate as the primary conductor of the action and sometimes as the chief arbitrator. In many instances, after the group has learned the objectives of the activity, a student can take over as leader; then the teacher becomes part of the whole group. Before a student assumes the leader's role, however, everyone must clearly understand the basic procedure. Usually, a trial run, interspersed with some rapid translations into the first language of the few who have not caught on to the idea as yet (either given by the teacher or by a fellow student) insures that everyone is participating. Above all, keep the mood light. Language learning can be enjoyable.

Although a "frontal" classroom plan is workable, in most reacting activities the nature of the lesson demands that the atmosphere should not be rigid. Movable chairs which can be loosely placed in a semicircle are always preferable to fixed rows. But even in the most conventional classroom setting, it is the spirit and tone of the group which stimulates language reactions, not the furniture arrangement alone.

a. Party games, group games, fireside games: All of the techniques which involve people as active participants serve as material to consider for utilization in the language class. Many group games demand quick responses; they require us to listen attentively and to utilize a limited range of vocabulary. They have simple, clear-cut objectives. They appeal to people of all ages and backgrounds.

1. Guessing games: Well-known examples are "Twenty Questions" and the many variations on that one idea. "I'm thinking of a famous person; who is it?" Or, "I'm thinking of an object in the room, what is it?" Guessing games can be varied by using a reverse pattern in which "It," or the guesser, goes out of the room while everyone else decides on the person or object which must be guessed. In this case, the whole group agrees on the item through free discussion. Guessing games can be structured so that only "yes/no" questions are asked, or the game can be based on asking either particular types or the whole range of *wh-* (interrogative) questions. The facilitator selects the rules of the game to fit the linguistic abilities of the group.

Another variation is "questions and answers." The teacher writes out questions with their appropriate answers, placing each on separate slips of paper. The questions are distributed to one-half of the room, the answers to the other. People take turns asking their questions, waiting to hear the right reply. The fun begins when more than one reply comes for a single question. The effective teacher exercises control over the grammatical structures and vocabulary items which appear on the slips of paper, introducing topical subject matter which is relevant to student interests.

2. Semantic Set Games: The teacher prepares lists of items which are commonly known and understood. Each list contains one item which does not fit with the others. Everyone listens and responds with an appropriate word or gesture when the incorrect item is named. For example: cabbage, lettuce, spinach, squash, endive. Which vegetable does not belong in the list? The answer is "squash" because, unlike the others, it is not a leafy vegetable. After presenting a few such models, students make up their own semantic sets and present them to the whole group. Other semantic areas might be: types of food, vocations and occupations, tools, electrical appliances, means of transportation.

3. Add-An-Item Games: This type is helpful for practicing both spelling and the alphabet. A typical example is the game "Geography." "I'm going to take a trip to *Bermuda*. What should I take along?" The reply must begin with the same letter of the alphabet as in the place name already given. In this case, it could be: *binoculars, bananas, books,* etc. Anything that begins with the letter *b*. The possibilities for expanding add-an-item games are amazingly vast. Experienced facilitators often keep card files of just such types of games.

Particularly useful for the language class is the variety which restricts the item to be added to a particular word-class. For example, the game "Adjective." Person A: "I have a *guitar*." Person B: "What kind of a *guitar*?" Person A: "It's a *mellow guitar*." In this example, questions and replies from Persons A and B are given according to the participant structure known as *chaining*. Chaining consists of each member of the group, in turn, asking another person a given question. Then, it is the answerer's turn to question someone else. The teacher's role in chaining activities is to help direct the line of questioning. Sometimes it is helpful for the teacher to suggest that everyone talk to someone on the other side of the room instead of simply turning to the person who sits alongside. In that way, shyer ones must speak up a bit louder. The action is always livelier when everyone hears what is going on.

4. Command Games: Although they appear simple, yet they require close listening attention. The general motif is based on "Simon Says." The leader performs a body, hand, facial, or head movement, accompanying the action with a verbal command. One command carries the meaning: "Do what I am doing." The other, "Don't do what I am doing." The possibilities for expansion are endless and so is the delight which participants usually experience in playing the game. The necessity for close listening and concentration is obvious.

5. Alertness Games: One type of alertness activity is related to "the joker is wild" idea in card games. A variety called "Buzz" is played with numbers. The leader announces that a particular number and all of its common multiples are "wild." For example, the number "seven." The first person begins with the number "one," and so on counting around the room. However, when it is a person's turn to count off the number seven (or any other stipulated "wild" number), that person must say "Buzz." The same applies to all multiples of seven (14, 21, 28, etc.).

Or, "Fashion," a game which is helpful for practicing color and clothing vocabulary. All learners cover their eyes. The teacher pulls one person's name out of the "hat." "It" keeps his or her eyes covered and must tell what the person sitting alongside is wearing today. The teacher varies the game by having "It" describe a person on the other side of the room, or even what the teacher is wearing.

6. Sensory Games: Those that focus on other faculties such as touch, taste, and smell are not as directly related to language competence as are games which involve listening and seeing, but because they can be hilarious classroom happenings they serve the end of stimulating talk.

Touching games are of the type in which teacher puts an assortment of items inside a pillow slip or a large paper sack. The items should feel different to the touch. For example: cold, smooth, rough, slimy, wet, etc.

Students take turns putting their hand in the sack, enumerating the items which they feel. Someone at the blackboard is the scribe, recording each person's guesses. Keep score and see who wins. While playing the game, students practice language, such as:

I can _____ it.
I think it's a _____ because I can _____ it.

Tasting games are played by blindfolding "It." With eyes closed it is curious how potatoes, onions, and apples or sugar and salt begin to taste similar. The language objective is to guess what we taste by talking aloud. Try putting sugar on the potato or salt on the apple! A followup to the taste game can be played by having students bring assortments of taste items to class.

b. Stimulus Aids: "A picture is worth a thousand words." This cliché is a reminder of the endless uses to which picture collections can be put. Along with collections of both object and action pictures saved from magazines, many teachers have had good results from using *color slides* to encourage language response.

A game based on the use of slides is called "Rumor." A slide is thrown on the screen, preferably one which contains numerous people performing actions. Before anyone sees the slide, three people are asked to step out of the room. The first person returns to the room, standing so that the screen is not viewed by him or her at any time. Each person in the group takes a turn telling that person one detail which appears in the slide. Members of the class, of course, are looking right at the slide, while No. 1's back is turned to it. Next, Person No. 2 returns. Neither Person No. 1 nor Person No. 2 have seen the slide, but No. 1 proceeds to tell No. 2 what was said about it. In turn, No. 2 tells No. 3. The hilarity and amazement come in because the rest of the people are still observing the slide itself. What is reported by Persons 1, 2, and 3 is usually a long way from what is actually there.

Magazine Advertisements also lend themselves to a wide variety of reacting activities. Some teachers collect ads which contain attractive, clear photos of objects for teaching useful vocabulary. Pictures of food, transportation, household equipment—all of these are fairly easy to find. Ads also serve as stimuli for games. For example, try cutting out the name of the product which appears in the ad. Place the ads, mounted on cardboard saved from empty boxes or packages, around the room. Each person has a chance to guess what the ad is trying to sell. Some teachers conduct "guess the ad," in the style of an art show. They put ads on the chalk board. Everyone walks around the room with pencil and paper, jotting down notes. Then, it is time to share guesses before the teacher reveals the correct answers.

c. Choices Based on Real-Life Problems: Everyone likes to give advice, so mini-situations are excellent stimuli for talk. Some teachers carefully collect appropriate items from newspapers. For example, advice to lovelorn columns such as "Ann Landers" and "Dear Abby" are filled with potential ideas. The teacher either reads the situation aloud or puts the item on dittoed handouts. Then, each person has a chance to offer advice by expressing his or her own view of the problem. Marriage, divorce, sex, money, in-laws, children vs. parents—the whole gamut of common human conflicts in which everyone is interested are sources for material. Let two people offer different alternatives to the same problem. Or, as a class, list the possible alternatives which are available to the unknown person who has sought advice.

One of the best ways to prepare students for later improvisation activities which involve role-playing is through first reacting to and then discussing (see section following) the very same problem. For example, here is a skeleton list of some mini-situations which one teacher has constructed from letters to a newspaper advice columnist as well as from selected news items. First, the full versions were used for reacting activities. Subsequently, they became material for discussions and improvisations. These particular situations all pertain to problems more typically found in American society, although many are universal in today's urban world. Teachers in other countries would want to be on the alert for specific real-life problems which are more commonly found in the particular region where the students live.

Mini-Situations: (1) A landlord sues a tenant for back rent. (2) Two drivers argue with each other after their cars collide in an accident. (3) A millionaire finds himself confronted by an irate internal revenue officer examining tax-returns in the upper, upper income strata. (4) A school board warns a group of striking teachers to return to the job or be fired. (5) A policeman arrests a middle-class teenager on charges of vagrancy. (6) A Pulitzer Prize-winning novelist is arrested for carrying illegal drugs as he is about to board an airplane. (7) An angry customer argues with a shopkeeper. (8) Two parents nearly come to blows because each one's child accuses the other child of fighting. (9) A conservationist tries to halt a housing project under construction in a wooded area by refusing to move out of his rural cabin for approaching bulldozers. (10) A pedestrian is stopped by a policeman for jay-walking. The pedestrian argues that the green light of the signal does not allow sufficient time for a person on foot to get across the heavily trafficked boulevard.

2. Activities for Interacting

Intended as encouragement for greater intrastudent talk in the new language, activities for interacting are explained to the whole group by the teacher who then usually does not enter into the action. As soon as there is general accord that everyone understands what will take place, the teacher's responsibility becomes that of judge or time-keeper. For the students, interacting as members of a team serves as important preparation for other, more structured small group activities. (See Section 3, *Activities for Sharing and Discussing*.)

Interacting activities are particularly effective in classes where attendance is uneven because of students' outside commitments. For example, they work well in adult education ESL courses or new immigrants' language programs in which, more often than not, participants come from many language backgrounds. However, there is no need to designate them exclusively to such groups. High school classes in EFL settings can use interacting activities, particularly when students are motivated to want to speak English within the classroom. Often, it is useful to introduce interaction activities by asking anyone who so desires to make a personal contract with himself or herself to try to carry out the activity without using the native language at all.

a. Partners: For most people it is less threatening to talk with one other person than either to speak within a group or before a group. The process of selecting partners becomes a language activity in itself. Names can be drawn at random from a hat; there can be duplicate numbered slips, then it is up to each person to find the corresponding number; everyone looks for a person who shares the same sign of the zodiac (month of birthdate). If the class is made up of speakers of different language backgrounds, the teacher should encourage everyone to seek a partner who does not speak the same first language. The teacher, of course, displays tact and awareness of students' feelings when any kind of pairing activity is undertaken. Be prepared with alternative plans before pairing begins if there happens to be an odd number of people present.

1. Interviews: A good activity to use at the beginning of a course. The teacher provides a list of questions either by dictating or by writing them on the blackboard. Each class member takes a turn interviewing the other. The list is designed with both the linguistic competence and cultural background of the students in mind. With low intermediate groups questions should be fairly straighforward pertaining to matters such as name, country of origin, length of time studying English, etc. When the pairs have finished interviewing each other, then the whole group reunites and everyone takes a turn introducing his or her partner to the rest of the class.

2. What Is It? Partners sit with their backs to each other and at a comfortable distance from the next pair. The teacher walks among them with a paper sack filled with simple objects, either household or classroom items. Everybody takes an object from the sack. Then each person asks his or her partner twenty questions about the other's object. The game is more fun if the partners wait until the group reunites for guessing what the object is. Then the partner can hold up the item so that everyone sees it.

3. Know Your Partner: This may turn out to be more interesting if each person has a partner of the opposite sex. The pairs have one minute to look at each other very carefully. Then all of the women are sent out of the room. The teacher presents a list of physical characteristics. For example: color of eyes, color of hair, shape of nose, pattern and color of dress, shoes, height, weight, etc. Each person completes the list based on his memory of what he had seen during the one-minute session. When the partners return to the room, each person reads his list aloud while standing next to his partner. Then, reverse the group who leave the room and also alter the list of characteristics.

b. Scrambles: Although they may appear chaotic, classroom scrambles give people the opportunity to talk with each other much as they would when they go outside during a class break. But there is a language-learning objective besides. People are free to walk around the room, to talk to whomever they wish. Indeed, to enter into the games, they must talk with other people.

1. Who Am I? Upon entering the classroom, everyone receives a name tag which is pinned onto his or her back. Under no circumstances should the wearer be allowed to look at the tag. It contains the name of a famous person. All of the students walk around the room reading the different names on everyone else's back. The strategy is to ask questions, to talk with other people and to try to guess the name of the person on one's own name tag. Limit the answers which can be given to a simple "yes" or "no". When everyone thinks they know who they are, the group reforms and each person takes a turn to tell the others: "I am _____ ."

2. Jumbled Songs: This activity is good for groups that have done some singing together. On separate slips of paper, write one line from the choruses of several songs which everyone knows in English. Each person takes two slips from a hat. First, everyone must trade slips with others until he or she has two consecutive lines to the same song. When everybody has accomplished that task, then they must try to team up with people who have the rest of the lines to the same song. If they are so inclined, when they find each other the members of the group may want to sing their song for everyone else.

3. Mixers: The teacher prepares a "treasure hunt" list of questions on information about members of the group. The facts should be available to the teacher through conversations with students or from enrollment data. For example: (1) Who comes from the largest city in Korea? (2) Who has four grandchildren? (3) Who knows how to type? (4) Whose telephone number begins with the numbers 971? Everyone scrambles; they walk around the room trying to find the answers to the treasure hunt questions. Then the class regroups and finds out who has discovered all of the answers.

c. Teams: The forming of teams can be organized by the teacher or it can occur by chance, for example, by having each person take a slip of paper

208

which contains a number or a symbol from the hat. Working in teams gives students an opportunity to interact in a new participant structure. Teamwork implies that each person tries to help the other members achieve a common goal. Often, teamwork involves making sure that each member understands the objective of the activity. If English is the only medium of communication, so much the better.

1. Treasure Hunts. Working within a team, participants must collect objects which are to be found either in the classroom or in the vicinity of the classroom. Be careful to prepare the treasure hunt lists so that they contain a few items which are relatively easy to find and a few which are more difficult. The lists might even require the members of the team to seek help from other people in the school. A variation of a treasure hunt can be organized around collecting information or facts. Frequently, the answers might be obtained from reading notices on school bulletin boards or by looking at posters in the neighborhood. Be sure to conduct treasure hunts within a specified time limit which is realistic for the demands of the list. Remember, too, to encourage teams to work together on finding answers or items on the lists.

2. Charades. Charades are games in which people act out meanings which must be guessed by others. They are excellent preparation for improvisational activities. There are endless varieties of charade games. Here are two examples which are compatible with the goals of a language class.

a. Paper Bag Charade. The class is divided into four or five groups. Each group receives a paper sack into which five unrelated items have been placed. For example, things like kitchen utensils and tools, erasers, buttons, hooks and eyes, plastic spoons, peanuts, etc. Each group makes up a charade "using" all the items in its bag. The others watch and then try to guess the contents of the performers' paper bag.

b. Word Charade. Working in several teams, each group either chooses a word and acts it out in syllables, or for a low intermediate class, picks a slip of paper containing appropriate words prepared by the teacher. Good words to choose are those which divide into syllables which by themselves have meaning. For example: message (mess, age); wonderful (one, dear, full); sausage (saw, sage); pillow (pill, low). A worthwhile procedure for a language class is for the teacher to first give the teams words to act out; later, each team thinks up its own words.

3. Party Games. Depending upon team effort, the variety of games which can be utilized in the language classroom is vast. Although those which make use of language are most appropriate, don't overlook the ones which are played for the sheer fun of it. Remember, shedding inhibitions is an important requisite for using a new language. All three of these party games require teamwork.

a. Ping Pong Football. No one can remain too reserved when taking part in this game. Two teams are formed. They have goal posts at opposite ends of the room. The team members get down on hands and knees in the center of the playing area. Then, an ordinary pingpong ball is put in the center of the field of play. The object is to blow the ball to the opponents' goal. No physical contact is permitted. If the ball touches any part of the player's body, the other side gets a free blow from the center of the field. Only English can be spoken.

   b. *Newspaper Jigsaw.* Two pages are taken from the same English-language newspaper and cut up so that members of a team all receive a piece from the same page. Then, the team members must put the pieces together again properly. The paper should be cut in irregular shapes. Provide each team with a jar of paste and a large piece of cardboard upon which to paste the pieces. The first team to reconstruct the pieces into their original places wins.

   c. *Chain Talking.* Choose two teams. Either the teacher or an impartial visitor gives each a subject to talk about. The first member of one team talks about his subject as long as he can. Then the next team member takes over and so on until the whole team has finished. Keep track of the time and see which team is able to talk the longest. Keep a supply of topics ready in order to use this game again, making sure that they fit students' interests. The more opportunities there are to practice, the longer most people are able to talk.

4. Reading.   Teamwork is also part of reading plays aloud. For example, the team must make internal decisions about casting, interpretation, cutting, etc. If the activity takes place over a number of class meetings, the team might be given the assignment of selecting its own material from sources in the classroom. (There are good paperback selections, for example, of well-known plays by both American and British authors.) On the other hand, if the activity will be conducted in one or two class sessions, then it is more time-saving for the teacher to hand out copies of the play and assign the parts. When each team does its reading, the rest of the class becomes the audience. Encourage interpretation and expression over correct pronunciation. Young people and adults particularly enjoy reading plays aloud since it gives them an opportunity to partake of material in the new language which suits their span of interests. The teacher should try to select plays with which the students already have familiarity by having read them or by having seen them performed, perhaps in a film or on television.

   A more elaborate form of team play-readings takes place when students write and then read aloud from their own efforts. This can either be done as a creative writing project, or more typically in a language class, as material which has been paraphrased from a film or television drama or musical with which everyone is familiar. (See the sample lesson plan in Section D on pages 222-223.)

3. Activities for Sharing and Discussing

The dominant participation structure now shifts focus from class interaction to each individual student's own actions. First, it concentrates on one person as the "expert," sharing information with the rest of the class. Second, it moves to the individual as a member of a small discussion group, answerable along with the other members for having the discussion take place successfully. When students have recurring opportunities to talk before the whole class on topics in which they hold special interests or enthusiasms, even those who initially showed reluctance sense their own growing assurance. Similarly, small group sessions improve as a class activity when everyone learns how to take part in a discussion.

Strategies for sharing and discussing have an important place in a program for advanced second-language learners because they depend more crucially on everyone being able to proceed on one's own. As such, they are important stimuli to independent thought. On the teacher's part, there are vital steps of anticipating and preparing which must be carried through; however, during the activities themselves the instructor's best tactic is to quietly merge into the background of the classroom prepared to intervene only at moments of stress.

Generally, "share and discuss" activities are more content-oriented than are "react and interact" activities. They hold stronger appeal to maturing young people as well as to adults. Important issues in the news, opinions based on one's own reading, personal experiences—all can be incorporated as themes for talks and discussions. Since they depend upon each person assuming the role of specialist in a particular subject, most of them require some amount of out-of-class preparation time.

But topics for talking assignments can be so universal that everyone will have something to say. For example, try incorporating themes from the whole scope of human relationships in life; men and women; husbands and wives; children and parents; the individual and the family; the young and the old; students and teachers; brothers and sisters; people and machines; people and nature; a person and his/her friend; employers and employees; people of high status and people of low status. In at least some of these areas, everyone will have something to say if the teacher prepares the activity by carefully explaining the topic to be explored.

a. The Individual Student as the "Expert":   For almost everyone, it is much easier to speak in front of others if we feel strongly involved in whatever we have chosen to talk about. As much as possible, students should be encouraged to make their own selection of topic. No one's pet interest or hobby is too trivial for inclusion.

1. Show and Tell.   What does each person make or do outside of the classroom that can be the subject of a short demonstration talk? Who knows a special recipe? Who does macramé or other handwork? Who builds things in the garage? Who can make wine? Who can repair a child's broken toy or a simple kitchen tool? For those who are less mechanical or less adept, there is always the necessity to ask questions. Recreational interests are also good topics: Who can show us how to carry a backpack, or how to change a bicycle tire? Topics can be based on personal experience: "The diet that helped me lose twenty pounds;" "How I stopped smoking;" "How I found an inexpensive apartment." Each person's presentation calls for a certain amount of preparation, but there are opportunities for spontaneous talking as well.

2. Gathering Information. These projects usually require that everyone interviews someone outside of the class. The interview may take place in person, or by means of the telephone. A high degree of role-playing can be built into the assignment: You are a newspaper reporter trying to write a story about . . . . ; or, you are a consumers' affairs specialist trying to find out about . . . . ; or, you are a researcher conducting a public opinion poll about . . . .

3. Debates. More formal debating style calls for a structured format: prepared talks pro and con, ad lib rebuttals, and carefully kept scores. Yet debates can be organized in ways which better accommodate the needs of language students for whom the experience of talking *per se* is more important than winning arguments. An informal debate between two students on a topic which they themselves select can often turn out to be an experience in which both gain new-found confidence in using English. Many of the themes which deal with human relationships can serve as subject matter. Two students might choose to speak on a topic such as "household tasks should be shared by both husband and wife," for example. After deciding on the topic, together they plan how to present their opposing views on the matter. Their presentation in front of the whole group requires at least one class period spent together in discussing their separate ideas.

The facilitator's important role in guiding informal debates is to help students narrow down a topic to a quite specific question. "Men vs. women" is hardly a specific topic. However, one such as "men should receive higher salaries than women for the same job because they must support families" might very well serve as a lively subject for two individuals to debate.

b. Small Group Presentations to the Whole Class: Both radio and television have popularized the format of the informal, small-group presentation. The teacher should know what programs are familiar to the students. Frequently, these shows offer many possibilities for classroom adaptations, thus expanding activities for sharing and discussing ideas.

1. Panels and Talk Shows. If there is a television or radio talk show with which students are acquainted, this activity can be even more effective if the participants appear as themselves, yet receiving all the necessary attention customarily accorded to well-known personalities. Or, the students may choose to take on the identities of famous people. The role of the moderator or host is a crucial one. To that person falls the job of querying each member of the panel about his or her work, goals, and opinions.

2. *Quiz Shows.* A variation on the panel format is the quiz show, or panel of experts. Questions for use on the show should be submitted by the audience in advance. It is often effective to plan quiz shows around specific thematic material which relates to students' active interests. For example, questions for the experts might concentrate on popular music or sports.

3. *The Press Conference.* Role-playing is a vital necessity for carrying out this activity. One member of the group is designated to be a famous person, someone who is currently in the news. A group of four or five journalists, representing important newspapers or magazines, comprise "the press section." It is their job to ask the "Very Important Person" leading and provocative questions. A moderator acts as chairperson to rephrase and interpret questions. After the members of the press have finished asking questions, then everyone else in the audience should have a chance as well.

c. The Small Group Experience: Student-Led Discussions. Small-group discussions differ from other interactional activities where the participation structure involved team effort. As team members, all of the participants performed the same task. In a discussion group, each person's contribution is unique. Yet, the overall success of the small group discussion rests upon each person being able to keep in mind both his or her own ideas as well as their impact on the group as a whole.

1. *Roles within the Discussion Group.* Too often student-conducted discussions falter because of insufficient preparation. To simply assume that everyone knows how to hold a discussion is an inaccurate estimation on the teacher's part. Taking time with the whole class to acquaint everybody with *how* to discuss topics in a small group—not merely *what* to discuss—is a vital preparatory step. For example, participants in a discussion should be familiar with the responsibilities which all the members share. Much like any communal effort, there are a number of separate jobs which must be taken care of. There are more than enough tasks to go around, so usually each person has more than one. The separate roles which people assume in the groups should be explained carefully before any small-group discussions take place.

Someone must initiate the discussion. Others must keep it going by giving and asking for information. Still others must give and ask for reactions, as well as restating and giving examples. All of the participants must come to the realization that an important function of members in a discussion group is to challenge other people's statements. A good discussion thrives on open confrontation. No one feels embarrassment. Both the challenger and speaker know that this interplay is a vital part of the discussion process.

Another function for members of a discussion group is the restating or rephrasing in one's own words of what someone else has just said. Summing up and bringing the separate threads together are additional tasks which must be done. Further, someone must be the timekeeper, keeping an eye to the clock, while another person is the moderator, making sure that the discussants stay on the point of the topic. When we realize that all of these tasks must be carried out spontaneously, then we appreciate the importance of learning how to discuss as a necessary and primary step.

2. Brainstorming. When people sit together to talk about a topic in which they are interested, their objective may be that of trying to think of many ways to answer the issues posed by that subject. This process, called brainstorming, rests on the assumption that three, four, or five people can produce better ideas if they do their thinking aloud, sharing thoughts as they come, than if each person had worked alone. The mechanism of brainstorming can be effectively incorporated as a small group discussion activity if the facilitator activates the process by first setting up a structure for the event. Since brainstorming is essentially a group effort at problem solving, questions that demand solutions work the best. Topics such as: "What should people do about _____," or "How can we go about changing _____," or "What should we do if _____" make suitable material for lively brainstorming sessions. The number of participants should be kept small enough so that each individual feels a personal responsibility towards the undertaking. But the groups should not be so small that there is a lack of sufficient mental stimulation within the group. Anywhere from three to seven members seems to work best.

Hypothetical problems make good material for brainstorming sessions. The following example has been used successfully in classes for overseas students at a university in the United States: Students are given a list of fifteen occupations. They are asked to rank the fifteen professions in order of most prestigious to least prestigious. Here are some possible occupations to include, but they could be altered to fit a particular group of students: author of novels, TV news commentator, policeman, banker, Supreme Court justice, lawyer, architect, rock-music star, motion-picture director, physicist, high school teacher, dentist, psychologist, ecology specialist, physician. If the activity is done in small groups, then the group must come to a consensus of opinion. After comparing the decisions of the separate groups, the whole class can discuss the cross-cultural differences that arose in arriving at the ranking of the professions.

3. Writing As a Small Group Activity. The experience of being part of a small circle for discussion sessions is an important building block for more complex group activities. Since the areas of speaking and writing are naturally linked together (see Chapter Six, WHAT, page 176), oral discussions are significant preparatory steps for group writing projects. A creative effort in the form of a story or narrative poem, for example, can develop as the culmination of a series of meetings with both the whole class and small groups.

The following schematic plan begins as an activity with the whole class, but evolves into a project for small groups by having three-person teams collaborate on the writing of the separate chapters of a full-length story. The steps in the plan have been adapted from the composite suggestions of a number of teachers who have successfully experimented with the technique:

a. *Phase one:* (1) General discussion with the whole class about personal experiences which can be used in story writing. (2) Discussion of writing techniques: plot, character development, chronological framework, dialogue, use of descriptive language, etc.

b. *Phase two:* (1) Work out plot with the whole class by having individuals offer suggestions. (2) Decide on main plot line, possible minor plots, and principal characters. (3) Draw time-line, divide time-line into possible chapters, talk generally about what may happen in each chapter. (4) List characters, place character appearance in chapters. (5) Discuss points of view of each character. (6) Taking one chapter at a time, decide which small groups will work on each chapter (three people per chapter is best).

c. *Phase three:* (1) Each three-member team writes its own contribution. Provide ample time. (2) Teacher moves among groups to make suggestions and give comments and encouragement. (3) Set a reasonable deadline for the first rough draft of each chapter. (4) Collect clearly numbered and labeled papers. (5) Teacher (or student aide) types each chapter, if possible reproduces them so that each person may have a copy. Needed changes are indicated.

d. *Phase four:* (1) Whole class discusses how to proceed from present rough draft stage to a completed work. (2) Copies are handed back to each student. (3) Small group teams discuss and write needed revisions and smoother transitions. (4) Teams read their separate chapters aloud before the whole group. (5) Teams meet again to incorporate further suggestions for revisions. (6) Set deadline for final versions.

Here is one teacher's comments about creative writing as a group effort: "This project takes time and planning, but the rewards are great. The students learn they can be creative in their new language. All are actively involved and proud of their story."

4. Activities for Improvising

With improvisational activities, learners come nearer to using the new language in lifelike communicative events. The classroom atmosphere for improvisations needs to be open and easy-going; this is not the time for attention to the details of correct language structure or correct pronunciation. A prevailing tone of "anything goes"—as long as the objective of communication takes place—is the only sensible way to conduct impromptu language activities.

Similarly, the classroom participation structures for improvisations are less constrained. Many involve small groups, but without the security which those groups offered during Interacting and Sharing-Discussing periods. Although some preparation takes place within the small group, when participants involve other group members in direct communication they do so while the rest of the class observes as the audience. For this reason alone, the feeling among the whole group must be accepting and supportive of each other's efforts.

The exercises themselves encompass a wider sweep of language behavior than do REACTING, INTERACTING, or SHARING-DISCUSSING activities. Now the participants practice the new language in contexts which take in expressive functions as well as the cognitive function. Language becomes more than a vehicle for conveying ideas. It must also be appropriate for particular social situations, role relationships, and topics. Gestures, body movements, facial expressions—all of the non-verbal elements which are a natural part of talking also come into play with improvisations.

a. Techniques for Role-Playing: In all of these free encounters, the participants must pay as much attention to the appropriateness of language behavior in the particular social situation as they do to the actual words and sentences which they use.

1. Ad-lib Skits.   Two, three, or even more participants can be involved. The complete sketch is explained beforehand, either verbally or in writing. Always use familiar places, people, and events. A most effective method is to bring in one or two native speakers to take part in the skits along with the learners themselves. Even if there are only a few opportunities during an entire course for this event to occur, the effort is well worth it.

An example of directions for an ad-lib skit with three characters: A customer (a newcomer to the community), the young man behind the counter at the _____ Ice Cream Parlor, and a second customer (you give him, or her, an identity). The first customer enters and takes a number. The counter-man calls his number. The customer orders three cones with chocolate syrup on top (add names of flavors). He pays with a one-dollar bill. The counterman gives back change by counting it aloud. The customer leaves with his cones in one hand, but just as he puts his free hand on the door someone enters by pushing the door inwards. The first customer drops his cones. He returns to the counter and asks for others. But this time he doesn't want to pay for them. In the trialogue, try to involve the third person, the one who pushed in the door.

2. A variation for ad-lib skits.   These can take in as many as five or six participants. The whole class is divided into three groups. Members of group No. 1 each write down the name of one character (for example, a fledgling lawyer, a deaf old man, an expensively dressed, middle-aged woman . . .). Group No. 2 writes down a location; Group No. 3 an object (for example, a telephone, a sports car, a man's tie . . .). Teacher collects the slips of paper. Each group of ad-lib players draws three characters, one location, and two objects. Allow the goups about ten minutes to prepare their skits. After each one is completed, the class gives comments and suggestions. As a means of checking for comprehension, ask a member of the audience to summarize the plot of the improvisation.

3. *Mini-situations.* Mini-situations are impromptu dialogues, trialogues, or even multilogues which participants are capable of creating because of prior exposure to the central topic of the conversation. Growing out of themes explored in other communication activities, they differ from ad-lib skits by having the players themselves create the story-line. For example, two students who took part previously in a debate on an issue which evolved from the men vs. women theme could transpose their ideas into a face-to-face dialogue between a husband and a wife who are caught up in a conflict over their respective roles. In this way the two have already prepared for the improvisation by thinking through their own viewpoints on the subject. Furthermore, they have already used some of the pertinent vocabulary that will be necessary in the improvisation. The exercise demands sensitivity to language behavior since it calls for the participants to shift from a discussant's point of view to that of a person who is emotionally involved in a controversial topic. In a similar way, topics which were brought up in other classroom contexts can become material for first-person, impromptu scenes. Letters from newspaper advice columns make excellent source material for mini-situations.

4. *Recreating a Story.* A movie, a television, or radio program, a story that most of the class has read, even a narrative song or ballad—any material with which the group is already familiar to the extent of knowing the outline of its plot and characters could serve as useful source material. Participants might even attempt an "original" story based on characters with whom everyone is well-acquainted. For example, many of the situation comedies and dramas from the world of television might fit into this type of activity. Creative students could enact their own Archie Bunker or Mary Tyler Moore scenes.

5. *Spinning a Problem Wheel.* This technique introduces a more elaborate device for creating impromptu situations which can be dramatized. On a large piece of cardboard, designate one section for "people," the other for "problems." The people section is marked off by family roles: mother, father, daughter, son, wife, husband, relative, etc. For the problem section, incorporate issues which touch the lives of the particular group of students. The following list, for example, may be suitable for an ESL class of adults in a large, U. S. city. Being laid off work, car breakdowns, in-laws moving in, overdrawn checking account, teen-age son or daughter leaves home, etc.

Each team of players spins the wheel to determine both the family roles of the characters involved in the improvisation as well as the problems they will face in their impromptu scene from real life.

b. Improvisations for Any Level: Spontaneous language activities are important classroom practices for learners at all levels. But when students are not yet ready to take part in the fully drawn events described in the preceding section, an apt facilitator could prepare them for those experiences by introducing impromptu language exercises which are somewhat less free. The following activities all call for creative use of language. However, the participants' language behavior is limited to a smaller range of actions and emotions.

1. Adverbs and Adjectives. One person, called "It," leaves the room while the others in the class choose an adverb or adjective. Then teams are formed of two or three people to prepare a brief sketch depicting an everyday activity done in the manner of the particular adverb or adjective. For example, if the adjective was "scratchy," a team could work out a skit with a customer, his wife, and a salesperson in a men's clothing store. "It" returns and calls on the various teams to perform. The teams can hold a conversation or use any other non-verbal means to convey the meaning of the chosen adverb or adjective, but the important part is never to use the word itself in the skit. After the round of skits, "It" tries to guess the correct word.

2. Who Is That? The class members work in teams of two or three people. Each team selects the name of a famous person without divulging who it is to the others. The person could be from the world of sports, the movies, rock music, politics, etc. The teams prepare brief skits in which the famous person talks with the other(s), giving clues as to his or her identity but without revealing a name. The audience tries to guess, who is that?

3. What's My Line? This impromptu activity is based on a popular television series of bygone times. Teams of anywhere from two to four members work out skits which involve a job or profession. However, they try not to reveal what that job or profession actually is. The rest of the group watches their performance and then tries to guess the job or profession they are attempting to convey.

c. Fantasy Activities: Fantasy is involved when we say, "what would you do if _____ ? or, "how would you feel, act, or behave, what would you say or do if _____ ? or, "what would you do if you could change _____ ,?" or "if you could have _____ ." The ideas which potentially could fill those blanks are what make-believe is all about; definitely, make-believe has a place in the language classroom. The fun lies in the fact that everyone knows the activity is a fantasy—and everyone likes to pretend. Imaginative activities which entice learners into using the new language in natural contexts do not need to be limited to one day a week time-fillers. A fantasy theme carried through many class meetings tends to spin out a number of related activities which take in various language skill areas.

An effective sequence of fantasy activities should begin with a gimmick, one that catches everyone's interest. The following series of classroom events is based on a teacher-inspired, imaginary situation. Variations of the sequence have been used with classes of both adults and high school students.

1. Preparation phase: Teacher introduces the fantasy theme, making clear that it *is* fantasy, using props such as a check and a letter, concerning an unknown benefactor who has offered $500,000 to be used for making a film. Benefactor has decided to invite members of this class to submit ideas. Who's interested? How will we prepare? Let's get ready for the project of creating a movie plot by talking about good ones we have seen at our next meeting.

2. Continuation of preparation: Each person describes a favorite old movie. Some are able to remind us of actors and actresses of whom younger members have never heard. Teacher tells group about theatres in the community which specialize in showing old films, art films, foreign-language films, after-midnight, inexpensive films, etc.

3. More preparation: Personal accounts of visits to various film houses. Discussion about viewing new films. Recommendations pro and con.

4. A mixing activity: "The Cocktail Party." Each person makes up a name tag (fictitious names encouraged) plus an occupation, either producer, director, writer, actor/actress. Everyone circulates at the "party". Object is to form small groups that will work together to prepare a story for a movie. At the end of the party, small groups announce their members and their company's name. (They may need a public relations person, too.) Acronyms and original names for movie producing companies are encouraged.

5. Central Casting: (location, teacher's desk.) All who did not join a company are asked to leave names and job sought with central casting. Write a brief description of the job you are seeking. Teacher makes sure that everybody becomes a member of some film company by arranging for "interviews."

6. On Location: Take a walk in the neighborhood (either as a class activity or in small groups) to look for good location shots. Before the expedition, talk about need for realistic background, effective scenery in the making of a film.

7. Sample script study: Read part of a sample shooting script for a well-known film. (These can be found in published books on filmcraft.) If possible, teacher dittos a few pages from a sample script.

8. Plot Outline: Small group sessions to work on ideas for movie plots. Set deadline for completing an outline. The outline should include suggestions for local color background shots, give information about proposed actors/actresses to fill the various parts.

9. *The Review Board.* Made up of teacher plus class volunteers, perhaps an outsider as well, the board will judge the proposals for film plots. The producer, director, and writer of each company take turns reading their story outline to the Board. The Board asks questions: "Can you make this film for $500,000", "Who are your actors?", "Will the story be popular with all audiences?", "Why do you think it's a good plot for a successful film?" The Board invites companies to have actors and actresses perform a scene. Set date for the event.

10. *The Big Day:* After seeing scenes performed by the various "companies", the Board decides which one will be selected to make the $500,000 film. Perhaps the whole group will be unanimous in their choice. This sequence might easily lead into organizing a class outing to attend a movie together.

WORKSHOP ACTIVITIES

1. A hypothetical situation can be created from people's accounts of their personal dilemmas. Use the newspaper "advice" column to find material for creating three hypothetical situations that could be used in small group discussions as described under the section on brainstorming. (See Section 3 above.)
2. Create a fantasy activity that could be carried out over a number of classroom hours in an intermediate level class of high school students in an EFL setting.

D. BROADER OPPORTUNITIES FOR COMMUNICATION

Practicing the new language only within the classroom has clearcut limitations. True enough, communication activities provide occasions for talking which are more realistic than are conventional drilling or translating procedures. But when creative facilitators begin to think of ways to enlarge the opportunities for natural language use by incorporating a wider scope, one beyond the bounds of the classroom itself, important questions arise: (1) Where can we go outside the four classroom walls to help students talk with native speakers of the language? (2) How can we plan extended activities and still maintain some of the controls which sound language pedagogy implies?

The direction is fairly clear for people who are in English-speaking countries. For them, just outside of the classroom there lies a virtual language laboratory which they can easily utilize. At this level the benefits derived from making use of the opportunities for actual language use within the community often turn out to be more fruitful than do hours spent with the mechanical equipment in an orthodox "laboratory."

The section following, *Talking Outside of the Classroom*, outlines some situations in which learners can practice language beyond the classroom. Sending students outside does not mean dispensing with planning and preparation. But some of the preparation has already taken place. Many of the activities which have become familiar in communication exercises lend themselves to further elaboration in new locales.

Teachers in EFL situations, along with those for whom it is less possible to arrange language practice in extended situations, will find there are still new avenues to explore. The final section on HOW to conduct meaningful language classes for the intermediate and advanced students gives ideas for making English-language-learning a dynamic experience anywhere. *A Unit for Everywhere* suggests ways to enrich a language program by incorporating the material of a musical show as a context through which to present both language and culture.

1. Talking Outside of the Classroom

Sending students out into the surrounding community to practice language carries responsibilities for the teacher of anticipating and preparing. Activities beyond the classroom need to be just as carefully controlled as do those within. (See page 184, One Step at a Time.) The teacher anticipates the assignment initially by knowing the potentials which lie within the community. Subsequently, the teacher structures the project so that the learners clearly understand how to carry it through. If students are going to achieve success in their share of the plan—participating and actualizing—they must be given more than a hazy suggestion to "find someone to talk with." The learner's assignment must be laid out quite explicitly.

a. Concrete tasks, some of them similar to in-class communicative activities, can be adapted for out-of-class plans. Treasure hunts, interviews, games, gathering facts, finding information around a central topic, these are already familiar techniques. Some of the tasks involve reading, some may involve talking with people or finding one's way in a new place. For example, sending students into an American supermarket with a list of questions to answer (appearing either in the form of a Treasure Hunt list or as a Gathering Facts project), will necessitate reading signs, reading labels on packages, as well as asking for information from store personnel and other customers.

b. Telephone calls as communication exercises open up a wealth of possibilities. Many communities list various information services with which students can be put in touch. For example, calling the local public library information service with a prepared list of questions helps the learner of

English become familiar with some necessary conversational skills connected with telephone talk. College and university communities often have all-night, "help-line" numbers, staffed by students and faculty to serve as a concerned but impersonal voice and to give information on community agencies and resources. Talking informally with a native speaker over the telephone might turn out to be a lively opportunity to ask bothersome questions about local customs and practices. All activities involving the telephone benefit from prior, in-class preparation. Later, the experiences gained, the information gathered, even the new friends made—all can be shared with others in the group through informal reports.

It is up to the teacher to plan telephone communication exercises which take advantage of existing local conditions. Expert facilitators are informed themselves about the telephone resources in their own communities. They have fairly accurate information about telephone rates. That calls to any United States long-distance "information" operator can be placed for a local unit charge should be made known to the learners and the fact incorporated into planned, communication activities.

c. Places to Go.   Each town and city has its own assortment, but parks, museums, and recreation centers are typically found in every middle to large-size community. Moreover, there are supermarkets, drug stores, and discount stores everywhere. In fact, they may all be in one place—the ubiquitous shopping center. We give language-practice tasks to students with a definite place specified. Whether it is to go to a theatre, a restaurant, a library, or a historical monument, there can always be an activity devised that will motivate language learners to try using their new skills in the larger English-speaking setting.

d. Services to Seek Out.   Both local and national government services are closely linked with peoples' everyday lives. Probably newcomers have already encountered some of them. The post office, the utility company, the social security office, the employment office—these are all public services where people must be able to ask for information and answer questions. There are numerous other services as well: legal aid, visas and immigration, insurance, medical and dental, motor vehicles. In schools and colleges there are principal's and counselors' offices, locker services, admissions offices. Potentially all of these institutions can be incorporated into talking activities in an English language program.

e. People to Talk With.   People have identities connected with their jobs. So, of course, there are postmen, landlords, garage mechanics, bus drivers, postal clerks, salespeople, policemen, market checkers, etc. But there are many other ways to categorize people in organizing a language-learning task. For example, people have physical characteristics: there are redheads or blondes, men with moustaches or beards, girls with ponytails or braids. People have dress characteristics and age characteristics as well.

Students can try to find people with special interests: someone to interview who believes in UFOs, or ghosts, or Vitamin E. Or, people who want to lose weight, or who want to stop smoking, or who want to travel. An activity could be built around talking with people who engage in particular recreational pursuits: bikers, runners, window-shoppers, browsers, hikers, joggers. An activity could be built on people's opinions on issues of the day.

f. Finding Language in Print. Aside from the conventional media sources such as newspapers and magazines, our communities are flooded with printed materials which can be effectively incorporated into a language-learning program: Menus from restaurants, brochures from public offices (example, driving regulations and social security information), timetables from buses and trains. There are free shopping newspapers to read, bulletin boards at markets and community centers to look at, as well as posters and outdoor advertisements to find. An imaginative ESL teacher even had students collect logos from the bumper stickers on automobiles. (Start off the activity by taking a walk in a nearby parking lot.) Their assignment included asking a local resident to help explain what each slogan meant. Students shared their findings with each other in class. Language in print seems to follow fashions. One year T-shirts bear tokens of language, but the next year bright epithets may appear somewhere else. Incorporating searches for topical language is an effective way to introduce advanced students to informal, contemporary English.

2. A Unit for Everywhere: The Musical Play

Throughout this chapter on HOW to create meaningful programs for advanced students, various techniques have been outlined. To be implemented to their fullest potential, many of them can be integrated with other skill areas in order to create a full and rounded program. There are few instances where it is feasible to build a course on communication activities alone. Good menu planning is not based on serving hors-d'oeuvres and dessert; sound course planning pays attention to all aspects of language use.

This section suggests a framework for incorporating the various skill areas within a larger unit. Listening-comprehension, talking and communicating, reading, writing—all are included. The selection of the context for the unit grows out of the belief that materials for language learning should be intrinsically interesting to the people who will use them. At the intermediate and advanced levels, the principle is even more urgent.

Both American and British musical plays boast a long tradition of combining literary values, songs, and settings into a whole which is more dynamic than are any of those separate parts. The whole is called "good theatre." Bringing examples of the form into the language classroom makes good sense because it opens up new ways to teach many skills in one unifying context. By examining a list of some of the outstanding productions of the musical stage we realize how many have been adapted from published writings which could be utilized in a language course. For example, "South Pacific," "The King and I," "Oliver," "Kiss Me, Kate," "My Fair Lady" are particularly well-known

Along with interesting plots, musical plays contain songs which offer rich material to enliven class sessions. If the teacher pays close attention to the resources in the surrounding community, it might even be possible to see a film version of the show which the unit is featuring. And perennial favorites are often produced by local companies.

The following outline for a unit on "West Side Story" was developed for a high school ESL class in a large United States city. In this sample unit, students have copies of the script for the Broadway show, "West Side Story." A phonograph recording of the musical play is also used.

I. Preparation for the unit: "West Side Story"

a. Use map of a large city (preferably your own) to introduce basic layout of a complex urban center.
b. Review necessary vocabulary: for example, suburb, inner city, slum, business section, recreation area, residential section, etc.
c. Individual activity: Create a new city. Use blank outline map of a large city. Develop color key and establish different sections. Who lives where? Locate the stores, schools, services.
d. Dicuss patterns of settlement in large United States cities: immigrant groups' contribution to American life; the "melting pot" ideal vs. "the salad bowl"; tensions in United States urban areas.
e. View educational films on city settlement and immigration. (For example, from Los Angeles City Schools, "Golden Temple on Mott Street," "The Golden Door," "Our Immigrant Heritage.")
f. Prepare family portrait reports. Use interviewing techniques, include information on language, country of origin, educational level, skills, income, ethnic and religious customs, family relationships.
g. Small group discussions: trace personal experiences in a United States city.

II. Selected Activities For Skill Areas

a. Listening Comprehension

1. Listen to a summary of the plot, scene by scene.
2. Listen to songs with word sheets. (Suggested selections: "I Feel Pretty," "Officer Krupke," "A Boy Like That," "America.")
3. Further listening to songs: leave out key words in song sheets.
4. Introduce new vocabulary through songs.
5. Relate content of each song to story line in which it appears.

b. Speaking and Talking

1. Read parts orally. Present play scene by scene. Characters are assigned after each class period; preparation is part of homework. Or, organize small groups to prepare parts of scenes. Everyone selects a favorite character to portray.
2. Check for comprehension through oral discussion of each scene.
3. Give oral summaries of each scene; paraphrase the action.
4. Tape scenes as read by different small group teams.
5. Dicuss important themes in the story: prejudice, sarcasm, grief, behavior in youth gangs.
6. Discuss personal experiences with in-group vs. out-group tensions.

c. Reading

1. Check reading comprehension through understanding of stage directions. Students draw sketches (use stick figures) of major scenes showing positioning of characters.
2. Use frequent short factual quizzes: "Who is a Jet?" "Where does the rumble take place?"
3. Read other Romeo and Juliet treatments; familiarization with Shakespeare's plot through reading and listening to a few selected passages.

d. Writing

1. Write summaries of each scene.
2. Write summaries of message content in songs.
3. Write compositions. Possible topics: What is prejudice? What characters show prejudice? What are your personal experiences with prejudice? What are your personal experiences as a member of a gang or a club?
4. Write sketches of main characters in the play.
5. Analyze symbolism in final scene: Is there "a place for us"?

WORKSHOP ACTIVITIES

1. Using the advanced level plan (see Section 1) write a lesson incorporating use of the telephone. The lesson, which will be conducted within the classroom, should offer students a wide range of role-playing possibilities.
2. Prepare a unit plan along the lines of the one for "West Side Story" using a musical play with which you are familiar.
3. Prepare a unit plan similar to the one for "West Side Story" using a contemporary play in English.

8

WHERE

The Facilitator Reaches Out

OVERVIEW

An amateur's efforts are different from a professional's approach. The latter person knows where to go to look for answers to questions. Becoming a professional English language teacher depends as much on knowing the aids and resources in the field as it does on knowing how to conduct classroom activities. The professional relies on a variety of people, on a large collection of resource materials, on journals and publications, on libraries, and on the information disseminated by organizations.

This final chapter of Part Two describes some further resources which are available to teachers. It complements the WHERE section of Part One by taking in additional possibilities for assistance. The facilitator reaches out first to other people; to aides, volunteers, and colleagues. A vital technique for augmenting the traditional classroom teacher-to-students ratio is through the growing practice of cross-age tutoring. In language teaching, where communication is the essence of the activity, bringing in other students to help both individuals and small groups holds out exciting potentialities.

The idea has been expressed more than once in these pages that the skilled facilitator works with a collection of textbook resources. Even if students use one core text, the teacher needs to have a variety of authorities to turn to. The second section of this chapter outlines some of the most important features to keep in mind when looking for additional textbooks either to borrow or buy for use in the classroom. Finally there is an open-ended list of publications and journals, professional organizations, and libraries which are available to English language teachers throughout the world.

A. INVOLVING OTHER PEOPLE

A significant characteristic of the modern classroom (see Chapter I, WHO) is the presence of various people who are involved in the teacher-learner relationship. They might be aides, volunteers, or student helpers. The benefits for students in language courses which are staffed by more than one person can be immense: they have more models of the target language to listen to, they have more people to interact with, they have greater possibilities for attention to individual needs.

From the point of view of the people who are responsible for the instructional program, any plan which uses either teacher-teams, aides, parent volunteers, or student tutors necessitates close attention to both external matters such as scheduling and internal matters such as interpersonal attitudes. A classroom teacher who is condescending or authoritarian with an aide or parent volunteer can cause more harm than good. A person who uses the team-teaching format as a convenient way to shed responsibility is undermining the spirit of cooperation which is essential in such an undertaking. Involving other people in the classroom can best be described as a high-risk, high-gain plan, one which is, in the end, usually worth the effort.

1. Team Teaching

When teachers work together the results can be immensely profitable both for themselves and for students. Team teaching is a means to conserve human energies for top-priority objectives. It is also a means to overcome the problem of insufficient self-evaluation by teachers in the classroom. Working as a member of a teaching team involves sharing ideas and accepting constructive criticism, for each person's efforts become more open to scrutiny by colleagues. Team teaching necessitates careful planning, but it also provides the possibility that a good plan can be modified or slightly altered for use with a larger number of students than when individual teachers are only working with one or two classes. In every way, team teaching makes good sense. But it requires sound leadership and real cooperation on the part of every person involved.

The possible ways for organizing team teaching will, in the final analysis, depend upon all of the variables in a particular school situation. One possibility for team effort has already been described in a previous chapter on individualization(see Chapter Five, WHO).When a language,curriculum for intermediate and advanced students is set up around classes in skill areas, the preliminary basis for teamwork has been provided. For example, in a program which calls for students to attend separate classes in various skills such as reading-vocabulary, syntax, and spoken English, team effort can exist if the teachers of the different skills who are concerned with the same level in the program regularly work together by preparing and sharing materials.

As an illustration, if the teacher responsible for directing activities in spoken-language work coordinates with the syntax teacher, then some degree of team teaching is taking place. A team effort can either be worked out in terms of a tightly drawn up course in which there is a week-by-week plan of topics to be covered, or the effort may be rather informal, one in which teachers work closely in harmony and closely in terms of contact hours with each other. The possibilities for reinforcing what one has covered from the point of view of another's specialty holds out important prospects for a successful program.

From the students' point of view, team teaching cuts down on some of the monotony of daily class attendance. A successful plan for team teaching has been carried out in short-term, intensive English language courses for overseas students who attend summer programs at a university in the United States. Since these programs, of five or six weeks in duration, call for the students to have six hours of instruction per day, team teaching makes it possible to add more variety than if one teacher stayed with one group for the entire day. Programs are usually organized so that a two-person team, a man and a woman, work together. For the more advanced levels, teams made up of three instructors have turned out to be quite workable. A benefit for the students is the exposure to more than one person's way of speaking English.

In these programs approximately twenty people are assigned to a group. They have one classroom as their base of operations, while the teachers move from room to room. This scheme saves the time and effort of having new people finding their way in unfamiliar settings. But frequently instruction takes place out-of-doors, with the groups sitting in shady, grassy places on the campus.

Teacher teams work together quite closely, sharing the responsibility of raising each student's scores on a battery of achievement tests. A two-person team might switch groups two or three times during the day. They repeat the same lessons with the different groups, making slight changes when necessary. If the activity ever warrants it, the entire group comes together with both or all of the teachers. These kinds of full group activities are held for class outings, trips to see local places of interest, or walks in the neighborhood. The teachers themselves divide the responsibilities for the objectives of the course: one person concentrates on activities for listening-comprehension while the other is mostly concerned with activities for oral production. The team members coordinate their efforts on a daily basis so that there is correlation of topics and themes covered.

Another kind of team effort, one which involves cooperation between an experienced teacher and a paraprofessional, takes place in many classrooms which have aides or volunteers. It is frequently the case in bilingual education programs in the United States that a classroom aide who is a native speaker of the students' first language works as an assistant teacher. One of the plans for individualized instruction illustrated in Chapter Five, WHO indicated how aides are utilized in a program built around skill stations in the classroom. In that type of program, one or two aides assumed considerable responsibility for supervising the activities which took place under their care.

The most fruitful programs involving aides do not rely exclusively on either scheduling or materials. For it usually turns out that it is the presence of a cooperative, understanding relationship between the teacher and aide which makes the plan work effectively. Teachers and aides must begin by showing respect for what the other person has to offer. Teachers and aides who work cooperatively are able to convey an attitude of mutual trust to their pupils. Such a display of real feelings between people of different ethnic backgrounds can be a vital part of bilingual-bicultural education. On the other hand, the objectives of a bilingual classroom are not met when the aide who models the students' first language is continuously placed in a role which is subservient to that of the teacher's.

A skilled facilitator's abilities to plan and coordinate classroom activities are needed in order to take advantage of additional classroom personnel. Grouping, individualization, co-teaching of the same lesson—all are techniques that can be carried out when two people share classroom responsibilities. In an important experimental bilingual education program carried out with American Indian children in a U. S. Government reservation school, a teacher and an aide were able to teach beginning reading in two languages by carefully coordinating their efforts. An English reading lesson and a Navajo reading lesson were held in opposite sides of the classroom. Later in the day, children switched teachers and had instruction in reading the other language.

2. Cross-Age Tutoring

In the days of the one-room schoolhouse, older students often had to help teach younger ones. Since then, in almost all parts of the world, schools have become much more elaborate. But during this decade, many educators have rediscovered the dynamic fact that younger students often thrive when they are taught by older ones, and the older students benefit from playing teacher. Frequently, a very special relationship can grow between a teen-ager and a younger person. Being a tutor reinforces what the older student already knows. In addition, it gives the older one an opportunity to grow intellectually and socially.

The subject content of language courses lends itself uniquely to cross-age tutoring. Tutors can serve as helpers with individuals or with small groups. In EFL settings, involving older, intermediate, and advanced students in classrooms with younger children affords special opportunities for speaking the new language which otherwise are difficult to arrange. Beyond speaking skills, tutors can be asked to help with many types of reading and writing activities. Working with younger students often instills confidence in older students. They are motivated to continue their study of English.

Another benefit from cross-age tutoring has been observed in ESL settings where native speakers of English, high school students, were brought into elementary school ESL classrooms. The experiment caused school administrators to realize the spinoff benefits which could take place. The presence of native-speaker high school students in classrooms with younger ESL students raised the social prestige of the non-native children in the eyes of their peers in the school. Social relationships with English-speaking children, which up to that point had been negligible, began to improve. Teachers noticed that there was a subtle change in the cross-cultural atmosphere in the school. No longer were the ESL students quite as isolated. On the playground they were entering into games with the others. They tended to mix more with American children and began to be accepted into their friendship groups.

A particularly successful plan for cross-age tutoring has brought together American high school students studying Spanish and elementary school children in ESL classes. In this case, the benefits in language practice for both age groups have been striking. The American high school students are able to use the Spanish they have been learning, and the Spanish-speaking children benefit from the attention of older teen-agers. Many of the activities involved setting up one-to-one interactional meetings between a tutor and a tutoree. For example, the high school students ate lunch in the school cafeteria with the younger students. The most successful part of the plan was the inclusion of sports. High school boys coached younger boys in baseball, football, and gymnastics. There was a great deal of natural use of whatever language either group could manage, just to make communication take place.

Whether cross-age tutoring is planned around extra-curricular activities or whether it involves actual tutoring in language skill areas, the possibilities it offers for fostering real communication between involved individuals is filled with exciting possibilities.

When older students are involved either in ESL or EFL settings, the facilitator's role is to prepare them with the necessary materials and background information regarding the younger students. But then, after the initial preparation has taken place, the tactful facilitator knows to trust the students to work out their own best ways to facilitate language practice by themselves.

B. SHOPPING FOR TEXTBOOKS

The attitude of professionalism which motivates us to seek out every possible resource for utilization within the classroom (see Chapter Four, WHERE) also makes us critical shoppers in the textbook market. Observe some experienced teachers browsing through publishers' displays, the book exhibits which commonly take place at large professional meetings and conventions. These people ask questions. Plenty of them. Above all, they know there is no *one* textbook which will answer all students' needs. Any choice will probably carry with it some kind of compromise, of buying some good features while at the same time giving up others. A book which contains good drill material might be weak in providing grammatical explanations. One which gives ample opportunities for writing practice may be sparse in lessons which include oral work.

What do we actually look for when we pick up an unfamiliar text? One highly experienced language facilitator said: "When I stand and browse through an unfamiliar book, I usually go through one of the grammatical exercises or drills to see if it really works. I look for things like substitution drills that are constructed so loosely that I can find words and expressions which, if they are placed into the slots, produce non-English sentences. Or, I look for drills which tell the user to turn a list of statements automatically into questions regardless of whether the question form would ever be asked. If I find any of these kinds of unnatural, unworkable drills I decide right there on the spot that the book is definitely not a good buy."

The person made that remark on the basis of a great deal of experience using language textbooks. The following checklist of features to look for when you are considering whether or not to buy a book is a place to begin to build that kind of expertise. It is meant to be an open-ended list of suggestions. As you, too, gain experience you will want to add your own suggestions to it.

1. Vital Statistics

a. Does the title give an accurate representation of the contents? For example: If it is a "quick and easy" method, does the title hold out more promise for success than the contents warrant? If it is called a "review" book, does it explain the basis upon which particular grammatical topics have been selected for review? If it is an "intermediate" book, does it explain the basis for determining who are intermediate learners?
b. What is the scope of the book? Is it part of a series, or is it a self-contained entity? Is the book accompanied by other materials or aids such as students' workbooks, teachers' guides, tapes, or cassettes? How many pages does the book or series contain?
c. Who is/are the author(s)? What are their professional qualifications?
d. Who has published the book? Is it distributed widely in non-English-speaking countries? Where is it available?
e. What is the date of publication? Is it current enough to include recent points of view in language-teaching pedagogy?

2. Audience

a. Who is the book intended for? Is it for children, young people in secondary school, or adults? Or is the audience so vaguely indicated that there is no recognizably situated point-of-view in the lessons?
b. Is the book intended for people of one specific language background, or is it for anyone who wants to learn the new language, English?
c. Is the cultural setting of the book clear or vague? Are the lessons set in an American English or British English background?

3. Language Structure and Language Skills

a. Is the English language presented systematically? Is there a table of contents of language structures?
b. Is the user of the book told the basis for the selection of the structures which are presented? (See Chapter Two, WHAT.)
c. Is the user told the basis for the sequence (order) in which structures are presented? (See Chapter Two, WHAT.)
d. Is there evidence of contrastive analysis? Has attention been given to particular structures which are more difficult for the book's audience based on their first language background?
e. Is there evidence of language control? Are new structures carefully presented and explained before they appear in drills and presentation materials? Are new vocabulary items listed as "new words" before they appear in dialogues or stories?
f. Is there provision for practicing all of the language skills? Is attention paid to listening comprehension? To speaking skills including talking and interacting? to reading? to writing?
g. What is the distribution of emphasis among the separate language skills?

4. Pedagogical Principles

a. Are topics relevant to the learners' interests, needs, and cultural orientation?
b. Do the authors hold a particular point of view on language teaching? Do they promote audio-lingual, cognitive-code, direct method, or any other pedagogical bias?
c. What is the focus of individual lessons? Are they primarily centered on graduated grammatical structures? Are they centered on pronunciation problems? Are they centered on vocabulary?
d. What kinds of practice materials are provided? What techniques do they encompass? translation, pattern practice (substitution), reading, writing? Are the practice materials inventive? Do they lead to creative use of language?
e. Does the book give the user an opportunity to review?
f. Is the internal organization consistent? Is it helpful to the learner?
g. Do lessons move from grammatical generalizations ("rules") to practice, or vice-versa? (See Chapter Three, HOW.)
h. Does the book contain a teacher's guide which helps people understand the internal organization of the book?
i. Is there a table of contents? Does it give an indication of where to locate specific structures? Does it tell where to locate drill or practice materials?
j. Is there an index of new vocabulary items? Does the index direct the user to the lesson in which the meaning of a new word is first glossed or defined?

k. Is the book visually appealing? Are pages attractively laid out? Is there use of color, illustrations, drawings?
l. Is it a thick book or a thin book? Are the contents set out sparsely over the pages or does each page contain a healthy portion of new material? In essence, are users of the book getting their money's worth?

C. HELPFUL INFORMATION

Whether concerned with students at the beginning or the advanced levels, all teachers who want to facilitate the learning of new languages are interested in keeping abreast of the field. The profession of English-language teaching boasts a growing body of authors, publishers, educational equipment producers, language specialists, governmental agencies, and professional organizations. This support system reaches both English-speaking and non-English speaking countries.

Alert facilitators make sure to have their names on as many mailing lists as possible. Publishers are eager to send notices about new books; professional organizations want to publicize activities such as meetings, conferences, and conventions. By keeping the lines of communication flowing, we make the classroom teaching job more interesting. Teachers who avail themselves of all of the professional resources are usually those whose students enjoy learning new languages.

Many people who teach language work in relative isolation from colleagues. Frequently there are only one or two ESL teachers in a public school. Private tutors in non-English-speaking countries often work as freelancers in their own homes. For these people who work independently, it is even more vital that they get to know other teachers in the same city, district, or country. Often the best strategies for classroom teaching emerge from sharing ideas and experiences at professional meetings.

The most important listings in this reference source will undoubtedly turn out to be those which you, the user of this book, provide for yourself. In many parts of the United States, in many places in the world where English is taught as a foreign language, teachers are getting together to produce journals and newsletters. The national organizations can often direct you to local chapters and groups.

1. Publications

California TESOL Occasional Papers. 558 Seventh Ave., Menlo Park, Calif. 94025.

English Language Teaching. 16 Alexandra Gardens, Hounslow, Middlesex, England. (British.) W. R. Lee (ed.).

English Record. Journal of the N.Y. State English Council. State University College, Oneonta, N.Y. 13820.

English Teaching Forum. USIA publication. 1750 Pennsylvania Ave. N.W., Rm. 212, Washington, D.C. 20547.

Florida FL Reporter. 801 N.E. 177 St., North Miami Beach, Fla. 33162.

Foreign Language Annals. Publication of ACTFL, 62 Fifth Ave., New York, N.Y. 10011.

International Review of Applied Linguistics. (IRAL) c/o Professor Gerhard Nickel, University of Stuttgart, Federal Republic of West Germany.

Language Learning. University of Michigan, North Univ. Bldg., Ann Arbor, Michigan 48104.

Linguistic Reporter. (Published by Center for Applied Linguistics), 1611 N. Kent St., Arlington, Va. 22209.

M.E.T. (Modern English Teacher). Modern English Publications, International House, 40 Shaftesbury Ave., London, W1V8HJ, England.

Modern Language Journal. Published by National Federation of Modern Language Teachers Assoc. Charles King (ed.). University of Colorado, Boulder, Colo. 80302.

TESOL Newsletter. School of Languages and Linguistics, Georgetown University, Washington, D.C. 20007.

TESOL Quarterly. School of Languages and Linguistics, Georgetown University, Washington, D.C. 20007. Ruth Crymes (ed.). Dept. of TESL, University of Hawaii, Honolulu.

2. Professional Organizations

Center for Applied Linguistics. 1611 N. Kent St., Arlington, Va. 22209.

English Speaking Union of the U.S. 16 East 69 St., N.Y.C. 10021.

TESOL (Teachers of English to Speakers of Other Languages). School of Languages and Linguistics, Georgetown University, Washington, D.C. 20007.

NAFSA (National Association of Foreign Student Advisors). 1860 19 Street, N.W., Washington, D.C. 20009.

National Federation of Modern Language Teachers Association. 62 Fifth Avenue, New York City 10011.

MLA (Modern Language Association). 62 Fifth Avenue, New York City 10011.

NCTE (National Council of Teachers of English), 1111 Kenyon Rd., Urbana, Ill. 61801.

ACTFL (American Council on the Teaching of Foreign Languages). 62 Fifth Avenue, New York 10011.

Libraries   (Found in many cities of the world, they sometimes have local names.)

The British Council Library.

The U. S. I. S. Library (in some places called by other names, for example, "Amerika House," "Hellenic-America Union," etc.)

WORKSHOP ACTIVITIES

1. Find out if there is a TESOL affiliate group in your state, country, or geographical region by writing to the TESOL organization, c/o Georgetown University, Washington, D.C.

2. *For EFL:*
   Find the names and addresses of two libraries in your city or country which have collections of books and materials for teaching the English language.

EPILOGUE

In no way do we wish to suggest that we have covered all of the ground, nor have we answered all of the questions. The challenge in language teaching, as in any teaching, is the creative process of finding answers to problems as they arise. The aim of this book has been to provide a framework within which decision-making can be effectively carried out. We want this framework to be used by teachers to develop their own answers to questions which occur in their own school situations.

Language is a multi-faceted domain of human experience. All research and tested theory agrees, at least, on one important tenet: there is no acknowledged or proven view of human language which justifies an application in the classroom of a "do it this way only" approach. The single unifying theme that can be derived from theoretical sources is the need for all second-language education specialists to be well informed.

Throughout, we have made a concerted effort to bring into these chapters on practice vital considerations drawn from theory. As much as possible, up-to-date research has been incorporated into the discussions of basic questions. If, at times, you have read statements which were contrary to your own ideas, it may now be the time to turn to the further sources listed in the Bibliography.

BIBLIOGRAPHY

I. Second and Foreign Language Acquisition

Allen, Harold B. and Russel N. Campbell, *Teaching English as a Second Language: A Book of Readings*. New York: McGraw-Hill Book Co., Second Ed., 1972.

Allen, J.P.B. and S. Pit Corder, *The Edinburgh Course in Applied Linguistics*: Vol. 1 Readings for Applied Linguistics; Vol. 2 Papers in Applied Linguistics; Vol. 3 Techniques in Applied Linguistics; Vol. 4 Testing and Experimental Methods. London: Oxford University Press, 1974.

Altman, Howard B. (ed.) *Individualizing the Foreign Language Classroom: Perspectives for Teachers*. Rowley, Mass: Newbury House, 1972.

Bright, J. A. and G. B. McGregor, *Teaching English as a Second Language*. London: Longman, 1970.

Burt, Marina K. and Carol Kiparsky. *The Gooficon: A Repair Manual for English*. Rowley, Mass.: Newbury House, 1972.

Chastain, Kenneth. *The Development of Modern Language Skills: Theory to Practice*. Chicago: Rand McNally Publishing Co., Second Ed., 1976.

Croft, Kenneth (ed.) *Readings on English as a Second Language: For Teachers and Teacher Trainers*. Cambridge, Mass.: Winthrop, 1972.

Finocchiaro, Mary and Michael Bonomo. *The Foreign Language Learner: A Guide for Teachers*. New York: Regents Publishing Co., 1973.

French, F. G. *The Teaching of English Abroad*. London: Oxford University Press.

Jackobovits, Leon and Barbara Gordon. *The Context of Foreign Language Teaching*. Rowley, Mass.: Newbury House, 1973.

Logan, E. Gerald. *Individualized Foreign Language Learning: An Organic Process*. Rowley, Mass.: Newbury House, 1973.

Oller, John and Jack C. Richards (eds.) . *Focus on the Learner: Pragmatic Perspectives for the Language Teacher*. Rowley, Mass.: Newbury House, 1973.

Paulston, Christina Bratt and Mary Newton Bruder. *From Substitution to Substance*. Rowley, Mass.: Newbury House, 1975.

Paulston, Christina Bratt and Mary Newton Bruder. *Teaching English as a Second Language: Techniques and Procedures*. Cambridge, Mass.: Winthrop Publishers, 1976.

Richards, Jack C. (ed.) *Error Analysis: Perspectives on Second Language Acquisition*. London: Longman, 1974.

Rivers, Wilga M. *Teaching Foreign Language Skills*, Chicago: University of Chicago Press, 1968.

Saville-Troike, Muriel. *Foundations for Teaching English as a Second Language*. Englewood Cliffs, N. J.: Prentice-Hall, 1976.

Schumann, John H. and Nancy Stenson (eds.). *New Frontiers in Second Language Learning*. Rowley, Mass.: Newbury House, 1974.

Valdman, Albert (ed.) *Trends in Language Teaching*. New York: McGraw-Hill Book Co., 1966.

II. The Modern Classroom

Gagne, Robert M. *The Conditions of Learning*. New York: Holt, Rinehart & Winston, Inc., 1970.

Glasser, William. *Schools Without Failure*. New York: Harper & Row, 1969.

Manning, Duane. *Toward a Humanistic Curriculum*. New York: Harper & Row, 1971.

Neagley, Ross L. and N. D. Evans. *Handbook for Effective Curriculum Development*. Englewood Cliffs, N. J.: Prentice-Hall, 1967.

Nyquist, Ewald B. and Gene R. Hawes (eds.). *Open Education: A Sourcebook for Parents and Teachers*. Bantam Books, 1972.

Postman, Neil and C. Weingartner. *Teaching as a Subversive Activity*. N. Y.: Delacorte Press, 1969.

Rogers, Carl R. *Freedom to Learn*. Columbus, Ohio: Charles E. Merrill Pub. Co., 1969.

Weinstein, G. and N. Fantini. *Toward Humanizing Education*: A *Curriculum of Affect*. New York: Praeger, 1970.

III. Introduction to Linguistics

Crystal, David. *Linguistics*. (a Pelican original.) Middlesex, England: Penguin Books, 1971.

Fromkin, Victoria and Robert Rodman. *An Introduction to Language*. New York: Holt, Rinehart & Winston, Inc., 1974.

Langacker, Ronald W. *Language and Its Structure: Some Fundamental Linguistic Concepts*. New York: Harcourt Brace Jovanovich, Inc. (2nd ed.), 1973.

Liles, Bruce L. *An Introduction to Linguistics*. Englewood Cliffs, New Jersey: Prentice-Hall, 1975.

Lyons, John. *Introduction to Theoretical Linguistics*. Cambridge: Cambridge University Press, 1968.

Wardhaugh, Ronald. *Introduction to Linguistics*. New York: McGraw-Hill Book Co., 1972.

IV. The English Language

Grammar

Bloomfield, Morton W. and Leonard Newmark. *A Linguistic Introduction to the History of English*. New York: Alfred A. Knopf, 1963.

English Language Services. *A Practical English Grammar*. New York: Collier Macmillan, 1974.

Jacobs, Roderick A. and Peter S. Rosenbaum. *English Transformational Grammar*. Waltham, Mass.: Blaisdell Publishing Co., 1968.

Jesperson, Otto. *Growth and Structure of the English Language*. Garden City, N. Y.: Doubleday Anchor Books, 1956 (first published 1905).

Quirk, Randolph and Sidney Greenbaum. *A Concise Grammar of Contemporary English*. New York: Harcourt Brace Jovanovich, Inc., 1973.

Rutherford, William E. *Modern English*. Vols. One and Two. New York: Harcourt Brace Jovanovich, Inc. (sec. ed.), 1975.

Stockwell, Robert and Paul Schachter and Barbara Partee. *The Major Syntactic Structures of English*. New York: Holt, Rinehart & Winston, Inc., 1973.

Phonology

Bowen, J. Donald. *Patterns of English Pronunciation*. Rowley, Mass.: Newbury House, 1975.

Jones, Daniel. *An Outline of English Phonetics*. New York: E. P. Dutton, Inc., 1940.

Prator, Clifford H., Jr. and Betty Wallace Robinett. *Manual of American English Pronunciation*. New York: Holt, Rinehart & Winston, Inc., 1972 (3rd edition).

V. First Language Acquisition

Brown, Roger. *When Children Talk*. Cambridge, Mass.: Harvard University Press, 1973.

Cazden, Courtney. *Child Language and Education*. New York: Holt, Rinehart & Winston, Inc., 1972.

Chomsky, Carol. *The Acquisition of Syntax in Children*. Cambridge, Mass.: M. I. T. Press, 1971.

Piaget, Jean. *The Language and Thought of the Child*. New York: World Publishing Co. (Meridian paperbacks.), 1955.

Slobin, Dan I. *Psycholinguistics*. Glenview, Illinois: Scott, Foresman & Co., 1971.

Vygotsky, L. S. *Thought and Language*. Cambridge, Mass.: The M. I. T. Press (paperback), 1962. Introduction by J. Bruner.

VI. Language in Society

Burling, Robbins. *Man's Many Voices: Language in Its Cultural Context*. New York: Holt, Rinehart, & Winston, Inc., 1970.

Burling, Robbins. *English in Black and White*. New York: Holt, Rinehart, & Winston, Inc., 1973.

Fishman, Joshua. *The Sociology of Language*. Rowley, Mass.: Newbury House, 1972.

Gigliolo, Pier Paolo (ed.) *Language and Social Context*. Selected Readings. Middlesex, England: Penguin Books, 1972.

Gumperz, John and Dell Hymes (eds.) *Directions in Sociolinguistics*. The Ethnography of Communication. New York: Holt, Rinehart, & Winston, Inc., 1972.

Hall, Edward T. *The Silent Language*. New York: Doubleday, 1959.

Hall, Edward T. *The Hidden Dimension*. New York: Doubleday Anchor Books, 1966.

Labov, William. *Sociolinguistic Patterns*. Philadelphia, Pa.: University of Pennsylvania Press, 1972.

Subject
Index

A

Achievement
    evaluation   121 – 124

Aids
    audio visuals   15, 110
    blackboard   106
    flannel board   106
    magnetic board   106
    pocket chart   106 – 107
    plastigraph   107
    overhead projector   108
    flashcards   108
    ABC chart   109
    letter cards   109
    sentence strips   109

Aims (objectives)   5
    see goals

Attitude
    of learner   26 – 27
    towards FL   132

Audio-lingual method   73 – 74

Auditory recognition   86

Aural-oral
    general approach   69, 72−73, 93
    stage   53
    discrimination   58

B

Behaviorism   73

Bilingual programs
    vis-a-vis ESL   9

Blackboard − see aids

C

Cards − see aids

Charts − see aids

Cognitive
    process   69, 143
    code   73−75, 93

Communication
    general   82
    speaker/hearer   35−36

Communicative competence   173
    reacting   201−205
    interacting   206−210
    sharing & discussing   211−214
    improvising   215
    broader opportunities   220

Competence/performance   36, 74−76
    the testing of   138−141

Comprehension   65−66, 138−139

Consonant system   48

Content words   47, 49

Contextualization
    general   42, 142−143

Contrastive Analysis   41−42

Controlled activities   76–82

Correctness   144

Cross-age tutoring   230–231

Curriculum—*see* syllabus

Cyclic approach   41

D

Deductive/inductive   69–72

Decision-making   46, 69

Descriptive linguistics   73–74

Diagnostic activities   137, 188

Dialogues   76

Discovery procedure   71

Dramatization—*see* role-playing

Drills—*see* controlled activities

E

EFL   2, 37

English—American vs. British   12, 13–15

Errors—*see* interlanguage

ESL   2, 8, 37

Explanation   157
     see also generalization

Extensive reading   97–100

Evaluation—*see* testing

F

Facilitator   21, 32, 130, 183

Fill-in exercise   88

Filmstrips—*see* multi-media

First language vs. second   10, 38

Flannel board—*see* aids

Flash cards—*see* aids

Form (grammar)   42, 76

Frequency of occurrence   40

Functional load   40

G

Games   203–205

Generalizations   77, 81–82
    over-generalization   156

Generative-tranformational   74–75
    see linguistics

Goals
    societal   12, 131–133
    school   133–134
    individual   135–136
    skills (instrumental)   135

Gradation—*see* grammatical structures, sequence of

Grammar
    general   6, 9–10
    rules   6, 157

Grammatical structures
    sequence of   43–45
    contextualization of   43, 153
    presentation of   76

Grammar-translation   6, 72–73

Group work   99, 212–215

H

Habit formation   74

Homework   28

I

Individualized learning   112, 145 – 148

Inductive – *see* deductive

Intensive reading   93 – 97

Interference – *see* interlanguage
         see contrastive analysis

Interlanguage   155 – 157

Intonation   47, 86
     see pronunciation

K

Knowledge – productive/receptive   10, 35 – 36

L

Language
     general   35 – 37
     substance   36 – 38

Language – lab   118 – 120

Learner
     individual   21
     young beginner   23 – 24
     adult beginner   31 – 33
     pressures on . . .   25 – 26
     personal involvement   28

Learning
     theories   70 – 75
     modes of   141 – 144

Lexical items   50

Library   87 – 88

Linguistics
     influencing teaching   10
     structural   73 – 74
     generative – transformational   74 – 75

Listening   52 – 58

Literature   16

M

Mass-media   191
    radio   191 – 194
    television & films   194 – 196
    newspapers & magazines   196 – 198

Mastery — *see* goals
      see testing

Meaning   50, 163 – 164
    contextual   42, 164 – 165
    lexical   169 – 171
    situational   168 – 169
    social   173 – 175
    and paraphrase   171 – 173

Mentalistic   74

Method   3, 4, 19

Minimal pairs   85

Modes of learning   141 – 144

Model of speech   228

Motivation
    general   27
    in adults   31
    motivating the unmotivated   143

Multi-media   120 – 121

O

Objectives — *see* goals

Objective tests — *see* testing

Oral composition   180

Organic planning   185 – 186

P

Paraphrase   171 — 173

Performance — *see* competence

Pictures — *see* aids

Planning
    a framework   75 — 76
    a reading program   61
    a lesson   94 — 97
    see organic planning

Productive vs. receptive   49

Programmed instruction   28, 110 — 113

Pronunciation   47 — 49, 83 — 87

R

Reading
    general   16, 89 — 97
    planning of   61
    intensive   93
    mechanics   96
    extensive   97 — 100
    — habits   94, 97
    aloud   97

Registers   174

Relevancy of theme   43

Repetition — *see* controlled activities

Replacement — *see* controlled activities

Rhythm — *see* sentence rhythm

Role-playing   206, 216 — 218

S

Self placement   147

Sentence rhythm	48, 85
Sharing responsibilities	114, 186–187
Situations	
see contextualization	
see themes	
Skills	36, 51–52, 53
speech skills	56–58
receptive skills	53
productive skills	58–64
integrative use of	64–66, 134
literacy skills	58
Social context	130
Songs	198–200
Sound-letter correspondence	62–63
Speaking	52–58
Spiral approach—see cyclic approach	
Stress—see word stress	
Student contract	186
Substance	36–37, 37–38
Substitution drill—see controlled activities	
Syllabus—example of	44
Synonomy	72

T

Talking	76, 221
Teacher	
decision making	3
native speaker	7–10
non-native speaker	10–11
as an evaluator	58
Teaching machines	112
Team teaching	228–230
Television	113–118
Testing	121–124, 137

Textbooks 157 – 159
    shopping for 231 – 236

Themes 166

Translation 7

Tutoring 29, 230

Vocabulary 49 – 50
    see lexical items

Vowel system 49, 84

Words – *see* lexical items
    word stress 47 – 48, 86
    content/structure words 170

Writing 65, 100 – 102, 187